EDINBURGH INTERNATIONAL

Reason and Emotion in Contemporary Art

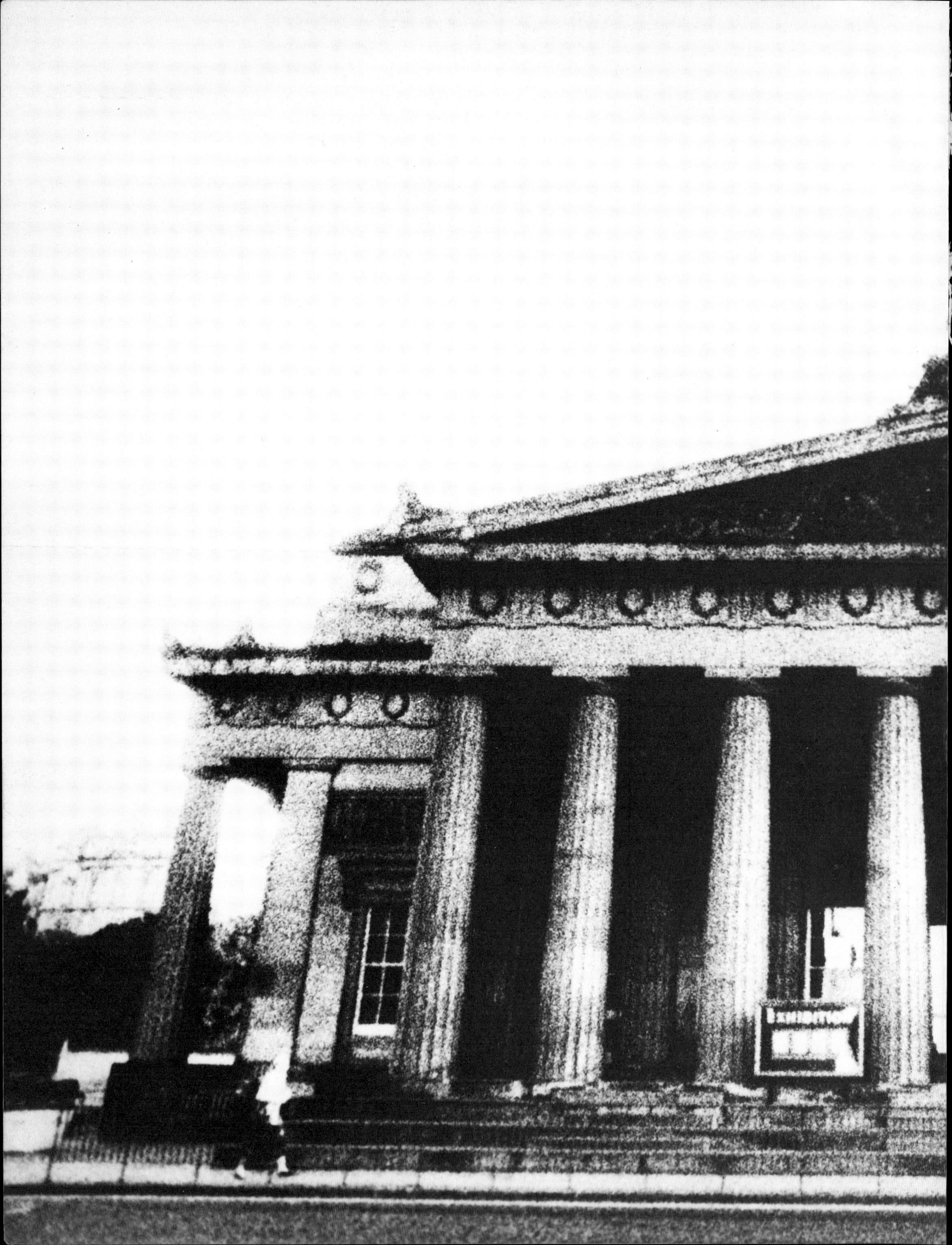

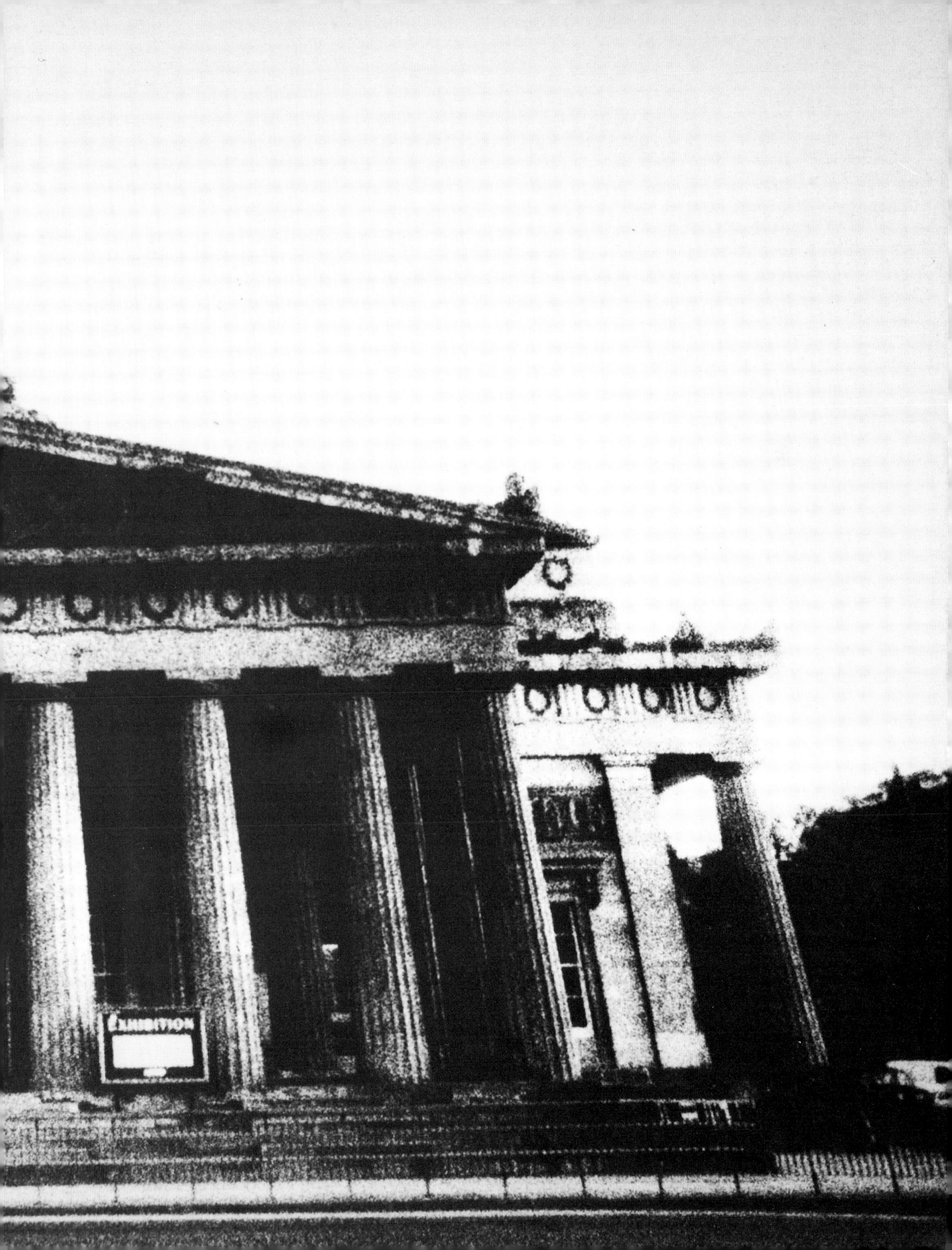
EXHIBITION

Selection Committee

Michael Compton
Douglas Hall
Martin Kunz

Secretariat

James Bustard
Elizabeth Cumming

Catalogue Editor

Douglas Hall

An exhibition organised and funded by the
Scottish Arts Council
with generous financial assistance from

Stanley Thomas Johnson Foundation
The Henry Moore Foundation
Moosehead Beer

Education programme supported by
The British Petroleum Company plc

EDINBURGH INTERNATIONAL

Reason and Emotion in Contemporary Art

Royal Scottish Academy
Edinburgh
19 December 1987 — 14 February 1988

SPONSORS

The following have given financial assistance to the exhibition:

Stanley Thomas Johnson Foundation
Henry Moore Foundation
Moosehead Beer

Adam and Company Group plc
Coopers and Lybrand, Chartered Accountants
FMC Corporation (UK) Ltd
Ferranti Defence Systems Limited
Murray Johnstone Limited
The Scotsman
Scottish German Centre, Goethe Institute, Glasgow
The Scottish Post Office Board
South of Scotland Electricity Board

The education programme is supported by
The British Petroleum Company plc

The following have assisted in realising the exhibition:

Air France
Appleyard of Edinburgh
British Midland
The British Philatelic Bureau
Bunnahabhain Distillery, Isle of Islay
Craig and Rose plc
Digital Equipment (Scotland) Ltd
Eastern Scottish Omnibuses Ltd
George Hotel, Edinburgh
Glasgow Herald
Der Kulturreferenten der Landeshauptstadt München
McIlroy Coates, Edinburgh
Radio Forth: Scotland's Central Independent Radio Station
Renault UK Ltd
Royal Mail Letters Edinburgh District
ScotRail

THE ARTISTS

James Lee Byars

Tony Cragg

Richard Deacon

Ian Hamilton Finlay

Gérard Garouste

Rebecca Horn

Stephan Huber

Axel Kasseböhmer

Sol LeWitt

Ann McCoy

Stephen McKenna

Carlo Maria Mariani

Michelangelo Pistoletto

Salvo

Andreas Schulze

Cy Twombly

Isolde Wawrin

Alison Wilding

Terry Winters

CONTENTS

LENDERS

Fondation Cartier pour L'Art Contemporain, Jouy-en-Josas
Tony Cragg courtesy Lisson Gallery, London
Richard Deacon courtesy Lisson Gallery, London
Liliane and Michel Durand-Dessert, Paris
Ian Hamilton Finlay, Dunsyre
Galerie Six Friedrich, Munich
Rebecca Horn, Bad-König-Zell
Stephan Huber, Munich
Mr and Mrs Isler, Auvernier
Galerie Kaess-Weiss, Stuttgart
Sol LeWitt, Connecticut
Ann McCoy courtesy Karen Amiel, New York
Stephen McKenna courtesy Edward Totah Gallery, London
Galerie Paul Maenz, Cologne
Mayor Gallery, London
Il Milione, Milan
Jackie Poncelet, London
Saatchi Collection, London
Jacqueline Sheinberg, New York
Mr and Mrs Sidney Singer, New York
Speck Collection, Cologne
Gian Enzo Sperone, Rome
Monika Sprüth Galerie, Cologne
Galerie Tanit, Munich
Isolde Wawrin, Düsseldorf
Galerie Michael Werner, Cologne
Alison Wilding courtesy Salvatore Ala, Milan and New York, and Karsten Schubert Ltd., London
Terry Winters courtesy Sonnabend Gallery, NYC

Private Collections

ACKNOWLEDGEMENTS

The Scottish Arts Council would like to thank the many people whose invaluable contributions have together realised this exhibition. To each artist: James Lee Byars, Tony Cragg, Richard Deacon, Ian Hamilton Finlay, Gérard Garouste, Rebecca Horn, Stephan Huber, Axel Kassebõhmer, Sol LeWitt, Ann McCoy, Stephen McKenna, Carlo Maria Mariani, Michelangelo Pistoletto, Salvo, Andreas Schulze, Cy Twombly, Isolde Wawrin, Alison Wilding and Terry Winters, for the work and time spent on the demands of this exhibition and publication. Many of the artists have visited Edinburgh to make new works for the occasion and we are grateful to them for their enthusiastic response to the project.

Our thanks go also to the selectors, Michael Compton and Martin Kunz, for the attention and thought they have given to developing the exhibition and for their important contributions to the catalogue. We would like to express a special debt of gratitude to Douglas Hall, who, as Chairman of the selectors and editor of the catalogue, has steered the project from its conception to conclusion. Equally, we are most grateful to the artists' agents and lenders for their support and loans to the exhibition. We would also like to thank the catalogue authors for their critical and scholarly essays.

The members of the Council's Exhibition and Art Committees, in particular Dr Duncan Thomson and Professor Myer Lacome respectively, have taken a close interest, and would like to join us in thanking the Director and Trustees of the National Galleries of Scotland and the President of the Royal Scottish Academy for permission to use the Academy for this exhibition.

We are grateful to the many sponsors and foundations listed in the catalogue for their support, in particular, the Henry Moore Foundation; the Goethe Institute, Glasgow; the Stanley Thomas Johnson Foundation, Berne; the British Petroleum Company plc for its support of the education programme to accompany the exhibition; and our major sponsor, Moosehead Beer.

Many other people have helped us in different, crucial ways, and we would especially like to thank the following:—

Karen Amiel
Robert Begg
Wilfried Dickhoff
Liliane & Michel Durand-Dessert
Julia Ernst
Mark Francis
Eric Franck
Karsten Greve
Keith Hartley
James Hofmaier
Henry Meyric Hughes
Irene Jack
Dany Keller
Naila Kunigk
Elisabeth McCrae
Ian McIlroy
Paul Maenz
James Mayor
Walther Mollier
Andrew Murray
Giles Ross
Nicholas Serota
Susanna Singer
Reiner Speck
Gian Enzo Sperone
Monika Sprüth
Edward Totah
Gerd de Vries
Michael Werner

PREFACE

This exhibition marks a bold and important initiative, which should not be judged only by international standards nor by national or regional ones. Both levels of success are equally important. The *Edinburgh International*, with the duality implied in the title, must be seen as a two-way affair based on the belief that we have something to give to internationalism as well as something to learn from it.

On a practical level the project represents an attempt to cater for an indigenous audience, however much it is hoped in Edinburgh to attract visitors at all seasons, all-the-year-round. Our decision to present the exhibition during the winter months was therefore a deliberate one. Edinburgh's importance as a tourist city and the concentration of activity during three hectic August weeks of the International Festival, have depressed the opportunities and the will to address the Scottish public as such. At another level the exhibition stakes out a small piece of territory on the international art map where, if it is successful, it may become a regular event. No regular series of large international exhibitions of contemporary art as yet takes place in the UK, in contrast to mainland Europe and North America.

The early development of the exhibition was quickly shaped by several local factors. There is a reasonably consistent exposure in Scotland to contemporary trends in British art—in temporary exhibitions throughout the country and in several permanent collections, particularly in Edinburgh, Glasgow, Aberdeen and latterly Ayr. Despite the programmes of several galleries in the cities, opportunities to assess current trends outside Britain are intermittent. A decision was taken therefore that the exhibition be international in scope. The physical restraints of space suggested an exhibition concentrating on fewer artists in depth, rather than any attempt to provide a survey.

The development of the concept of the exhibition, evolving by a synthesis of the notions of post-modernism, classicism and tradition, platonism and primordial forces, culture and objectivity, itself reflected the original impulse to find a starting point for the exhibition in the enlightenment philosophy and architecture of Edinburgh. The site of the exhibition itself, the Royal Scottish Academy with its ordered spaces and classical facade, contributed in no small part in developing the leitmotiv of classicism which characterises the project. There have been a number of 'international exhibitions' in recent years, but few have identified and examined the issues which cross international boundaries. The reinvigoration of the classical tradition and the dialogue with classicism is one of the most notable strains in the art of the past ten years. It is especially fitting therefore that an exhibition which deals with these issues take place in Edinburgh.

Classicism and traditionalism have acquired a special importance in the post-modern situation. For those who have grown up in the 'tradition of the modern', it has meant that a confusing range of possibilities is now open to them. Some artists have taken that as a sanction for the most extreme forms of personal expressionism. Others, sensing the loss of consensus about art, in society at any level, have looked back to see what can be learned from times when there was a much stronger consensus, stronger in fact than we have known in our lifetime.

This exhibition therefore presents classicism, not so much as a source of image and style, as a means of looking at the problems and dilemmas of art in the post-modern climate of recent years. In understanding the relevance of classicism to modern artists today, four aspects have been identified.

First is the use of images directly taken from classical art or art in the classical tradition. However, as these images are no longer part of the general culture their use is somewhat ironical or abstract for being 'out of time'. Carlo Maria Mariani and Gérard Garouste are 'classical' in this sense.

A very different sort of classicism is one that has been present all along in modern art, because it provided a philosophical basis for abstract art. By this interpretation, the classical, or the Platonic, expresses itself most purely through mathematics which are in turn expressed visually in geometry. This is the perfect order which allows also an infinite number of variations. Sol LeWitt represents this mathematical classicism in the exhibition.

Contrasting with both these interpretations is one that is more interested in the primitive or primordial aspects of the human soul that underlie them. Although fully explored only by modern psychology these were also painfully and terribly known to the ancient world in its rituals. This has been a rich field for recent art. Some artists such as Ann McCoy use traditional representation to objectify myths they are interested in. Others like Rebecca Horn continue to use the visual devices of modernism.

Going beyond these quite narrow interpretations is a fourth and more general one. By this interpretation, classicism is not a matter of a particular style or motivation but of rescuing art from its self-circumscribed role and making it again part of the general culture. This might mean a use of images from classical tradition (Ian Hamilton Finlay or Stephen McKenna) but can also inform the spontaneous draughtsmanship of Cy Twombly.

No group of artists chosen for their quality and reputation today, is likely to fit neatly or meekly into such categories as these. Even the few examplars cited here are disputable, no doubt. These aspects of classicism are not mutually exclusive and an artist's work may be justly considered under more than one. In short, classicism is not an easy key to the way the most interesting artistic minds work in the 1980s. We believe only that the artists brought together in this exhibition are among that number, and that all have an underlying relation to the theme discussed by Michael Compton in the essay that follows.

The exhibition has a sub-title, *Reason and Emotion in Contemporary Art,* which describes its contents with a very broad brush indeed, but does suggest the dialectic that underlies the work of artists today. In the present climate of post-modernism, art must look to its roots if it is not to degenerate into a mish-mash of stylistic and media devices. Since reason and emotion are twin roots of human behaviour, we have favoured this way of defining our field, rather than the possibly misleading term 'classicism'.

James Bustard
Douglas Hall

Four Aspects of Classicism

Progress and Post-Modernism

The Edinburgh International this year, with its sub-title and the range of artists it includes, may be seen as a commentary on Post-Modernism, although it includes artists who have been working creatively from the Fifties and have been associated with movements of the past. The theme, or rather the immediate context, of the exhibition is discussed below under the heading *Aspects of Classicism*, but the polemical background is that which has been given the name 'Post-Modernism'.

The implication of the prefix 'Post' is of course that something called Modernism is over or perhaps that something else is seeking to overthrow and supplant it. 'Post' implies in addition that this something else is a development of or a reaction to Modernism. It may even imply further that whatever stood against or apart from Modernism during the era of its dominance, was peripheral or ineffectual. So the notion of Post-Modernism assigns a great importance to Modernism, possibly even in excess of what was attributed to it by its own protagonists.

Some of the early formulations of Post-Modernism in relation to painting, including *Transavantgardia*, were directed against a specific Modernism, the one formulated and maintained by the critic Clement Greenberg and those influenced by him in the Forties, Fifties and Sixties, whether artists, critics, curators or others in the art world.

Crudely stated, the Greenbergian theory of Modernism is that the best artists of more than a hundred years past have, each in turn, studied the art of their immediate great predecessors and, finding in that work elements not essential to the medium of painting (the flatness of the canvas for example), have sought ways of eliminating them. Art is thus seen to proceed by a kind of dialectical criticism in a prevailing direction although it is not directed to an end point in view. The obvious terminus—the quite monochrome canvas had been achieved by the Russian artist Rodchenko in the early Twenties. But this move was considered merely as a gesture, lacking the necessary dialectical relationship with what went before and therefore the necessary degree of difficulty. (The Greenbergian matches the public view in its esteem of difficulty.)

The oppositions to this theory of Modernism in the later Seventies, which were to be brought under the aegis of Post-Modernism, were often regionalistic in that they contested an American dominance. As in the case of many of its political counterparts, the campaign became more insistent as its target became tired and less worth attacking with the revival of Europe as a centre of art and the diminishing power of the rhetoric of Modernism in New York. Greenbergianism survived as a creative practice perhaps most strongly in that museum of traditions, England. It still survives as a theory in that other museum of ideas, Marxist criticism—naturally as a demon—a suitable fate for what was in origin a sort of Trotskyite aberration.

As formulated by Greenberg himself, Greenbergianism was or purported to be, simply a way of characterising what had been common to the best painters of the period described. The prescriptive element of it—though disavowed or dissimulated by the critic himself—was felt by friends and enemies alike, as was also its pointed disregard for most of the art of the time, which it called 'easy', 'minor', or 'kitsch'. Consequently the opposition to Modernism has been itself rather exclusive, even though it opposes the simplifications not only of Modernism itself but of the Minimal art that was a reaction to it.

One may consider then, a more generalised post-modernism, without capital letters. This could be merely the feeling that an historic advance has halted and that contemporary art is going in no particular direction. Such a more diffuse post-modernism is not directly opposed to any style or theory nor can it justify its own achievements by reference to a prescriptive critique. But it does confront other tendencies in the art and criticism of the fairly recent past. One of these is the recurrent view that a new form of art replaces or makes obsolete a post form—as Futurism claimed to do in the first decade of the century—or that only the art of today is appropriate to today and what was done yesterday can be forgotten. I doubt whether any great artist or serious critic has ever held such a view in its extreme form, but the Minimalists in the mid-Sixties did come close, especially in their repudiation of what was considered a European tradition. In its weaker form this attitude is no more than a doctrine of progress, which, like the culture of science, does not pretend that a new artist (or scientist) is better than an old one, but only that his work is more developed, being built on an understanding accumulated in the work of the past. There is however an important difference between the role of the individual artist and scientist in the doctrine of progress.

Although science has as its heroes individuals who are credited with advancing science and even with influencing its principal directions of development for long periods, the individualism of a heroic scientist is only an ancillary part of the myth and not its essence. In contrast, in painting individualism had indeed become virtually its essence, so that expression in painting was referred back to the artist: it was self-expression. Criteria of judgement were likewise referred back—the artist determined his own ends. Who then was the great artist? Why, the one who opened the doors of perception to the new age. This is the paradox of Modernism—both self-justification and justification by the future. Post-Modernism likewise seems to refer quality back to the artist. The difference is that it is not then confidently expected to be established by the future. Rather it is found by a continuing voyage of exploration on the part of the individual members of the audience who show one another what they have discovered.

So this exhibition may be considered as a post-modern exhibition only in a very general sense: its artists value tradition, they are not creating an art purely of today nor is the criterion self expression. They are to be discovered by a journey of exploration (more figurative than real since all are wellknown) and they are not grouped together as a leading cadre.

Representation

The antagonists of Modernism convinced themselves mistakenly that abstraction had been dominant for decades and, consequently, that a reversion to figuration would be a heroic act of regeneration. They likewise convinced themselves that this dominant art had been without social or cultural significance and even without metaphor (in spite of the historical fact that nearly all the great abstract artists of the twentieth century, from Kandinsky to Rothko, were concerned above all with the subject of their art—with the human spirit; their consciousness of the medium arose from the need to find an adequate means of representing this). Conversely the antagonists of Modernism imagined that figurative art had been repressed—even in Britain, where figurative art was dominant in the 1940s and had been revived in various manifestations at least five times since. On the other hand, as far as I know, no artist who has newly embraced representational art as part of the post-modernism of the 1970s and 1980s has addressed the problems of representation opened up by Cézanne, Picasso or Matisse, Bonnard or Giacometti. They have not learned or striven to understand for themselves what they see nor to find a way of fixing it that is communicable in a medium. The way they have adopted most often is to use representation as a vehicle and to *invent* what is to be represented (since this may be invisible) and to tell a story, to construct an allegory or to dramatise an effect. Consequently the manner of representation often appears primitive, even deliberately primitive, or else it is a borrowed style, in sculpture, even a borrowed form—a cast from an earlier work. Can post-modern figurative art proceed on the basis of an unoriginal epistemology? I think not, but then I think the return to figuration is not the driving force behind Post-Modernism.

So, although we are looking at an art now that is made in the context of a history of abstract, Minimal and Conceptual art, together with Arte Povera and other vital manifestations, the conflict with abstraction is not the theme of the exhibition and the selectors have chosen rather, to think in terms of classicism.

The Four Aspects

The aspects of classicism which have been used to give a form to this exhibition are not by any means exhaustive of such a rich theme, nor is it claimed that the individual artists take them as precepts or illustrate them in their work. In so far as these artists do illustrate such aspects it may be found that they exemplify more than one. In discussing them here I only mean to draw out some of the features or qualities of the works by presenting an outline of a context.

The four aspects which have principally concerned the selectors are moreover not related in a simple structural way—one is not the obverse of another. Briefly, they are:

- i The device of quotation of traditional classical styles, subjects and images
- ii The evocation of the primordial and irrational drives and imagery of which classical styles are the rationalised and culturally conventionalised mask
- iii Classicism as a logical order
- iv Classicism as the standard and compendium of civilised values and practices

Naturally any art which is founded on notions like these is in our time precarious. The styles and subjects of what is usually called Classicism (generally, of course, those derived from what Greece and Rome have bequeathed to us) are no longer the basis of our education, nor the commonplace of our expression, nor the immediate disciplines of our thought. They have become exotic and anachronistic. Their assumptions concerning the relation of image and object have been dissolved by criticism, overlaid by innovation and alienated by semantic contextualism. If they are to be used again, parallel assumptions will have to be reconstructed or made provisionally. On the other hand, the disorder or strangeness underlying the order of Classicism has been a prevailing theme of Romanticism and twentieth-century art. Myth and magic have superseded the painting of the Parnassian goddesses and heroes. The unreason beneath our own political systems continually breaks through when it is not the very source and material of those systems themselves.

In spite of the dominance in our culture of science and technology, logical systems guaranteeing truth or beauty have not prevailed in painting or sculpture. They have taken on the role of generative devices and are more often used to show the gap between idea and object—a gap that many think of as a fatal flaw in our culture. And finally, the idea of offering or exemplifying standards for modern society seems presumptuous and, where it is attempted seriously (as for example by religious fundamentalists), crass, simplistic and even frightening.

The precariousness of all modern art is expressed by the symptom of its multifariousness, ambiguity and mutability. But there is a peculiar irony that Classicism should be as precarious as Expressionism or Conceptual art whose unpremeditated individualism and dissociation respectively are definitive of their very existence. In all ways, therefore, any contemporary classicisms will be an adventure, its references to the past no easy conservatism.

Quotation

The most obvious manifestation of Classicism, common to many of the artists in this exhibition, is the use of classical images, styles and references. Since this form of Classicism is no longer the common language of art, these quotations and allusions may present themselves as arbitrary. Being used out of context, they may seem to signify that context as much as a particular object or idea. In this they may resemble the citations of popular or industrial art that were the stock-in-trade of Pop Art. In addition, they largely lack the visual naturalism of classical Greek, Roman or Renaissance art and so do not have the air of dealing with the 'real' world. The classical prototype appears as a metaphor for a traditional art of high expectation, complex reference and wide resonance. It may even connote the humane. But we remember the use of

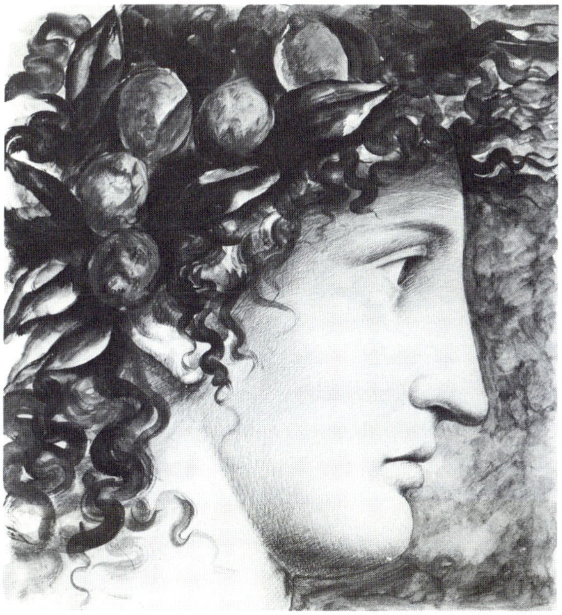

Carlo Maria Mariani, *Gigantic Head* 1986
Courtesy Marco Carrara, Vada

classical forms, especially in sculpture and architecture, by the most oppressive regimes of the century—Communist and Fascist. Their classicism in monumental sculpture depended on the metaphor that a well-proportioned and muscular body stood for moral and social virtue. It depended likewise on elementary theatrical gestures, raised fists, joined hands, striding bodies.

The contemporary art of classical reference is apparently without that instrumentalism. Nevertheless it does allude to the art of more distant peoples for whom beauty could be uniquely identified with a physical type. Nature was not so much explored as improved on the basis of systems and conventions. Such a medicine cannot be offered morally or plausibly to our contemporaries and so its forms appear always in quotation as something commented on, criticised or enacted. Alternatively a work may be reconstructed from elements that are not culturally specific and so cannot be considered dangerous. Classical styles, themes and objects are presented therefore today in an ambivalent way. They seem to express at least a regard for stability and a mode of right thinking of the past—at most a determination to re-integrate reason, feeling and nature in a culture that knows how to honour the best. But in the obvious absence of such a culture today, the expression is tinged with irony or desperation. There is always at least a hint that the order sought for may be too deterministic or may go wrong.

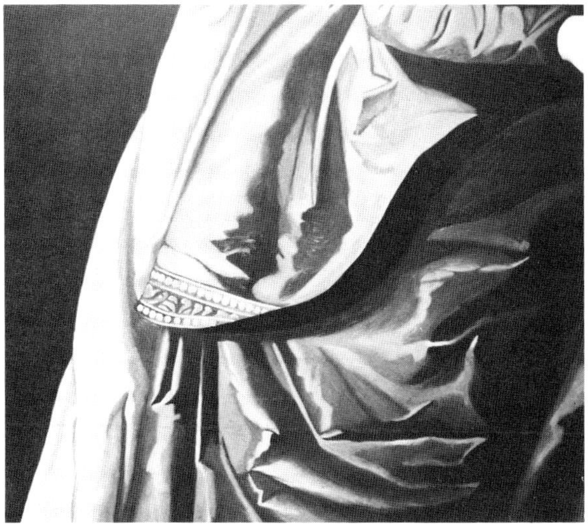

15 Axel Kasseböhmer, *Drapery* 1981

Arcana

The sculpture that has survived the two thousand years since classical times is often finely proportioned, its gestures restrained and balanced; the poetry is measured with careful rhetoric. But the stories told express rapture, fear, awe and all the primitive emotions. Indeed the classical images and myths, as they have come down to us, may be considered as a means of giving a rationalised or social expression to what was hidden, irrational, pre-rational and primordial. This has been a theme of European thought from Nietzsche to Freud and Jung, who gave classical names to the drives, complexes and personalities they found beneath the cultural behaviour of the citizen. And in Fraser's *Golden Bough*, the most ancient stories and rituals are shown as

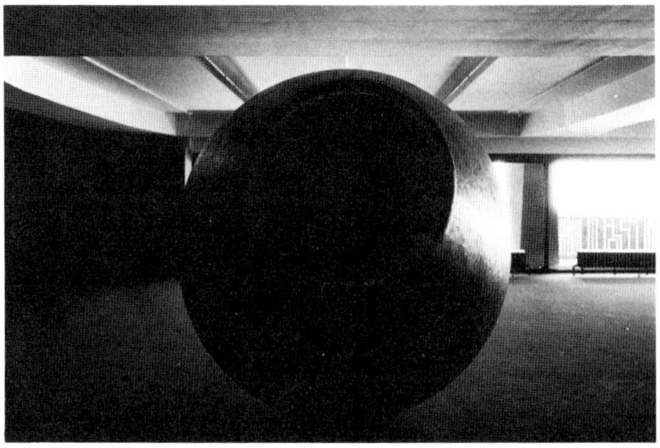

James Lee Byars, *The Spinning Oracle from Delphi* 1986
Courtesy Galerie Michael Werner, Cologne

giving dramatic form to the universal stresses of survival in the world, of social and sexual relationships.

That writers in the nineteenth and twentieth centuries should give classical names to new perceptions was itself, of course, a neo-classical phenomenon. It was a means of giving an air of rationality and respectability to what was being said. Greek and Latin are still collaged continually to make names for the concepts and hardware of our technological culture, even though little of these languages is taught in school today. Yet the artefacts and legends of Greece and Rome, of Egypt and Mesopotamia, of China and Japan, of Mexico and the other most elaborate civilisations, would not have their power if they did not truly embody the deepest and most fundamental drives of the human species under a mask of culture—a mask that cannot be pulled off without taking the flesh beneath. The sense of the inseparability of the mask and the life beneath has been a vehicle for painters and sculptors at least since the Renaissance, but it has had a new inflection with each age.

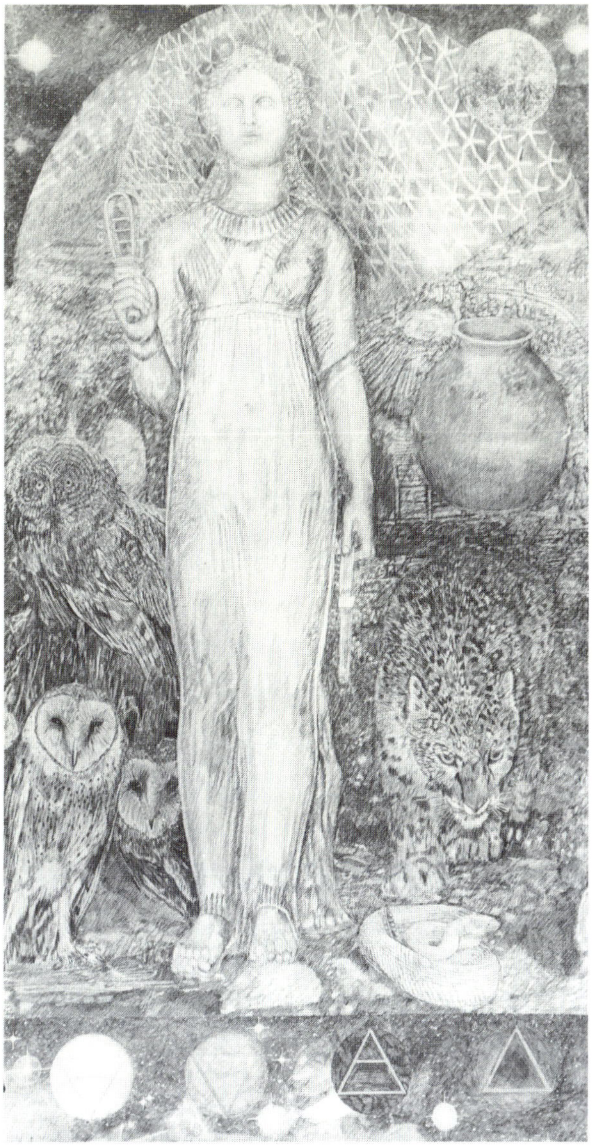

Ann McCoy, *Isis* 1986
The Artist courtesy Karen Amiel, New York

However, following as it does the media-conscious devices of Pop and Conceptual art, even the pre-rational aspect of art today has a sort of semantic and political self-consciousness. As is also the case with the more evidently neo-classical art, this pre-rational art cannot rely on conventions being sufficiently strongly embedded in the culture to appear natural and direct. Neither can it always rely on images drawn from a collective sub-conscious being allowed to pass through to the viewer unhindered by that critical consciousness. Such an art therefore has to proceed from the personal insight to the public statement by means that are often theatrical or which require the viewer to intuit a mode of invention and a context. That these may be arcane is not an arbitrary exclusiveness. On the contrary a sense of mystery is a human requirement and the specific character of the art is to simultaneously hide and to reveal. In the absence of contemporary universals, the richest means of doing this is to work with those that have been inherited from Mediterranean and more distant cultures and which, without explaining or analysing, embody the most poignant constants of human experience. Rituals cannot be easily revitalised but images have their immortality even when broken, defaced or deracinated.

Subterranean feelings are much easier for a modern artist to deal with than a prescriptive style of beauty or an established code of reference. This may be because, for two hundred years, artists have chosen or been compelled to disrupt or revise consciousness and to seek its roots, but also because necessity and even the most basic elements of western political structures require us to test continually the organs and formulations of power and order. This can no longer plausibly be done by individualism, bohemianism or expressionism, but must seek more universal means.

There is in particular an ever more pressing urgency to resolve the conflict between our civilisation (if it can be called that) and nature, whether that nature is inside us—inherited from countless generations of creatures, or outside us—our environment. The magic that once sought to picture and control nature and to identify the powerful bonds between the elemental forces and humanity now seems rather to express our guilt in having over-controlled, in having elaborated a view of the world so dependent on abstract theory and computation that it cannot strengthen those bonds. We are continually creating counter-cultures and political parties, adversarial groups to protect humanity from mankind and to protect nature from culture. They are factional rather than integral. An art which is dedicated to celebrating nature and to celebrating humanity as its epiphenomenon is not merely an expression of the Dionysiac converse of the Apollonian face, but a revolution in the making. It seems more than ever a necessity to foment this revolution by invoking the human case in art, since every attempt to describe it in the terms of science and politics only seems to threaten us the more with crass and manipulative domination. The probability of terrible errors, or things blowing back at us all with catastrophic effect becomes even greater. Art will not function as a placatory fetish against this power, so artists must find a way of representing the world that can change the culture without threatening itself.

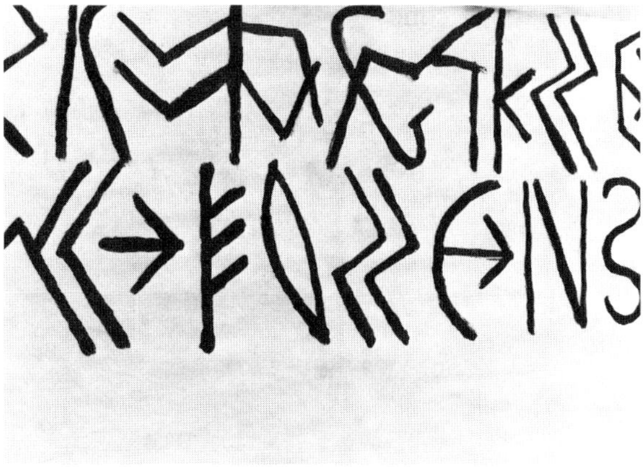

47 Isolde Wawrin, *Untitled Drawing* 1987 (detail)

It is in the nature of the visual arts—being without the formal structures of language—to deal with the world by means of mimesis and symbolic action. Thus all the artists in this exhibition, like all original artists, must in some way manifest the shamanistic power. However, some approach closer to the specifically classical in their techniques, styles or iconography, while exhibiting also what lies behind the mask, expressed as chimeras, monsters, compulsion, madness and death. Others seem to seek the roots and stems of the biological universe, the generative forms and processes that are at work in our own bodies and are imprinted by genetics in our minds. We inherit these forms as the basis of our intuition and our means of communication, always giving them new names and features in spite of the fact that they are perpetually the same. Yet other artists employ the most basic human marks: circles, crosses and spirals or the forms of objects universalised by the constants of human usage.

Order

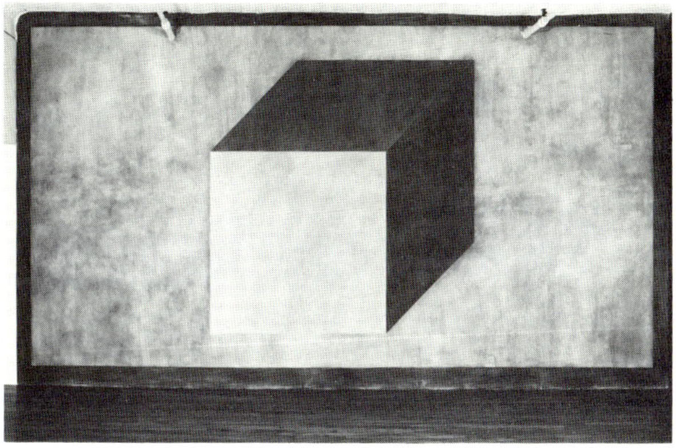

Sol LeWitt, *Wall Drawing # 380*
Courtesy National Gallery of Australia, Canberra

Reason has always been a means of controlling the world—a particular sort of magic. Like magic its power has sometimes seemed to derive from metonymy. If nature, diverse, dangerous and unpredictable as it presents itself, could be shown to be only the imperfect or corrupted realisation of some vast, godlike reason then a little application of human reason might control it: the skin of a tiger, suitably worn by a shaman, may control the hostile power of the animal itself. But the wonderful games of reason, logic and mathematics, when elaborated to a serviceable degree, have come to seem rather the pictures of the human mind than of the world.

The only artist chosen for this exhibition whose work exemplifies reason in the context of classicism, also demonstrates the gap that exists between an idea or concept and material objects. He has particularly proposed that the apparently simple and logical drawings that he devises should be executed not on dissociated pieces of paper but on other human constructs, walls, where they take their phenomenal form as much from those gritty realities as from the imagination of the artist. At the same time he specifically puts the thought before the realisation, notionally independent of any mutuality. The thought then models as a generative force, almost as a Platonic form, but human and physical interaction give it its contingent reality. The effect is to raise awareness both of the nature of the reality and of the ideas, which is itself born in the matrix of human language and in the context of the traditions of art. The language elements which he uses in stating the concepts (expressed in his instructions which are used as titles) are among those which seem to be most primitive or most fundamental in relation to the description of objects in space. They are found both in the theorems of Euclid and in the phrases commonly used to direct a visitor about the town.

The Standard

My last aspect of classicism is the most difficult to describe. It is also the most complex, including as it does the other aspects described here and still more, which, for the sake of simplicity, the selectors have chosen not to invoke. It is the one closest to the original definition of Classicism: that which is the standard, as the art of Greece is (or was) the standard, as Shakespeare or Mozart are the standard, as a Bugatti is the standard.

The general public has no difficulty with this idea: it is only, perhaps, too generous with it. But we, the 'Art World' certainly have difficulty. We wish to say that there are good and great artists. When pressed, we may even assert that one is better than another. On the other hand we would like to say that the artist sets his or her own aims and standards. The idea of an artist, even Picasso or Matisse, setting the standard for all painters or for a generation is too much like saying that all must imitate him, in any case it is too authoritarian. But if we wish only that artists should aim at such quality (without imitating style or subject) we are left with no serviceable notion of quality to apply.

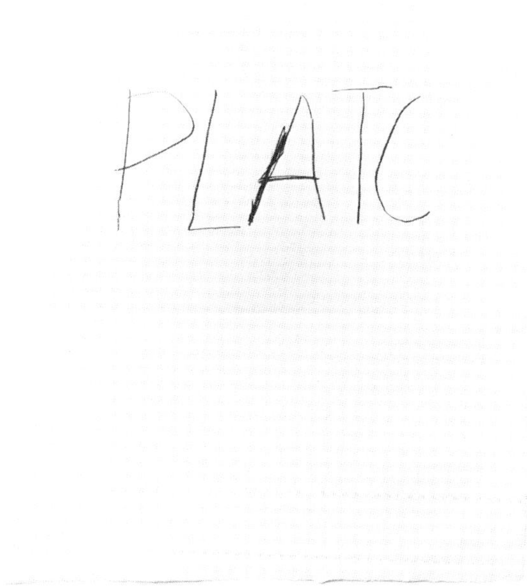

Cy Twombly, *Five Greek Poets and a Philosopher–Plato* 1978
Courtesy Speck Collection, Cologne

'Truth to nature' was such a quality but we have learned that, even in mathematics, there may be infinite different truths, and, in other forms of symbolic expression, it is known that there always have been. If there are so many truths—then there may be so many realities. An artist may use a new set of axioms of expression in each picture and even, plainly, several in one picture. All the same, I would like to reiterate that there can be a truth in art. Such a truth could be full humanity. Artists may beg a few questions while they build it up (or re-build it) and perhaps, after a certain point, it will sustain itself, it will become classic. But since one cannot and must not determine the ends for artists, nor even the means, then perhaps one may offer instead the notion of decent or reasonable behaviour in art, a notion that combines (but not too stringently) the moral, the professional, the craftsmanly, the serious, the thoughtful, the feeling, the learned, and so on what one may call the 'civilised'.

Can we indeed have a civilised art? Then can we have a civilised art when we know very well that we are not civilised? Can we have it when the assumptions that underpinned understanding and behaviour have been unravelled and left in a tangled heap? We cannot just go on or go back from there. We cannot just ignore what has been said and done. We must somehow collect and reassemble what we can out of fragments, binding them together with care, and hope that they will eventually acquire their own cohesion and generative power. For the moment the act of doing this will be a sufficient symbolic act—an act of piety.

One of the characteristics of this sensibility is therefore complexity. The quality achieved does not arise from the perfect expression of a thought or from a decisive gesture or from a masterly technique. Those would be lesser, journeyman skills, unbecoming to a civilised artist. If they are practised, it is only to show their limitations. Conversely, an apparent roughness of technique or conceptualisation has very often been the mark which distinguishes art from craft (decoration) and was carefully cultivated by, for example, Kandinsky for this reason. A polished accomplishment also suggests determinism—not the freedom expected formerly of the high-born, and, later, of the artist. Those works which are lapidary in their execution express their freedom by irony.

However, to many, roughness also necessarily expresses a lack of accomplishment which does not seem to match the ambition to set or achieve a high standard and is therefore odd in the context which I am trying to describe here. But painters and sculptors have often shown or tried to show that they are doing something so difficult that it cannot be perfectly achieved. The art which conceals art cannot be too completely exercised by the artist, who does not want to be a prestidigitator. Too neat a match between aim and achievement shuts out meaning. It also indicates that there is nothing more to be done. It is especially an axiom of an art that has the ambition to be more fully humane and civilised that there is much more to be done although no Utopia can be designed for the future.

At any rate this characteristic roughness belongs not only to the manual skills but to all the means of expression including the choice and organisation of images. The artist cannot now behave like the 'creative' team in an advertising agency, communicating visually a new truth, or more probably, an untruth, by means of elements whose meaning is guaranteed by their currency in our culture. The advertiser's novelty, therefore, depends on a conservatism that the critical efforts of many conceptual artists have failed to shake. On the other hand, the analogous currency of meanings that sustained traditional art has been taken apart by Modernism. Artists may re-establish it by constant reference to the stock of human understanding but the reconstruction of the shattered devices of meaningful composition is more difficult. It may only be achieved by a process of teaching: the artist sets out paradigms that may be perceived and, when comprehended, used to decipher the more complex and subtle statements. It may be this didacticism, together with a certain unpalatability of what is being asserted that gives the roughness of structure to this art.

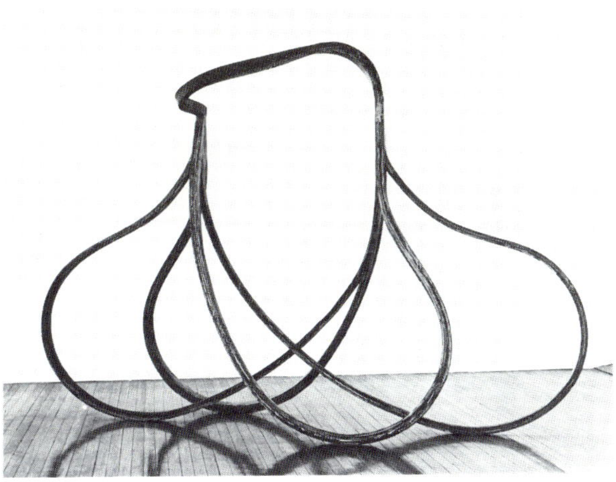

Richard Deacon, *For Those Who Have Ears No. 2* 1983
Courtesy Tate Gallery, London

One of the basic elements of the idea underlying the selection, is that the present can or should not be separated from the past and that certain achievements of the quite distant past remain valuable and potent, among them specific skills and images. Some of these have been alluded to in the previous sections. More important, perhaps, is the faculty of imagining and constructing metaphors or representations that are both immediate enough and ambitious enough to encompass what is vital to us and our culture—that which is the conscious and unconscious preoccupation of people. At the same time it will not be sufficient to feed back to them the matter of some public preoccupation which has only been reinforced by renewed statement.

Painting and sculpture do not have the means either in themselves or in the manner in which they are exhibited, traded or published, to deal with public topics on demand. One hears from time to time, for example, that the television companies want more plays on multicultural and feminist issues or more on Northern Ireland and unemployment. Such topics do, of course, properly preoccupy certain artists, but they are self-selected and moreover, most of the artists do not use a pictorial language likely to be of very wide public acceptance. Nor do they deal with such subjects in a way which suggests that they are expressing a generally experienced feeling: their medium and content are both antagonistic. The case is once more what I have described above. The conditions of visual art seem to force it always to present itself as novel and elite, in other words, as avant-garde.

However the classical art of today in the widest sense should be at the very least: comprehensible, authoritative, humane, mythopoeic, intelligent and moral. It need not resemble or quote the classic art of the past but it should express for our time and with the same responsibility what stems from the same universal and essential human drives and predicaments. I think that the artists in this exhibition have not yet achieved, and perhaps in the present circumstances cannot yet achieve, a mode or form that will last as a standard of practice for a long period.

But I do think they practise art in a way that may be considered civilised. They maintain a standard in concerning themselves with serious matters; with the most fundamental bases of humanity as well as their cultured expression. They draw on the wisdom of the past and work in the present.

Michael Compton

The Edinburgh International and Contemporary Developments

If we investigate the *Edinburgh International* Exhibition to ascertain whether aspects of a classical or classicistic approach are manifested in the works shown, we can establish that a spontaneous and unequivocally positive answer is found only in a minority, in which classical elements of form or content are used in a classicistic fashion. In all other cases, any evident and immediate reference to classical forms and content is absent. Accordingly, not all the participating artists would attest to an intentional reference, direct or indirect, to a classical artistic concept. If we take the concept of the exhibition primarily as an attempt to emphasise the significance of a new perception of a classical approach in contemporary art, and if we confront this with the markedly classicistic 'temple' of the Academy, then the corresponding selection arises primarily from our interpretation and only partially from the explicit artistic intentions of the artists in question. To label the theme as 'Aspects of a Classical Approach in Contemporary Art' would amount to a violation of the intentions of most of the artists. We have therefore refrained from applying this label and have merely drawn attention to the general principle of classical ideal, namely the perfection and harmony between the mind and the emotions. Hence the sub-title *'Reason and Emotion'*. The disadvantages of this generalised definition are that it does not provide a tangible definition and that it is too nebulous to explain the selection and disposition of the exhibition. Nevertheless, we decided on this title in order to avoid violating the majority of the artists through a one-sided interpretation with an equally misleading label.

An outlined explanation of the guiding principles and considerations of our interpretation of their works and the reasons for their selection will, however, be useful to both the viewer and the participating artists. By this it becomes clear that we were thinking about a *contemporary interpretation* of an originally *'classical'* approach, without, however, charging all the artists with any intentional, explicit reference to classicism.

What were the parameters of our selection and what made us think of them?

The first priority and aim of the instigators of the Edinburgh exhibition was to show a selection of contemporary art different to the usual ambitious, provincial imitations of a *Documenta* or a *Biennale* in miniature which are common all over the world. Secondly, the Academy's architecture and original function as an art gallery clearly limited the selection mainly to paintings, or wall-related works. The dimensions and number of the galleries was also a spatial restriction which led to the decision to limit the number of artists. In addition, the artistic needs of Edinburgh precluded a concentration on the work of very young artists as this would have necessitated a wider knowledge of contemporary art in the Seventies and Eighties than can reasonably be expected. Thus our committee of three had to find a thematic focal point which would take these factors into account and enable us to create an interesting, clear-cut cross-section of recent art history up to the present day through the work of a limited number of artists. The classicistic building—which, by the way, shows a slightly exaggerated, mannerised classical severity—posed another question. Apart from the tendency to combine classicistic fragments with fragments of other traditional styles in the fashion of the post-modern movement in architecture, can we see a different, less superficial form of reference to classical artistic ideals? Might this signal the arrival of a more profound '*Zeitgeist*'?

Since we expect to find this trend towards tradition and general classicism in our interpretation of the situation in art, and since we see an expansion taking place in the immediate neo-classicistic and 'post-modern' aspects through other aspects which are less dependent on style, we were finally able to agree on an exhibition concept of this kind. Attractive as a post-modern 'show' might seem, I personally would have considered it a distortion to emphasise this trend, which is frequently enlisted today to justify arbitrariness. I regard it as the task of the exhibition curator not only to underline the tendencies that are already creating a furore in our *Zeitgeist* but also to track down those which exist beneath the surface and which fail or succeed in surfacing according to our capacity to understand them.

The important questions now are the following: what do we mean by the translation of classical principles today? To what extent is it possible to realise classical ideals in the guise of outward similarity to classical forms and historical-classical content? If they are to be classical, is it not perhaps necessary for today's artists to liberate themselves entirely from outward form and dependency on historical stylistic forms in order to realise the ideal of classicism—i.e. to *be* classical instead of merely *appearing* so?

According to the platonic concept, a 'classical ideal' of this kind would be the '*embodiment of the pure idea*', which is more than the purely analytical definition of an idea as understood by the pioneers of conceptual art. The embodiment of an idea in all its purity would, in my opinion, represent an extreme reduction to a spiritual concept, a rationally comprehensible method which is nevertheless *sensually* accessible as a visual image through the harmony between the idea and the sensually materialised image. To demonstrate this we chose a single example, the work of Sol LeWitt, since we have grown to realise how rare such a pure realisation of this concept is today. Sol LeWitt forms as it were the backbone of the exhibition.

Another, less platonic, classical 'ideal' is that of perfection understood primarily as a *wholeness*, or *entirety*, which, rather than aspiring towards the fulfilment of a pure idea through the greatest possible reduction of sensual embodiment, brings the two poles *idea* and *materialisation* together in order to arrive at the embodiment of a human ideal: the perfection of the human being. Thus a synthesis of all sensual, emotional and rational factors is created of which the concept of unity between man and nature is also a part. This concept strives against the domination of one pole over the other and aspires towards harmony and the embodiment of man and nature in one structure, in contrast to the concept of man-dominated nature of later Christianity and materialism.

The embodiment, the extremely sensual expression of a spiritual religious world through visual art, endows the artist with an important function as mediator of religious mythology. It seems to me that this concept of art is realised most strongly today in works which do not necessarily refer consciously to the classical Greek art tradition, but which create an equivalent ideal through harmony between the polar opposites in a new humanity. Ethical principles connected with this would be, for example, no priority of man over nature and the earth (in contrast to the dominating tendency of the materialistic epoch of modernism), and no hierarchies of social, racist or sexist claims to power within the human category. This represents a balance, which, rather than referring to primeval prehistory or the paradise of primitive peoples, is already demanding a historical development which will be possible only after conflicts and struggles for power have been fought and won, and which can be consciously achieved only through reason, experience and spiritual awareness. A balance of this order would correspond to a high classical perfection which presupposes a consciously developed artistic awareness.

Such ethical artistic ideals are not part of the dominating tradition of modernism. There is, however, a connected, centuries-old tradition which, although influenced by the development of the avant-garde, never counted directly among its impulse-generating, innovative, spiritually inventive ranks, but was obliged to lead a subliminal, borderline existence. Today, in my opinion, this way of thinking is coming to occupy a central position. Works of art are being created which show a high degree of harmony between spirit and sensuality, as well as a more ambivalent kind of sensuality expressed through androgynous, or universal, sexuality. This has an effect I may call strongly erotic since, unlike sexuality, such an eroticism also presupposes a strong spiritual fascination and can, in a holistic sense, personify an artistic ideal. Time and time again, we find eroticism of this kind in the works of a few leading twentieth century artists (Picasso, De Kooning, Twombly). There are also a number of other artists who, although they are by no means unknown, are not yet counted among the most important because they have renounced all claim to revolutionary inventiveness in favour of realising and developing this ideal of erotic perfection. It would be possible to gather the most interesting of these artists together into a new, as yet unproven, developmental history consisting of names such as Georgia O'Keefe, Milton Avery, Arshile Gorky, Barnett Newman (from the 1940s), De Kooning, Elsworth Kelly, Louise Bourgeois, Francis Bacon, right up to the present with artists like Richard Deacon, Terry Winters, Alison Wilding.

The work of the last three artists is represented in the Edinburgh exhibition—which does not, however, aspire to bear witness to the thesis of a specific development of a different approach outlined here. This is my personal theme, and it cannot be expounded solely in terms of this aspect of a classical ideal. Nevertheless, in the framework of this aspect of the classical ideal that we have pursued for the Edinburgh exhibition, we find an unacademic, artistic and socio-political progressive tendency of vital interest to a number of artists today—a trend towards a new and different realisation of wholeness and perfection. They are concerned with an approach to tradition that was thrown overboard by the prevailing criticism of twentieth-century modernism. The avant-garde preferred to orientate itself according to pre- or extra-artistic visual language (primitive art, fantasticism, the ingenuousness of children's art, 'Art Brut'). Thus it repudiated classical harmony and sublime artistic heights, largely because these had lost their vitality and intensity through the academic usage of the bourgeois nineteenth century. Today, one hundred years later, the open artistic concept and the breakneck development of innovation upon innovation for their own sake have themselves become a kind of academicism. It is possible today for a concern with classical ideals and their interpretaion in our culture to disassociate itself from the 'academicism' of the avant-garde. The selection of a group of artists that aspires towards the ideal wholeness that I have outlined can only be fragmentary and may indeed seem arbitrary owing to the fact that no comprehensive study of the hidden 'tradition' that I am postulating has yet been undertaken.[1]

The same thing applies to the selection criteria mentioned here. Naturally, the aspects already elucidated as 'classical ideals' do not exclude a connection with classical mythologies with references to classical forms as subject matter. On the contrary, Cy Twombly, for example, constantly quotes the names of Greek heroes, authors of antiquity, works of antique epochs, or lapidary place names which play a part in classical history. These names do not say anything important or illustrative about this classical tradition. They are simply references which the viewer fills with the ideas he associates with the specific works and names. And the more Twombly's formulation of his pictures realises the erotic perfection already mentioned, the more the picture becomes as it were a sensual membrane which triggers off vibrations in our spiritual imagination. These quotations of classical names and concepts still have the power to excite the imagination of today's viewer and breathe life into history and tradition. As long as we aspire towards new realisations or original concepts of classical ideals it is impossible to avoid contradictions in our endeavours to achieve total, whole art and the artistic unification of polar opposites.

Not for the first time in its history, art today is developing away from an archaic situation which recognises neither artistic concepts nor autonomous artistic activity, towards a specific, acutely conscious ideal image, similar to that of the development stage of the Greek High Classical period. Since then, art has been through a complex history, parallel to the development of the world, which has led it further and further away from its social connections into an autonomous sphere, to the point where it could almost be said to have achieved a magical, subversive detachment from its bourgeois social context—which nevertheless continued to be the guarantee of its existence. The striving towards innovation and autonomy in an ever-increasing acceleration brought about the tautological self-definition of *'art is the definition of art'* which, as a cul-de-sac, blocked all possibility of escape in the continuation of this development. It is impossible to imagine what the situation would have been like without this whole historical process, or to conjecture about what would have happened if it had been replaced by a new and uncontradictory *'pure ideal'*. As it is, some artists integrate the dialectic counter-positions in a *'classical ideal of today'* in their overall ideal artistic concept. Anarchy versus order, the satanic element versus the ethical ideal, the materialistic revolutionary approach versus idealistic fiction. But when artists try to formulate a new image from the sum total of the mythologies of man, they can no longer succeed in creating a new 'ideal image' which, absurd as it may sound, would be pure and 'immaculate' and absolutely valid by virtue of its mediating cultural level. The experience of the *arte povera* group, from which Pistoletto and Salvo derive, or of Cragg and Schulze, shows as much. What is happening now in contrast to the beginnings of modernism is not a complete change of direction but the inclusion of tradition in a new and active relationship which will become an important factor for new utopias. Other scientific disciplines, particularly ethnology, linguistics and philosophy, have also experienced a similar conscious return to previously taboo traditions, and this, too, has had an influence on art. As regards art itself, it will thus be possible to reconcile approaches that have hitherto been regarded as diametrically opposed, such as romanticism and classicism, within the concept of an 'actual classicism'.

Artists who research into the psyche, and thus into dreams and the mythologies which occur in them, may be seen as connected with the classical ideal—in a sense of a perfect image of mankind—in so far as they are not concerned with their own psyches for romantic or narcissistic reasons, but because of their wish to convert the sum total of consciousness and subconsciousness into an ideal unified human whole. This would embrace not only the intellect and the emotions, but also deep psychological reality and the collective history which is stored in the subconscious in the form of myths. Such an idea is not new to art, and it was in fact a conscious theme long before Freud, but it is nevertheless worthwhile drawing attention to the change in the interest of today's artists in the period around the turn of the century, and in the methods of the surrealists. The surrealists' experiments with automatic drawing and the interest by Art Brut, and a majority of the post-war avant-garde, in the art of the mentally sick, children's drawings etc. demonstrate an interest in the psyche and its reactions to extreme situations which attributed to it an important, central role. Connected to this was the attempt to recapture a retrograde stage of development in art which was supposed to be pre-conscious and untutored, and thus in a pre-artistic phase. The difference between the surrealists and artists introduced in this exhibition (such as Ann McCoy, Rebecca Horn or James Lee Byars) becomes particularly clear in this context, for these artists try, in a maximally developed, subtle, sophisticated and thus artistically highly developed language of form and material, to recreate consciously and as optimally as possible the mythologies taken from the resources of depth psychology as *ideal images*, as artistic works of art. This finesse and artistry, and also a religious aura surrounding their work that is now once more accepted on a sublime level (and perhaps even justified), presents a contrast to the 'primal scream' that is characteristic of the rough, direct quality of the early twentieth century avant-garde which gave expression to the *weltschmerz* of the time.

Since the clearly classicistic aspects have been comprehensively discussed elsewhere, I do not propose to elucidate them here. I should, however, like to point out that there are approaches to 'classicism' which I personally regard as dangerous because they are opposed to all emancipatory aspirations in art. Tendencies of this kind are often evident within the framework of the fashionable classical 'post-modernism', which is not surprising since classical formal principles—and especially their interpretation in architecture—were never free from usurpation as the means of a legitimation of power. The typology of Roman monumental architecture served over and over again as an image of legitimation. The role of classical art and architecture in the French Revolution is a case in point. In more recent times, the visual structure of classicism was usurped by Fascism in Germany and Italy. In Italy, for example, in spite of a breakaway from classicistic detail, the tradition and the effect of 'classicism' was usurped by means of imperial monumentality under the guise of modern forms. There is evidence elsewhere today of a leaning towards this 'modern classicality' which radiates the absolutely dictatorial claim to power we recognise in Fascist architecture. This is classicism as a symbol of power in a modern disguise, but it is the power of uncontrollable self-imposed dictatorship, in the guise of a 'people's tribune', rather than the *Civitas* of the free citizen. It is a dangerous kind of playing with fire which, in my opinion, is not mastered by its authors.

But why do 'classical ideals' conceived in this way have such a fascination for some of today's artists and public, a fascination based on apparent ideals, on perfection, but really on a chauvinistic type of power demonstration? Insecure individuals may thus lay claim to the hierarchical principles of power, by usurping traditional classical forms in the belief that they are still valid and effective. I do not believe that a 'macho' obsession with power has much future in the field of art. It is not a coincidence that the more complex artistic personalities, those who are possibly less restricted by the ideal of exaggerated maleness, thus *female* artists too, are actively seeking the more subversive 'classical ideal' I am postulating. If our parameters hold good for those people, who are searching for a possible, ideal conception of art and contribute towards the discovery of isolated roots at the basis of a different artistic development of tomorrow, then they have served us well. They remain, however, no more and no less than that which they were meant to be: aids towards an understanding of the arbitrary character of the manifold directions which constitute the vitally interesting trends in contemporary art.

Martin Kunz

[1] I have already started work on this theme as the subject of an exhibition. It is a delicate matter which requires a greater degree of 'intuition' from both the artists and the interpreting viewers than has previously been necessary for an understanding of the main lines of development in twentieth century art.

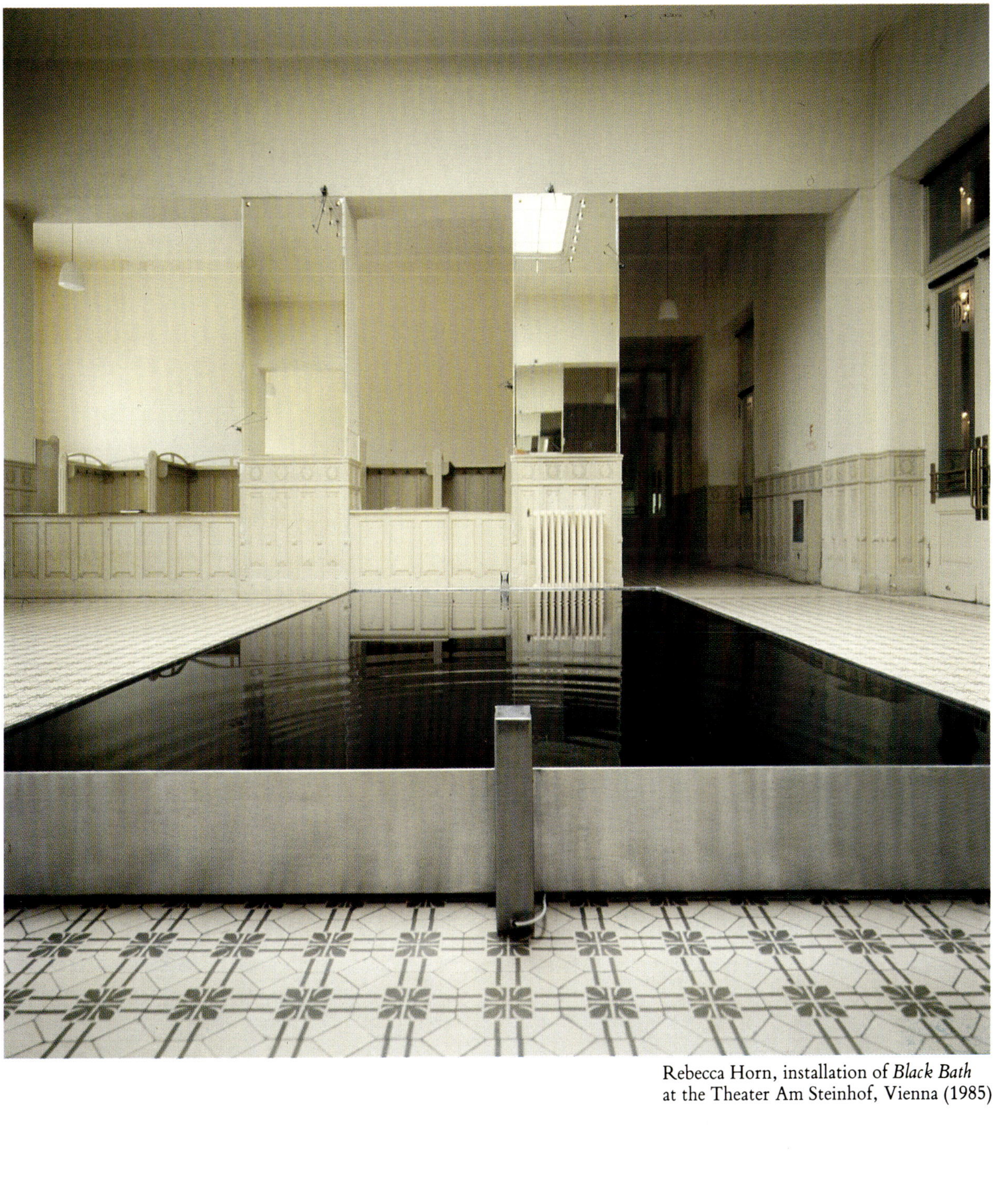

Rebecca Horn, installation of *Black Bath* at the Theater Am Steinhof, Vienna (1985)

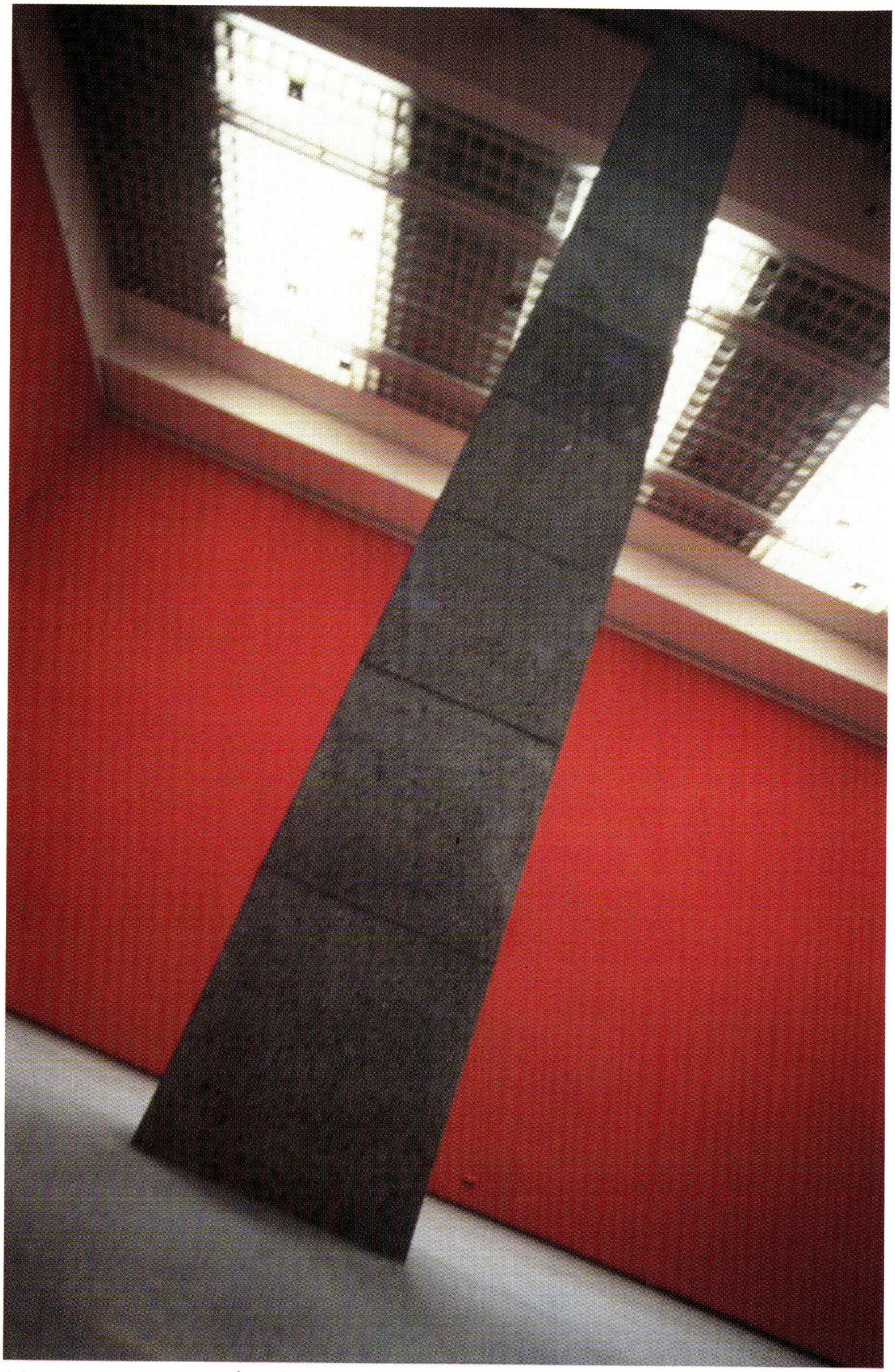

1 James Lee Byars, *Figure of Death* 1986

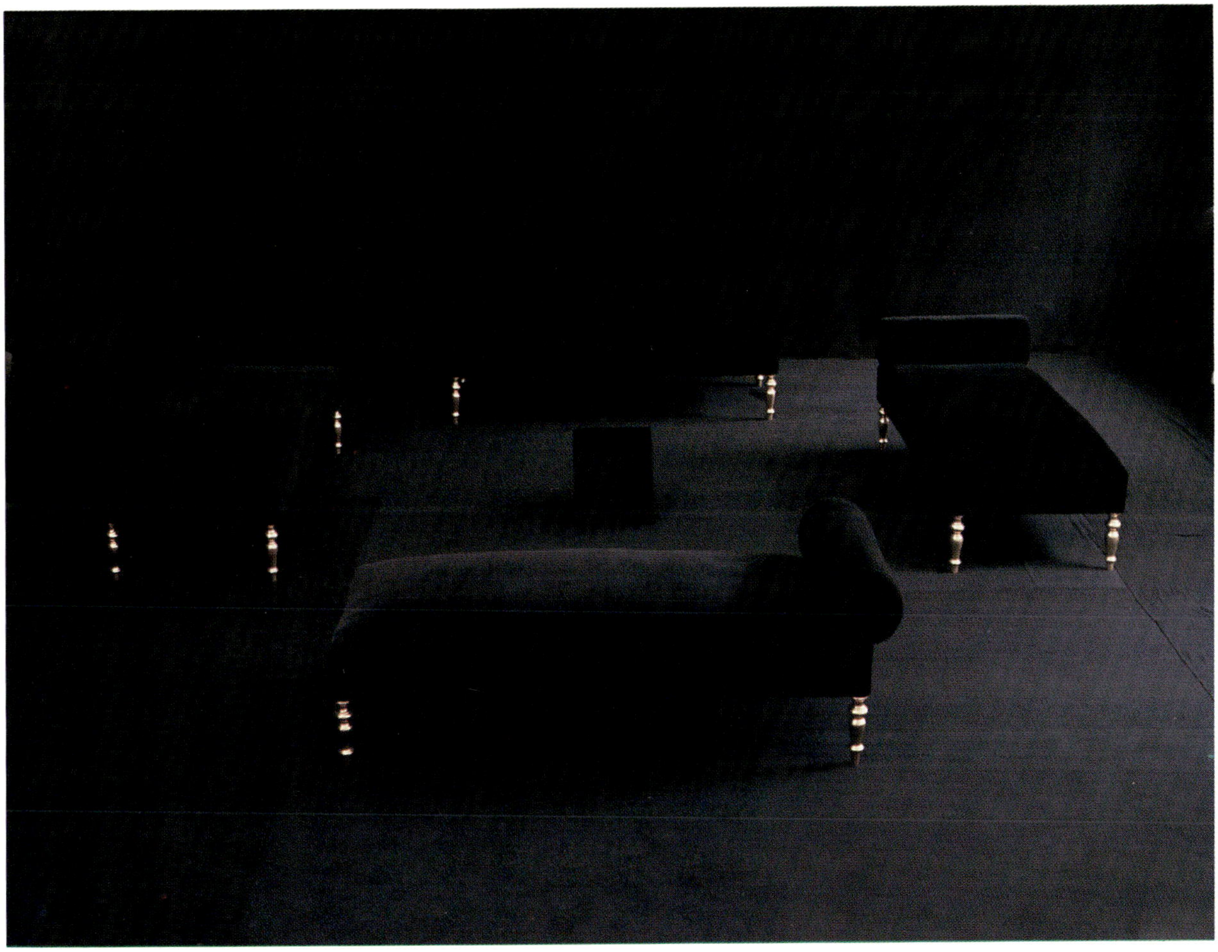

James Lee Byars,
THE BOOK OF THE 100 PERFECTS 1985
Courtesy Galerie Michael Werner, Cologne

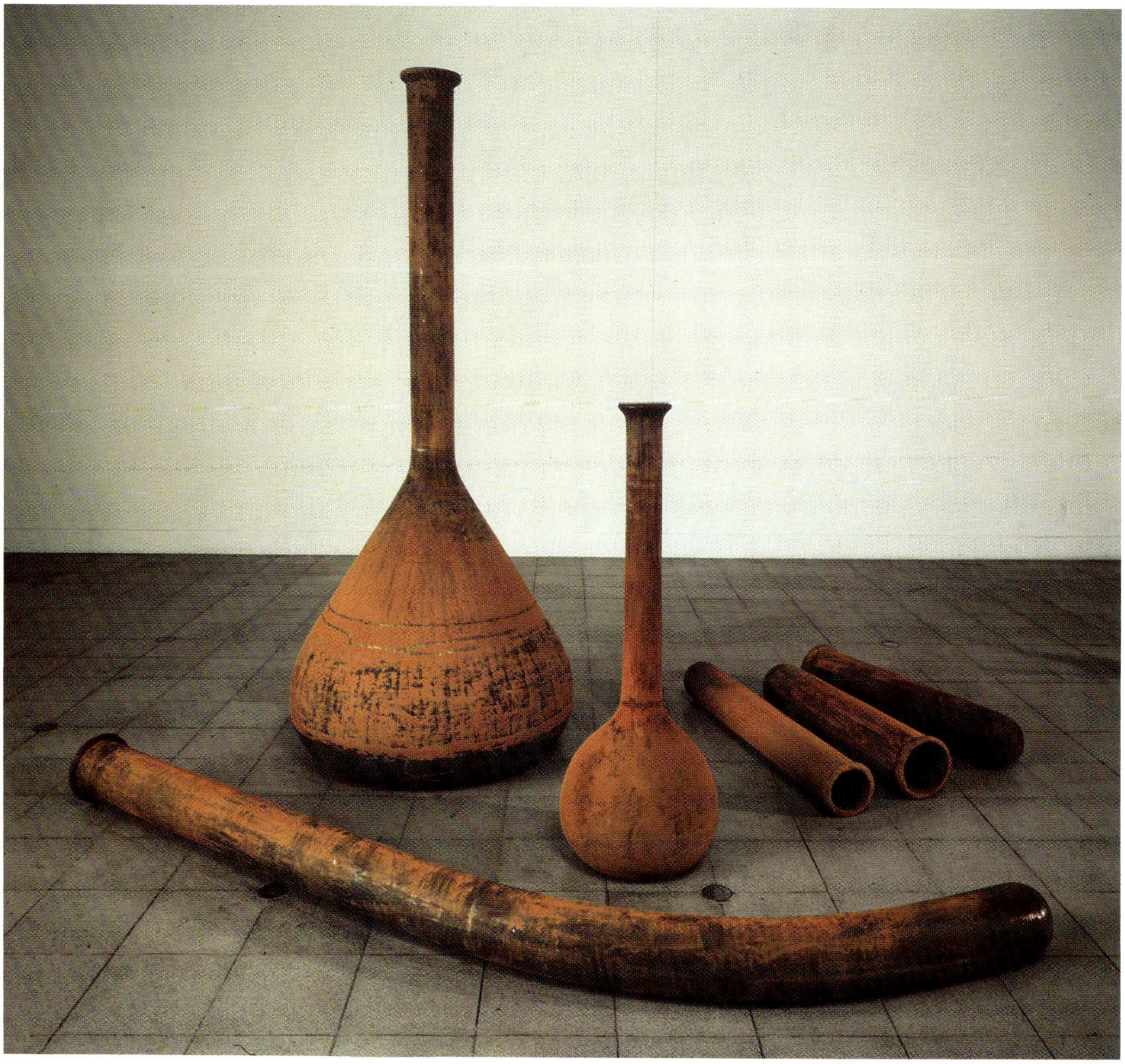

3 Tony Cragg, *Instinctive Reactions* 1987

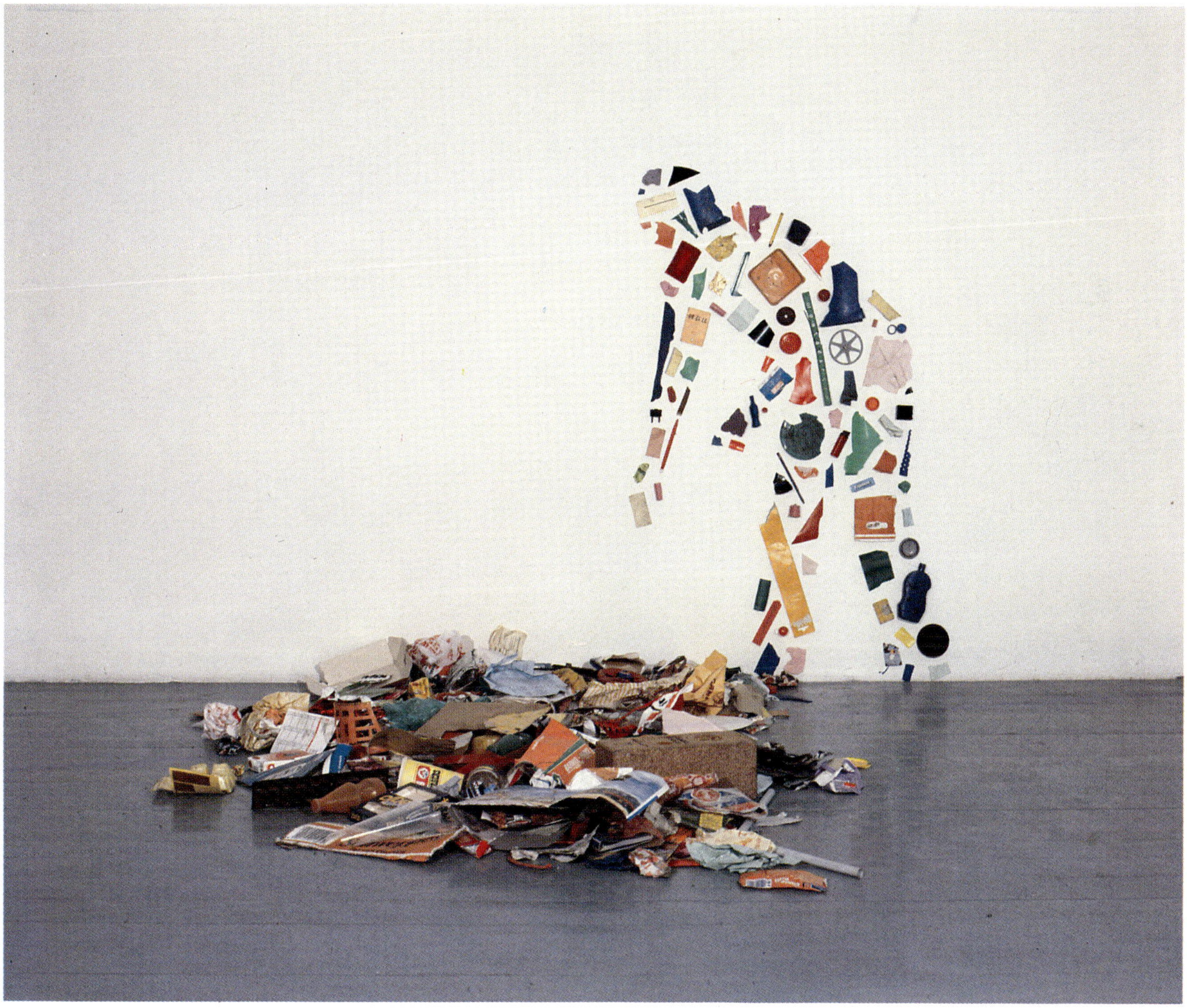

Tony Cragg, *Self Portrait* 1981
Courtesy Bernd Klüser, Munich

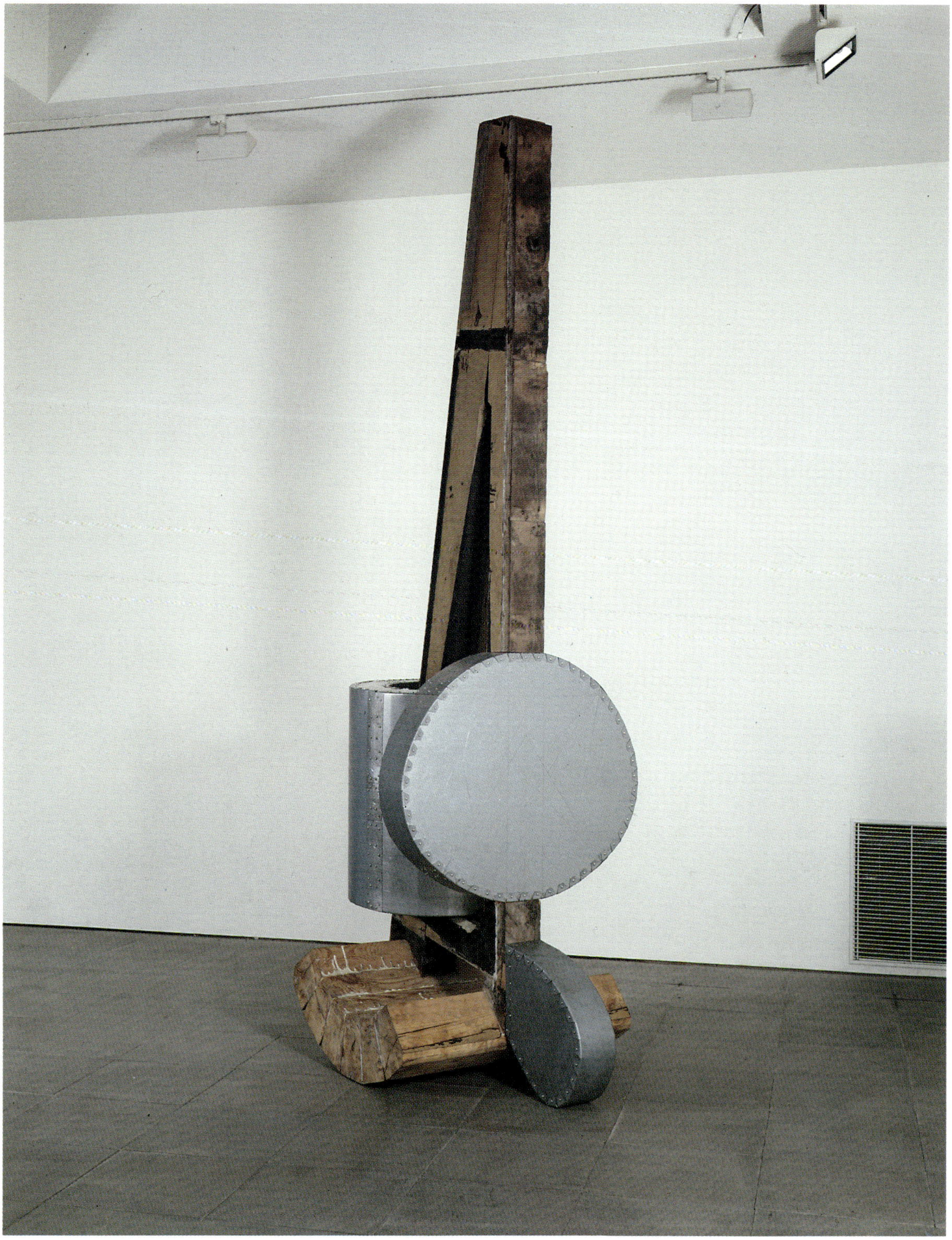

5 Richard Deacon, *Troubled Water* 1987

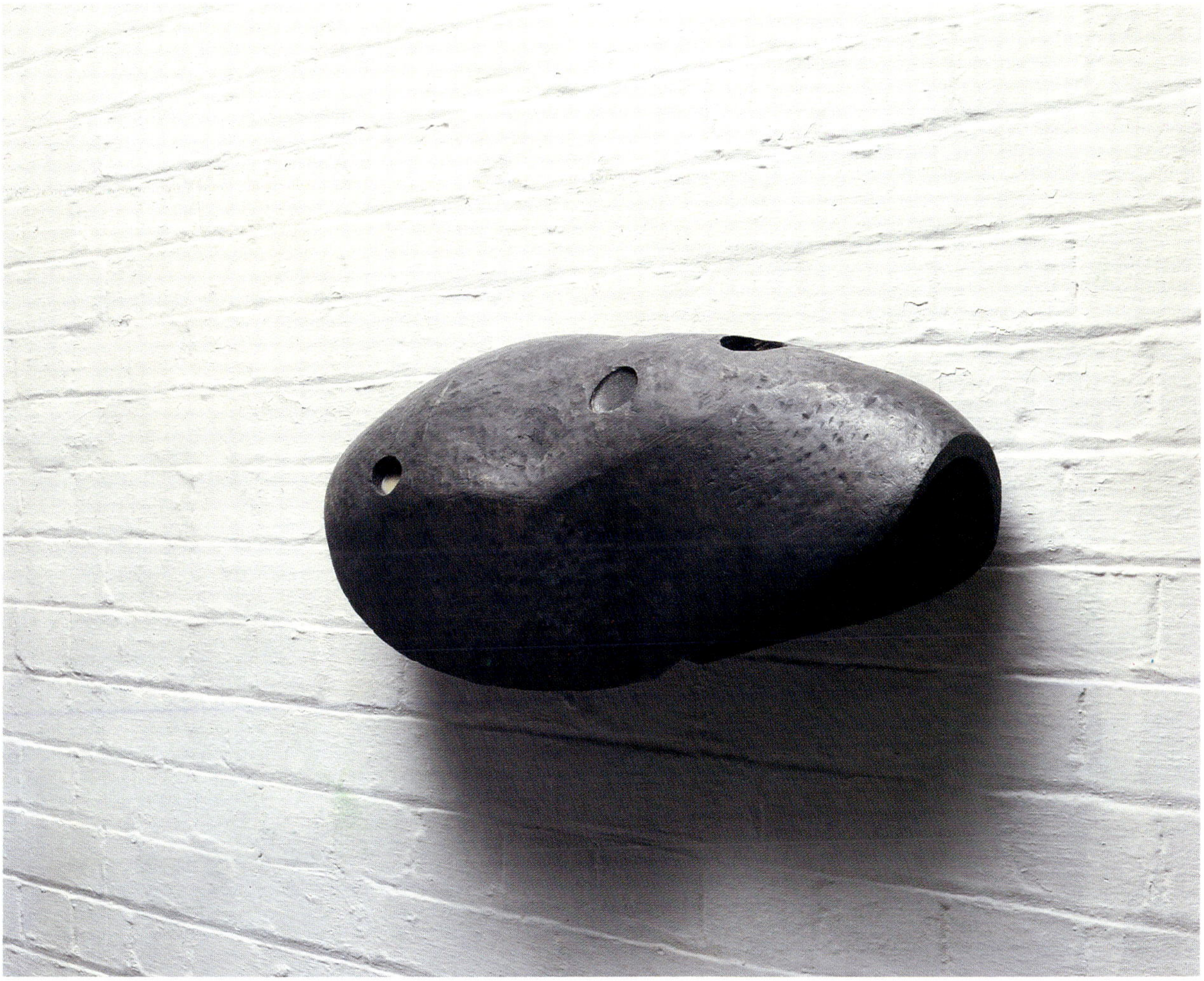

51 Alison Wilding, *Beneath the Skin* 1986

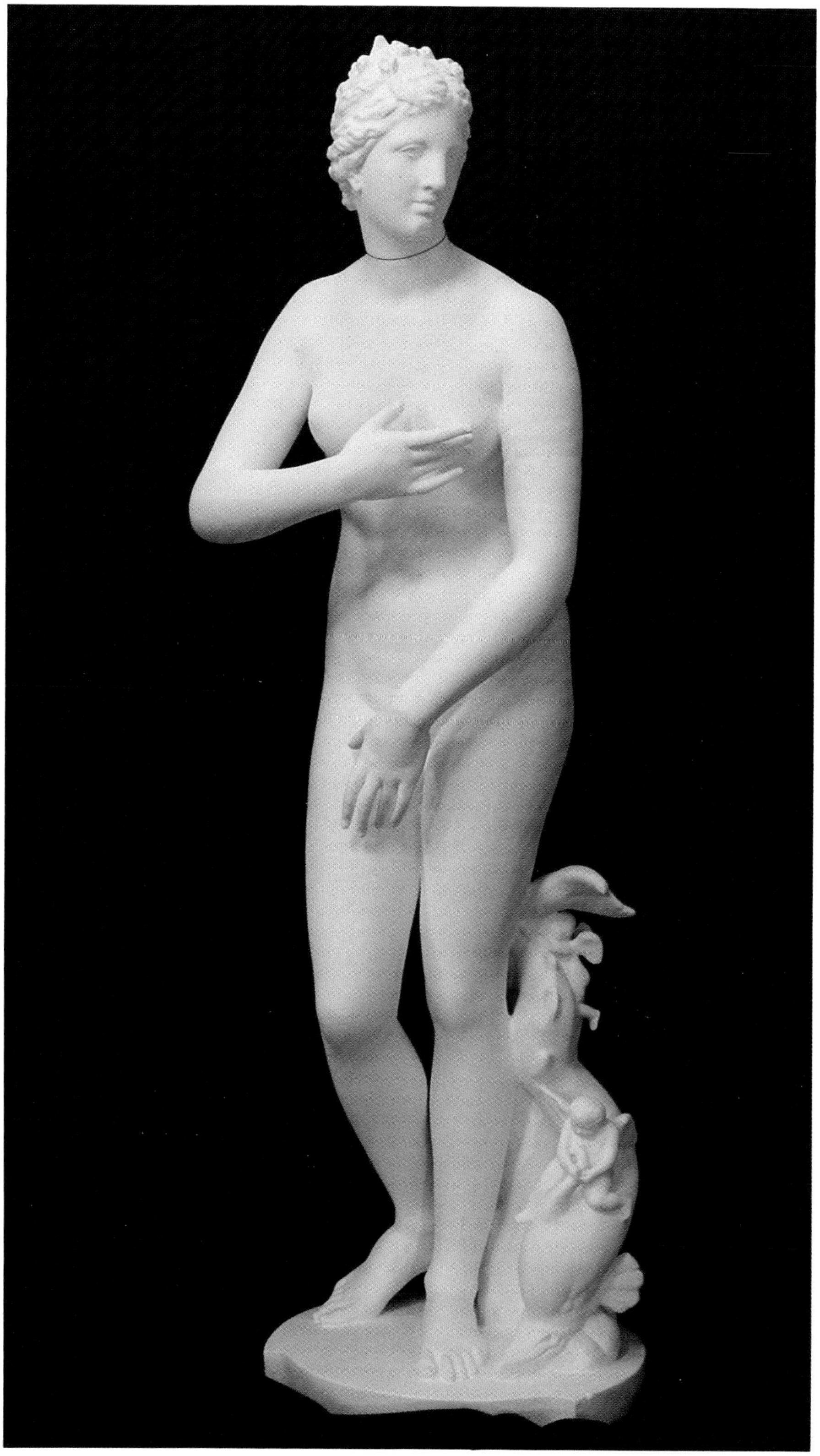

10 Ian Hamilton Finlay, *Aphrodite of The Terror*, 1987
In The Terror, a red silk thread worn around the neck intimated that friends or relatives had been lost to the guillotine. Aphrodite (or Venus) being a goddess, the same adornment signifies the loss of Olympian relatives and refers not the Revolution's 'Sublime' Terror but rather to the subsequent, secular Terror directed against The Ideal. *Ian Hamilton Finlay.*

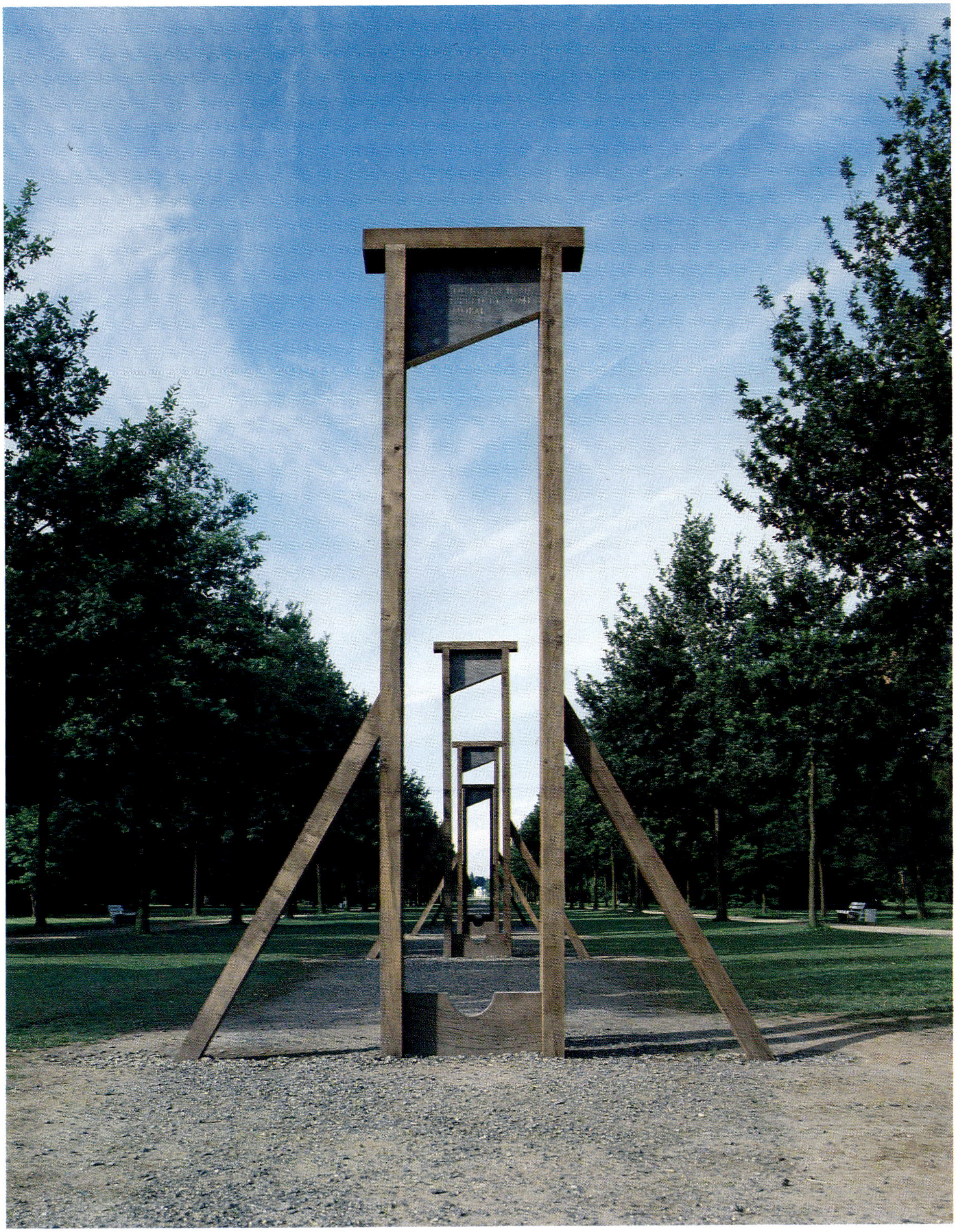

Ian Hamilton Finlay, *A View to The Temple*
Documenta 8, Kassel, 1987

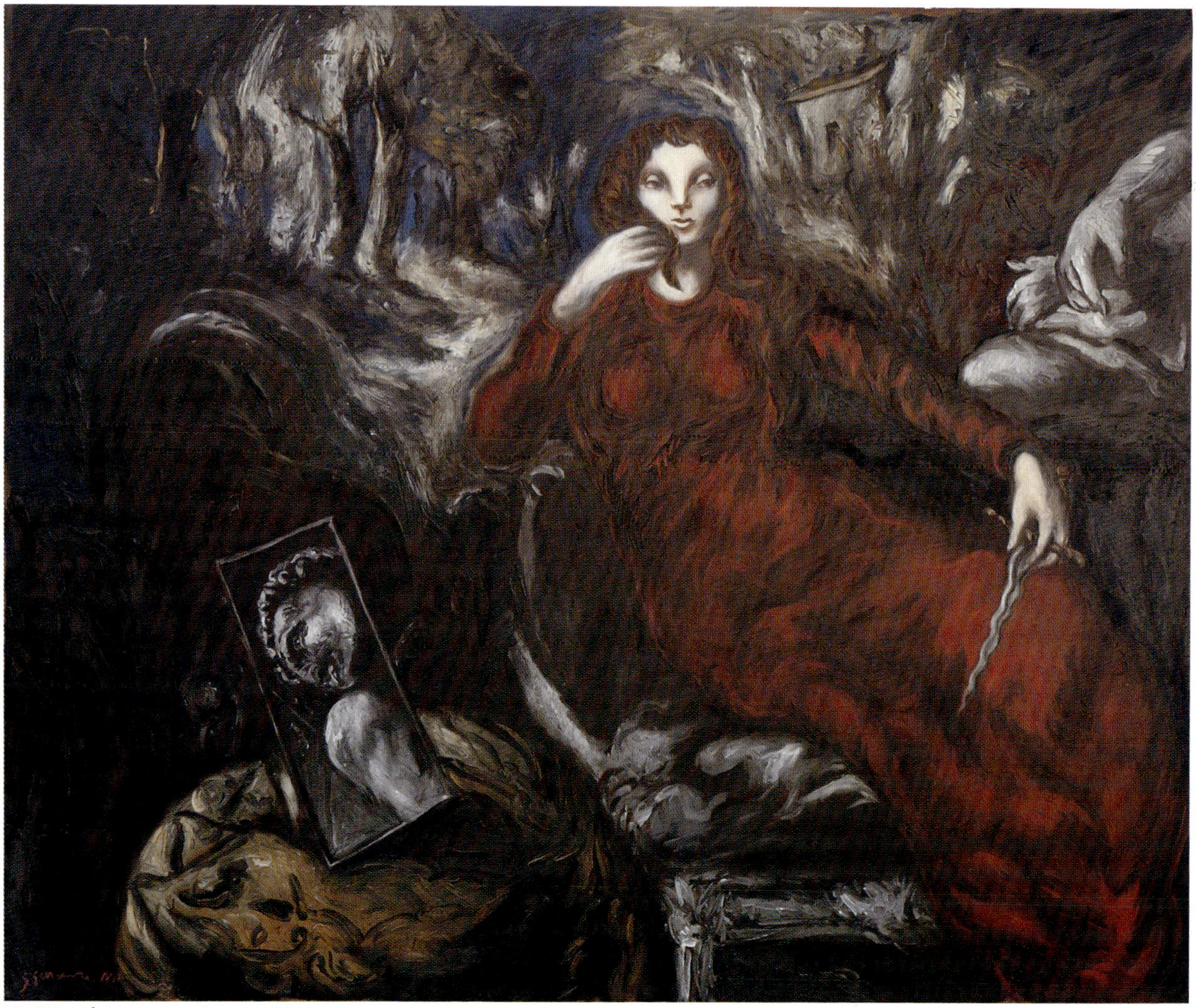

12 Gérard Garouste, *Lucrèce* 1983

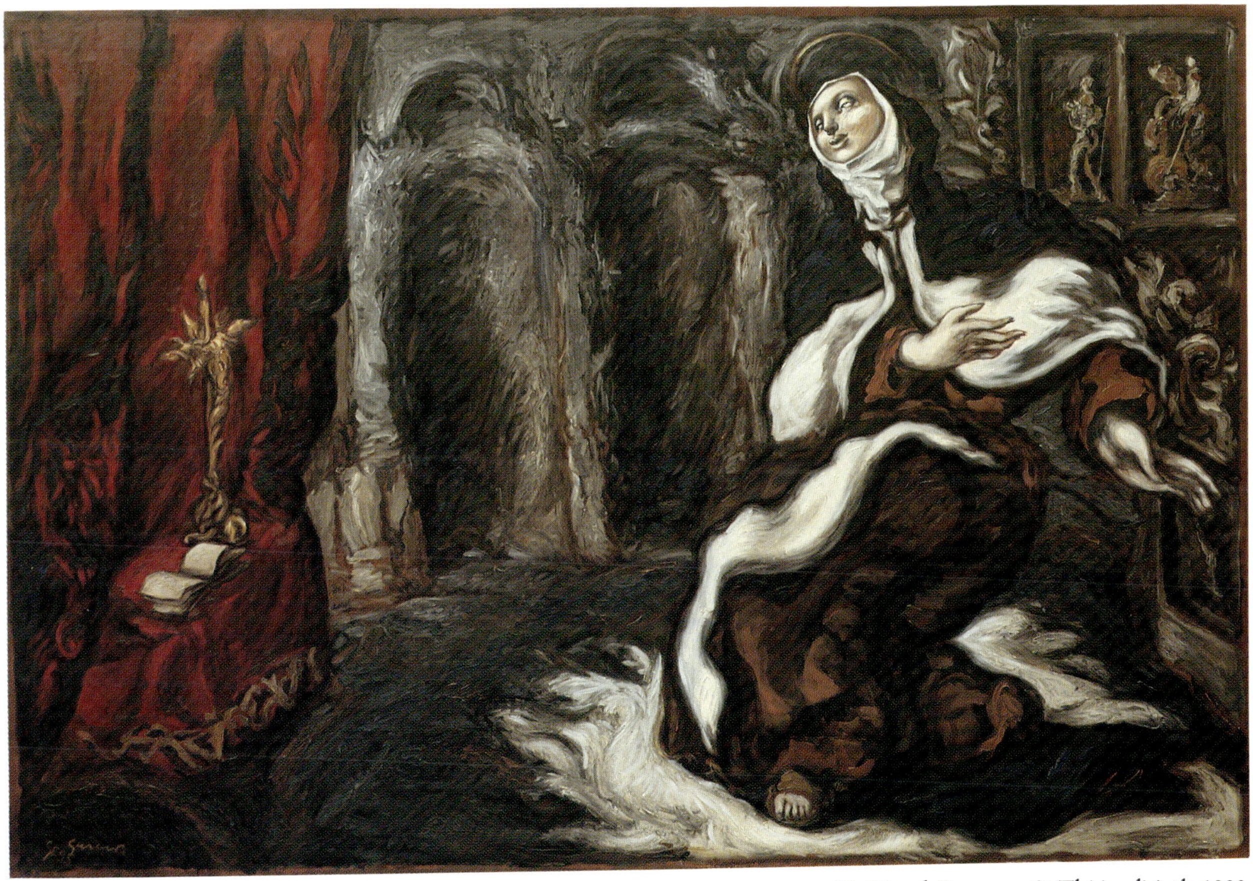

11 Gérard Garouste, *St Thérèse d'Avila* 1983

Stephan Huber, installation at the Galerie Dany Keller, ▷
Munich (1986)

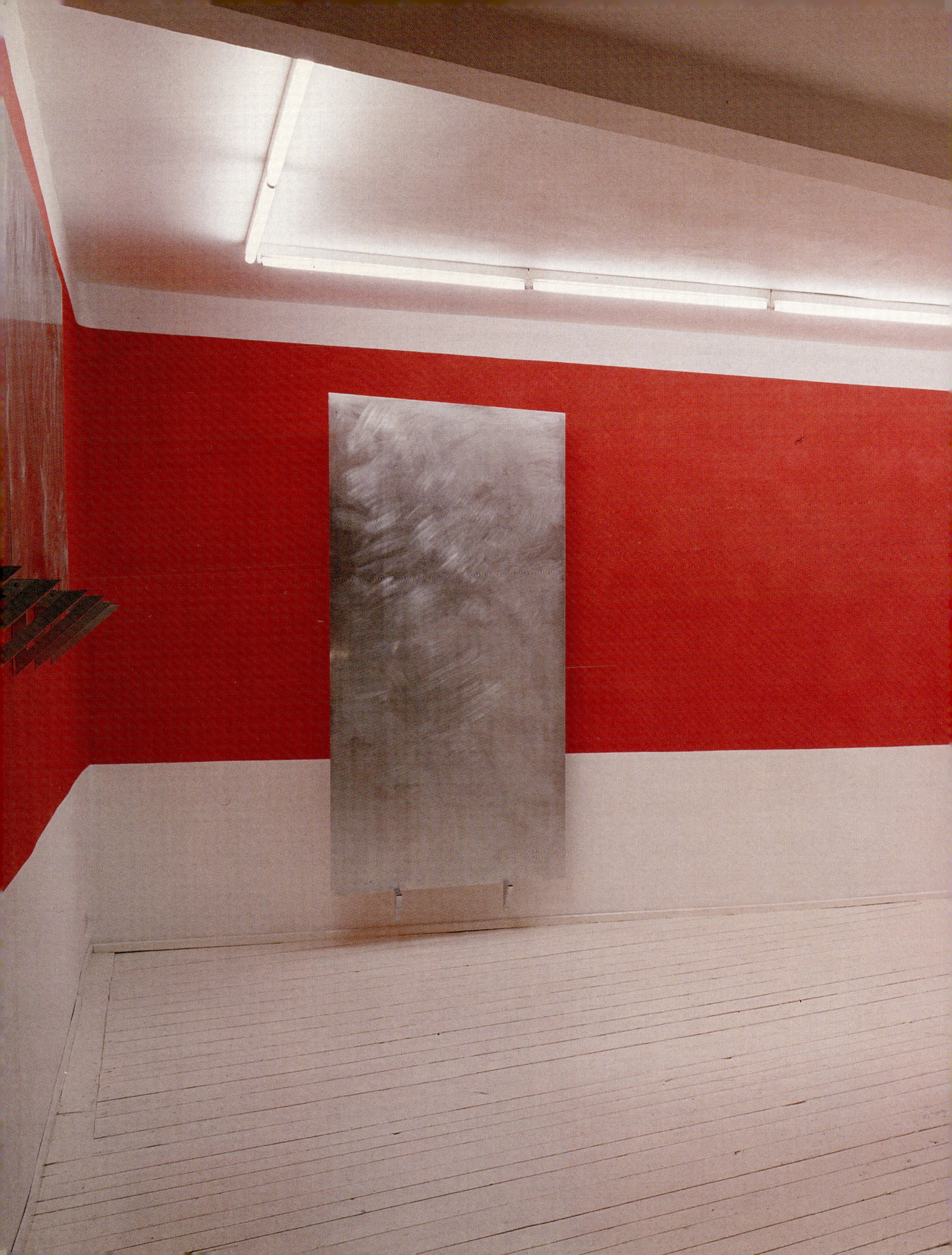

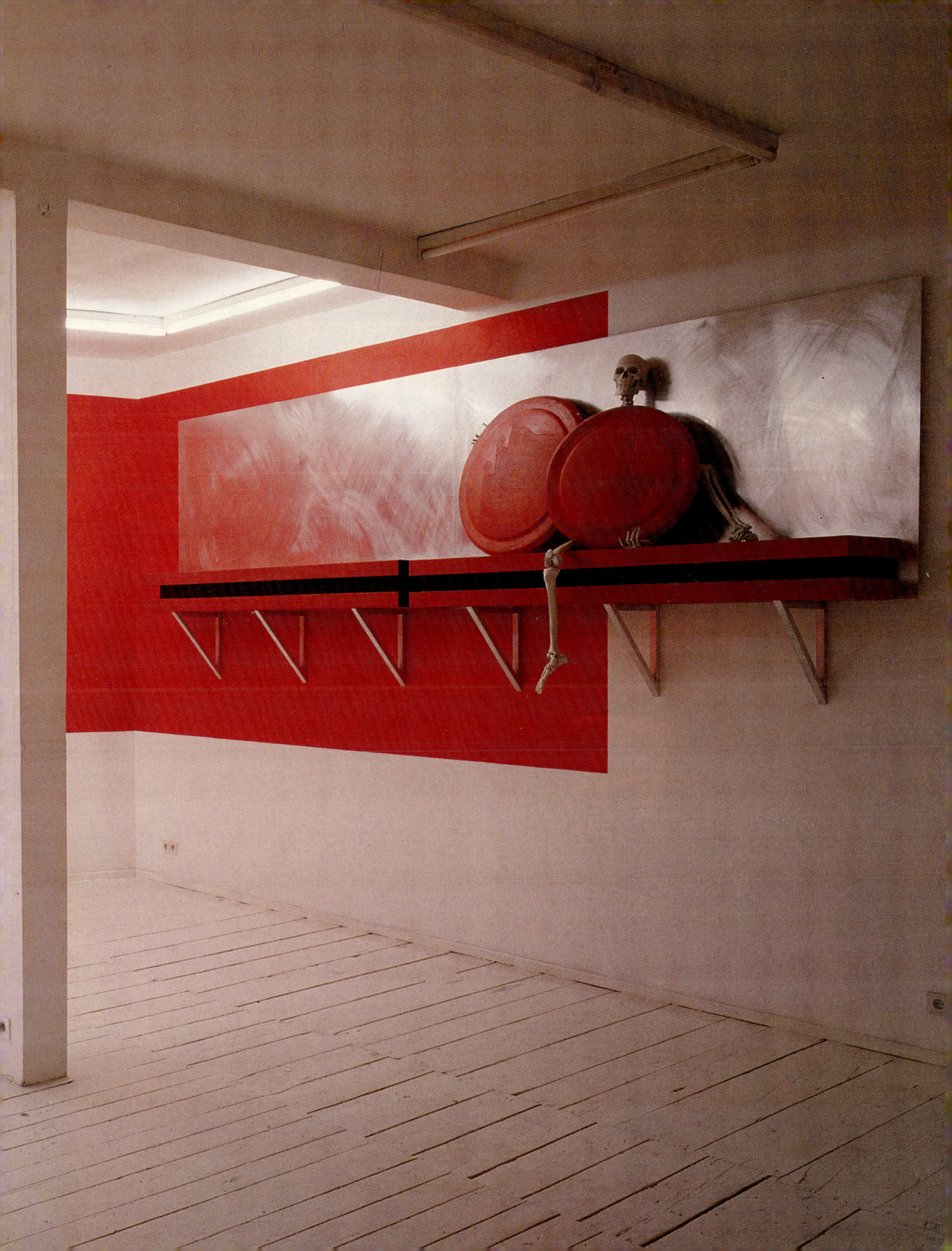

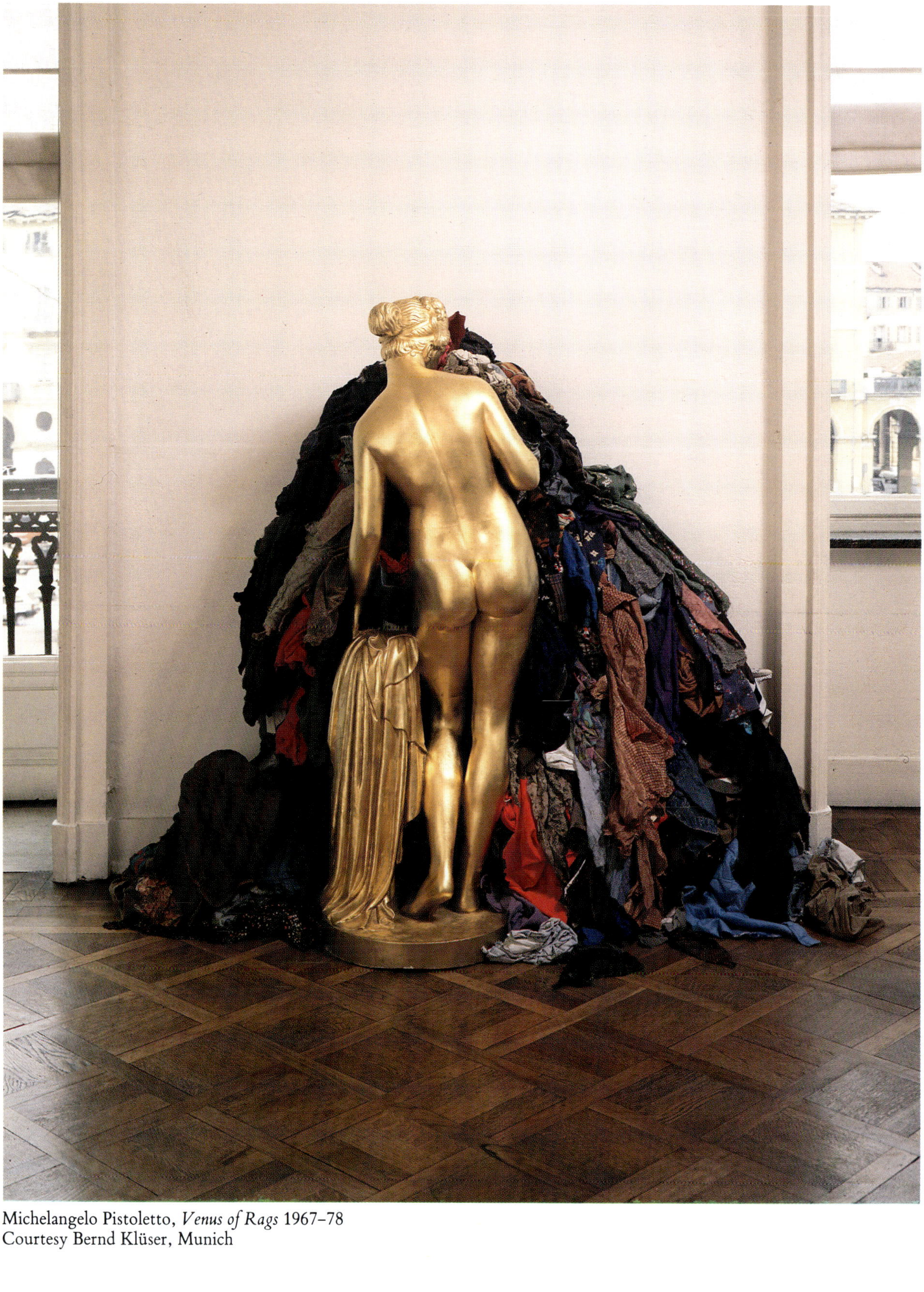

Michelangelo Pistoletto, *Venus of Rags* 1967–78
Courtesy Bernd Klüser, Munich

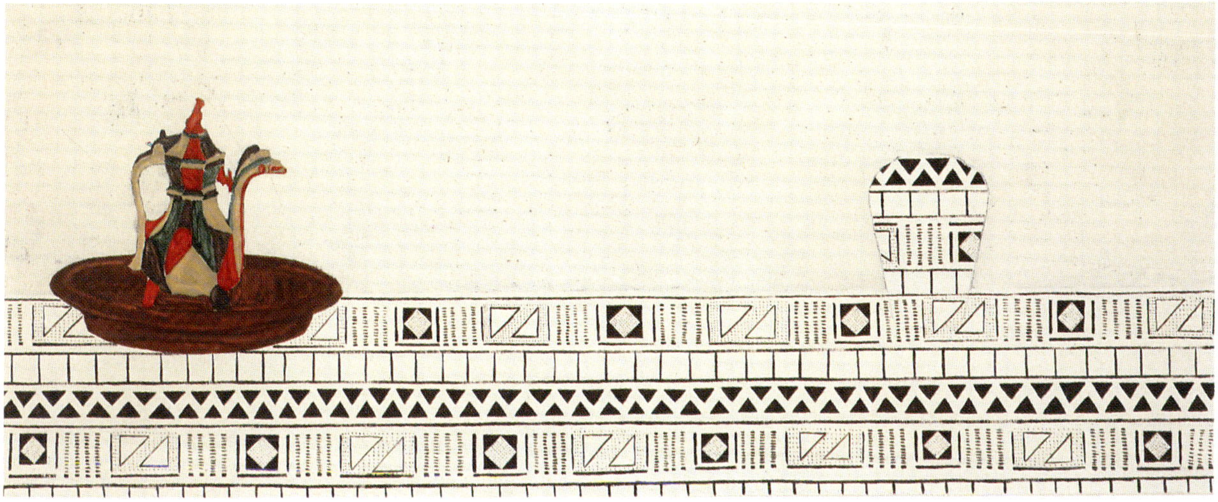

19 Axel Kasseböhmer, *Still Life with Ornament* 1987

Sol LeWitt, *Wall Drawings Tilted Forms*
colour ink wash
First drawn by: Andrea Marescalchi and Anthony Sansotta
First installation: Yvon Lambert Gallery, Paris, October 1987 ▷

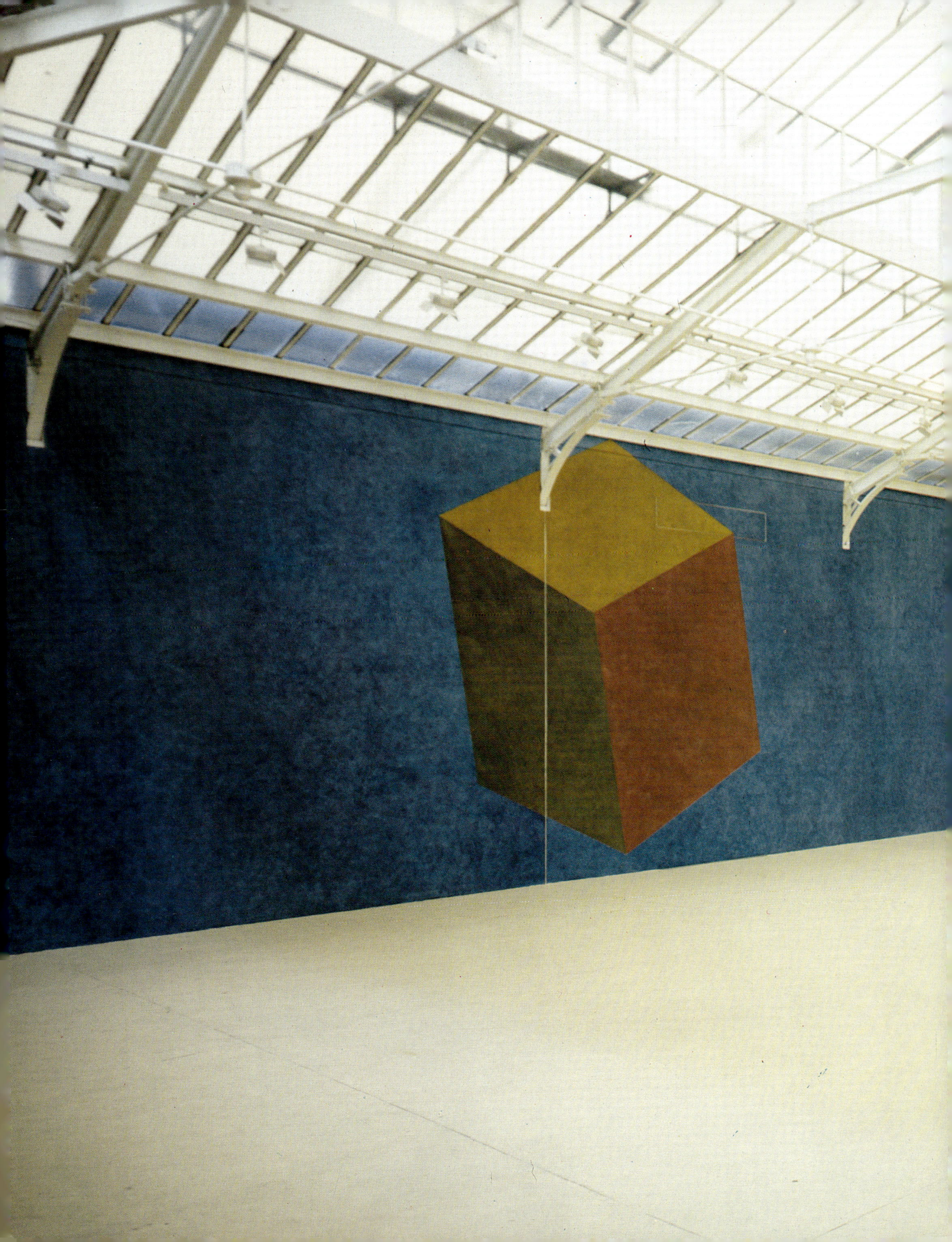

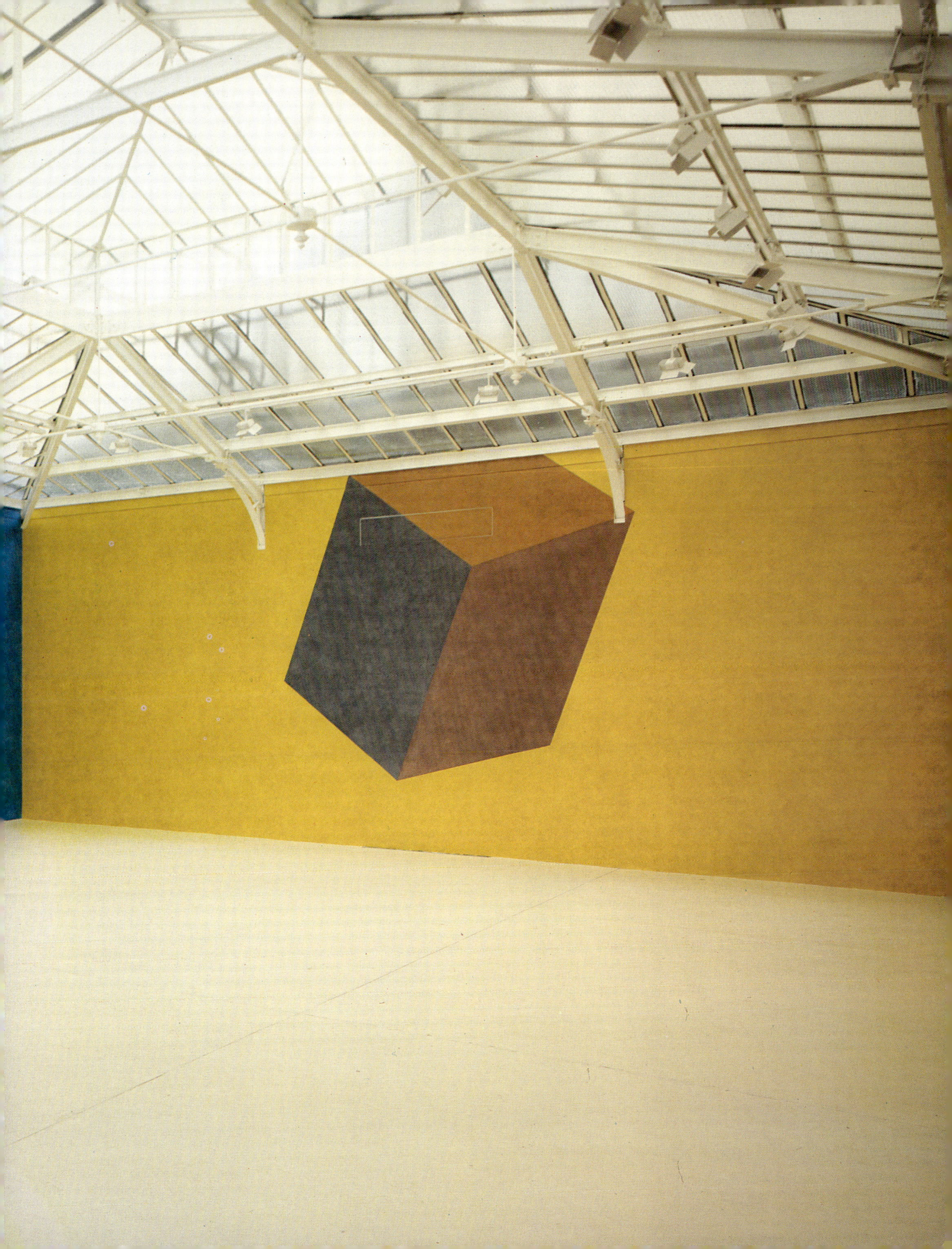

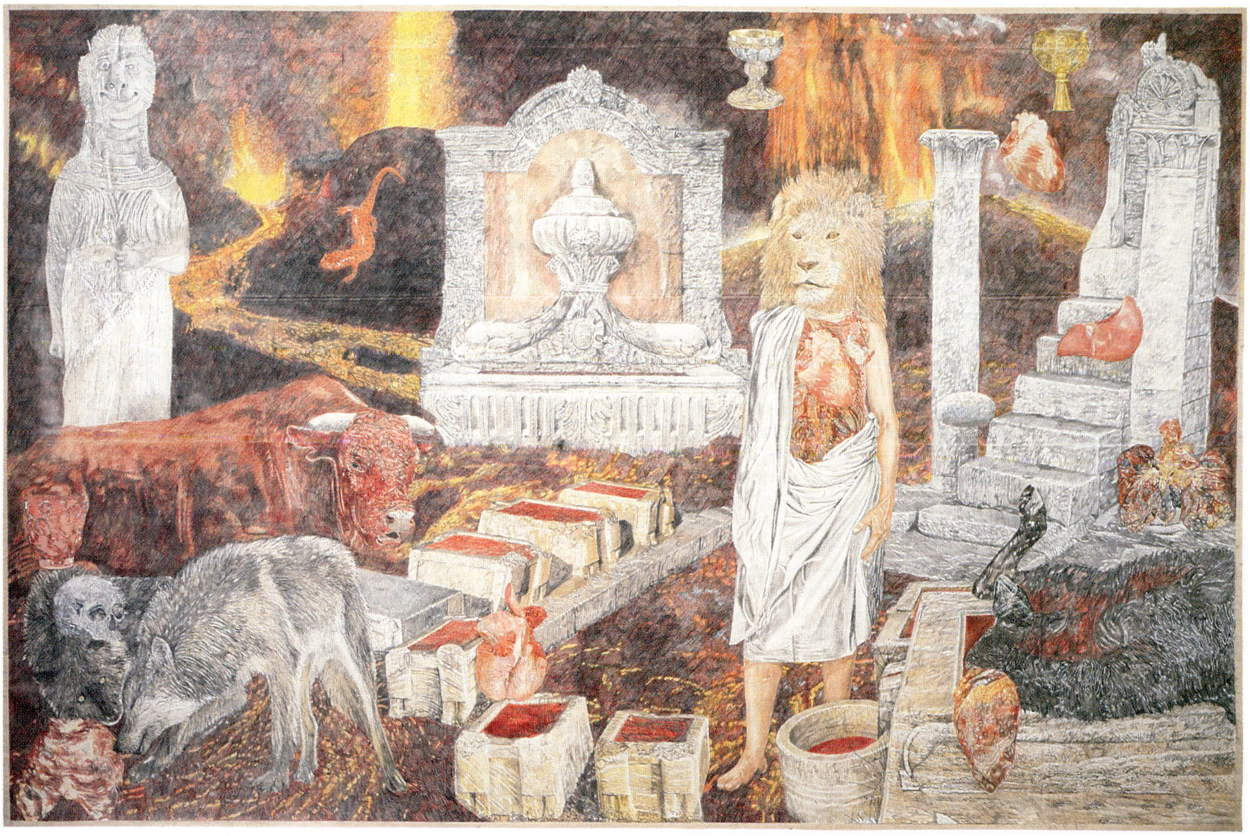
22 Ann McCoy, *Coeur de Lion* 1985

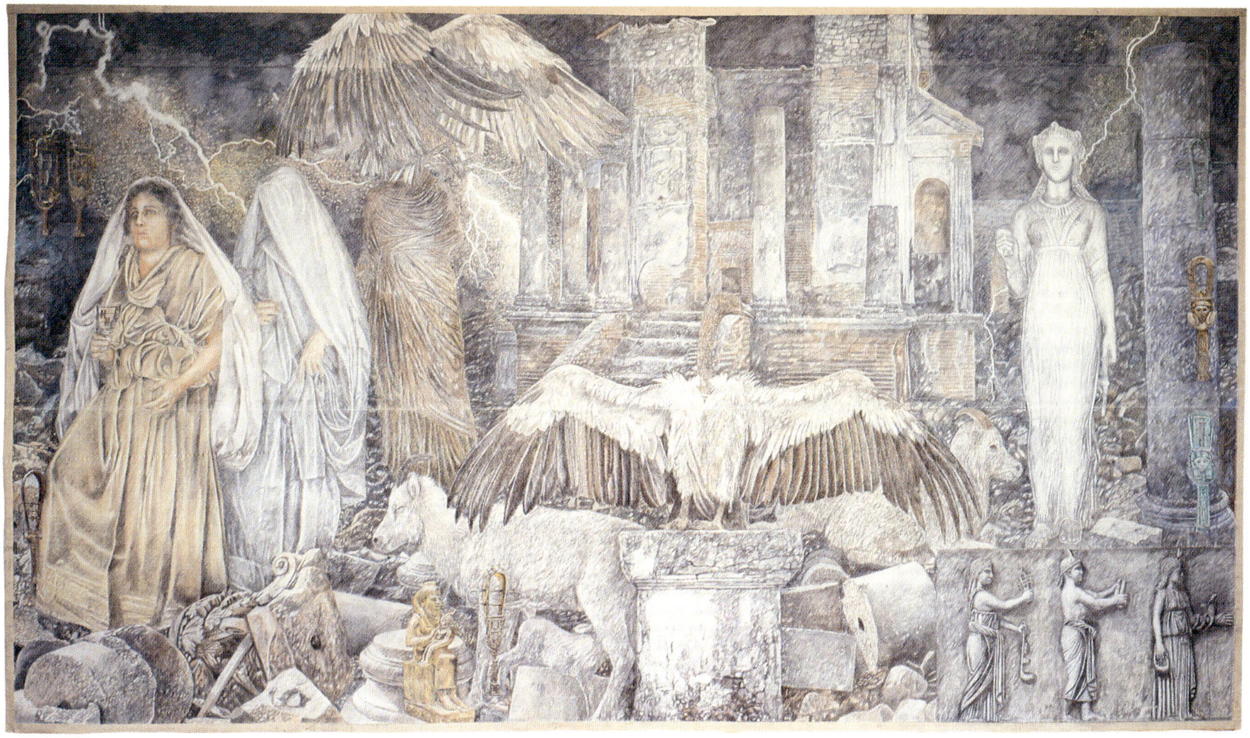

25 Ann McCoy, *Temple of Isis, Pompeii* 1987

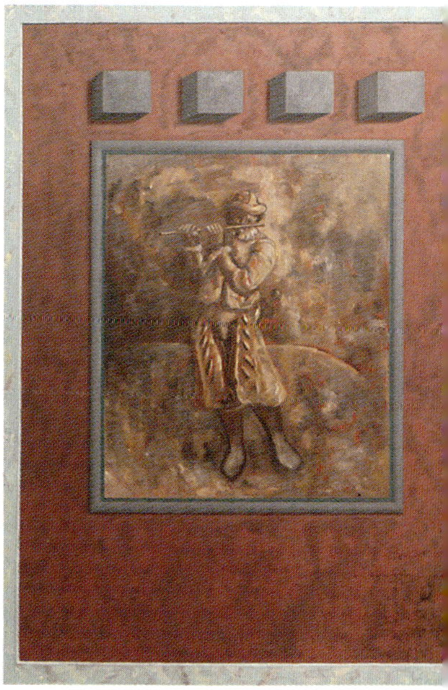

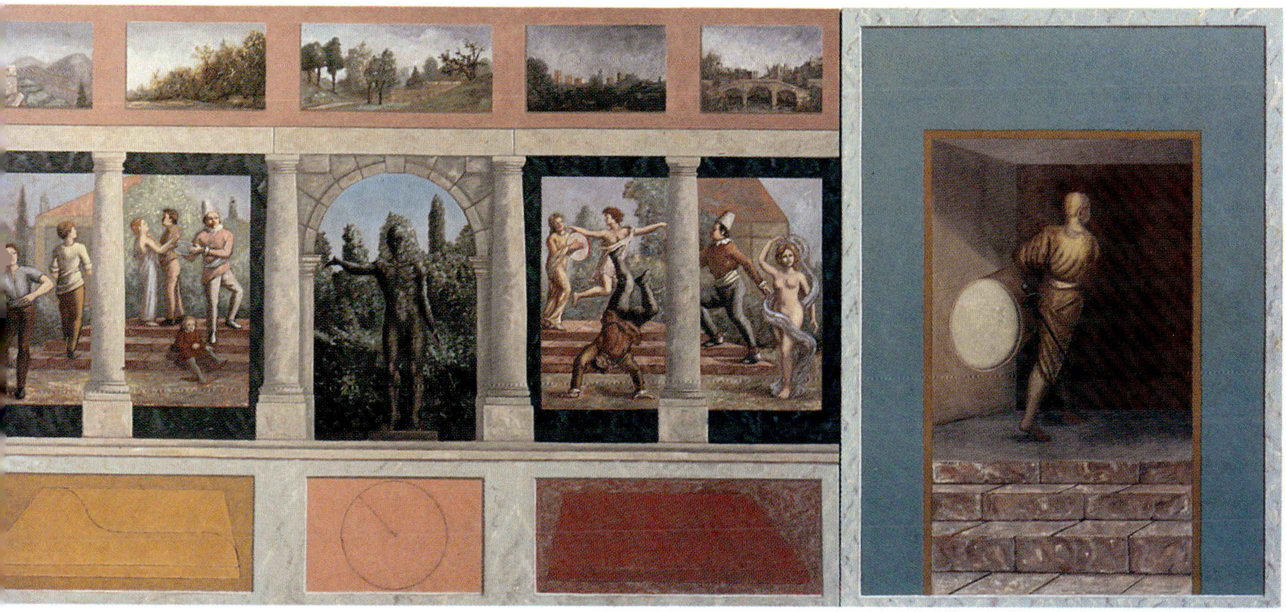

26 Stephen McKenna, *The Tuscan Order* 1987

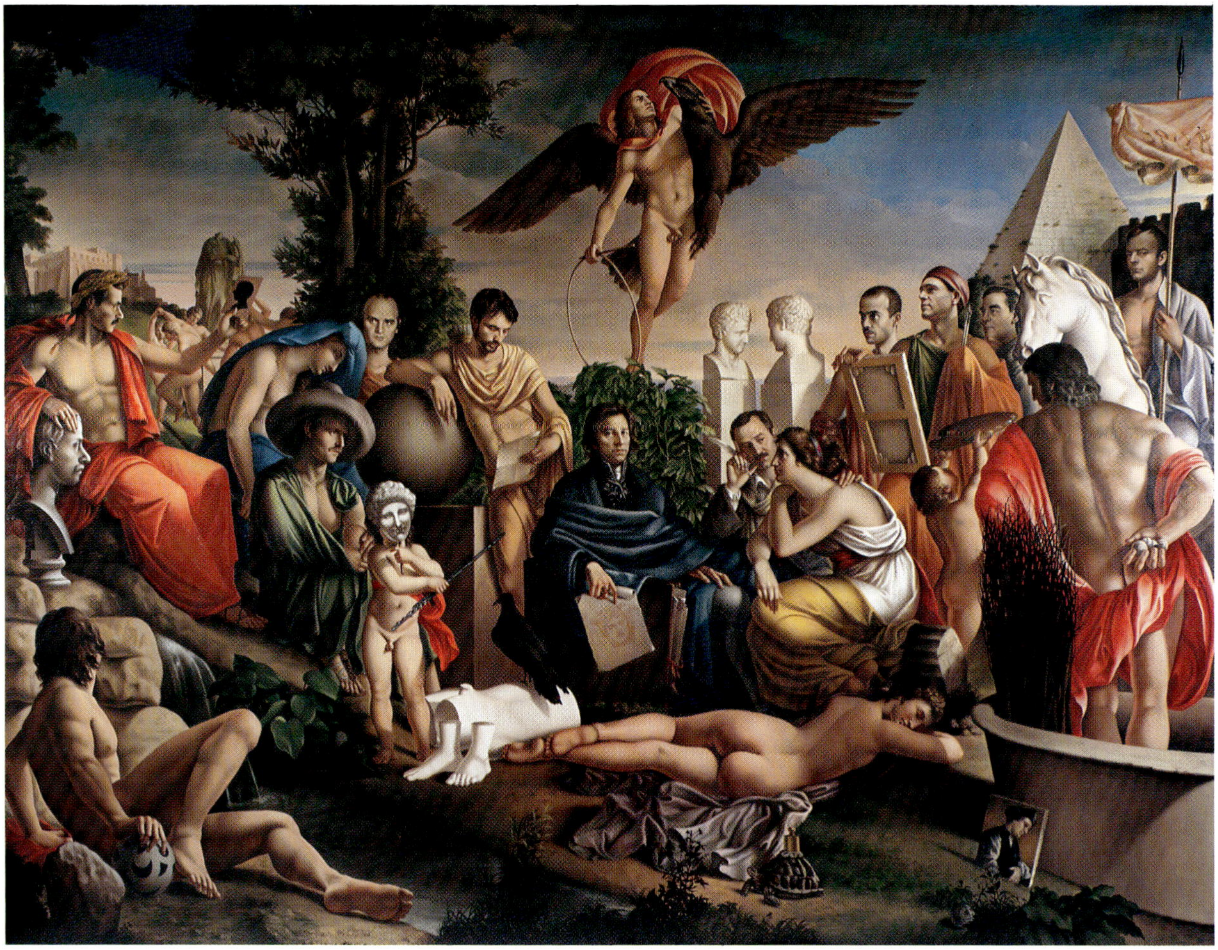

Carlo Maria Mariani, *The Constellation of Leo* 1981–82
Courtesy Gian Enzo Sperone, Rome

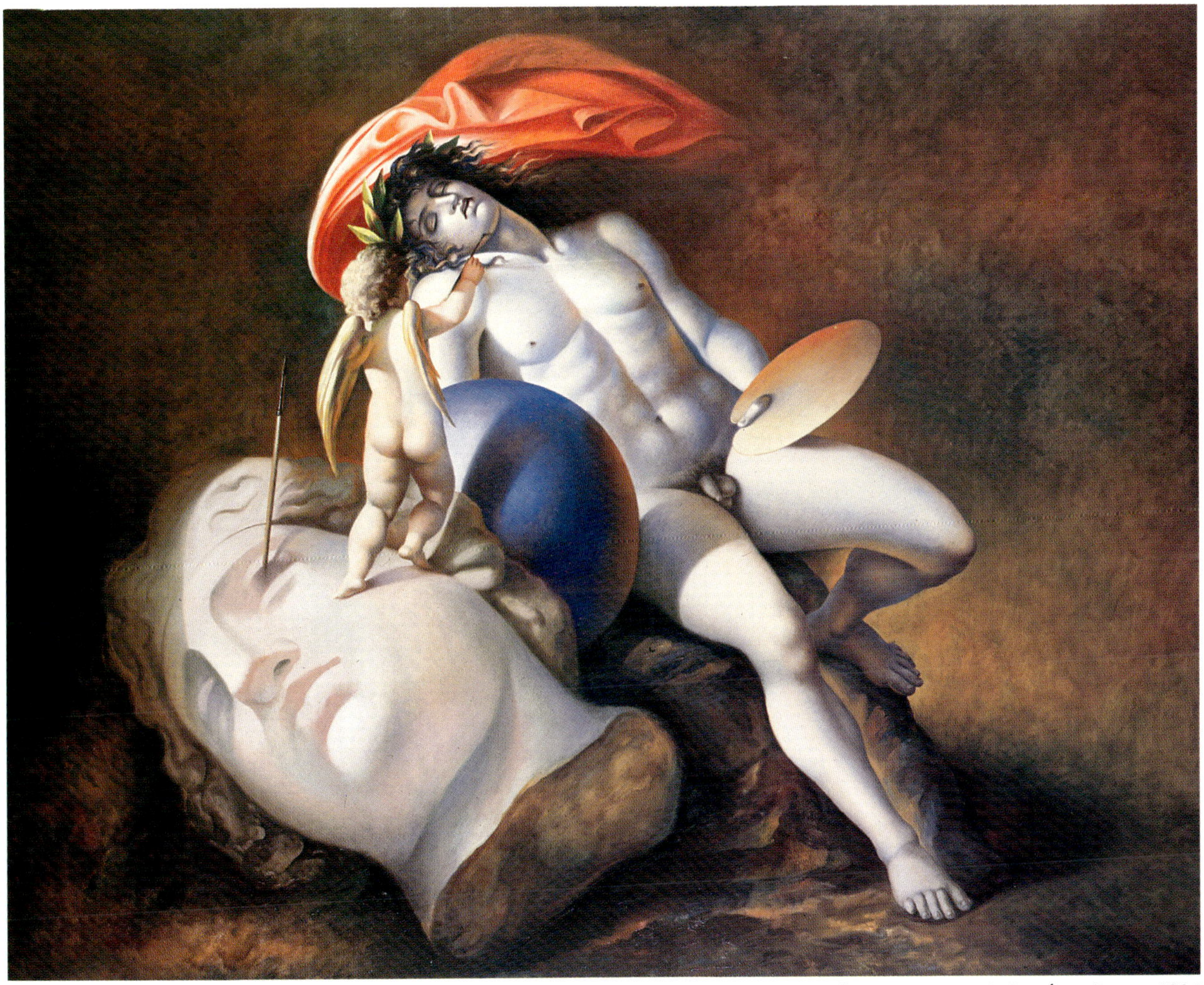

33 Carlo Maria Mariani, *Prophetic Dream* 1984

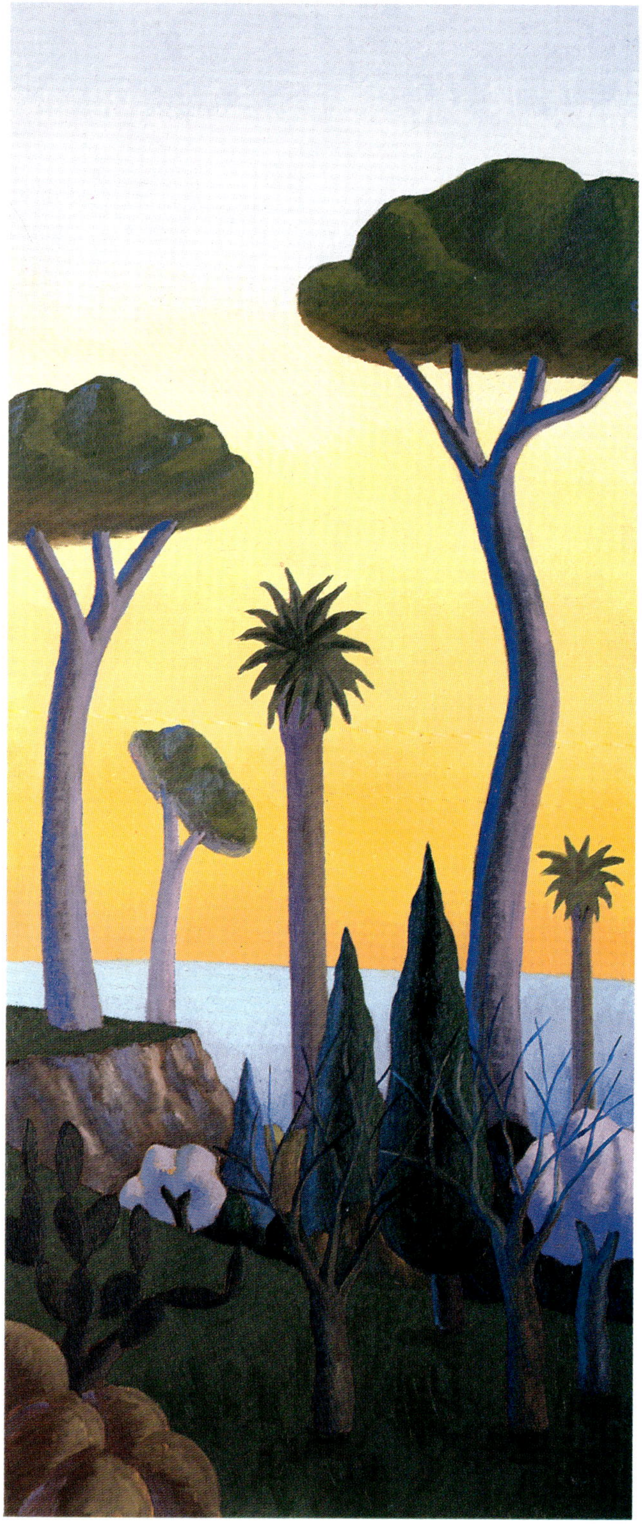

39 Salvo, *Untitled* 1986

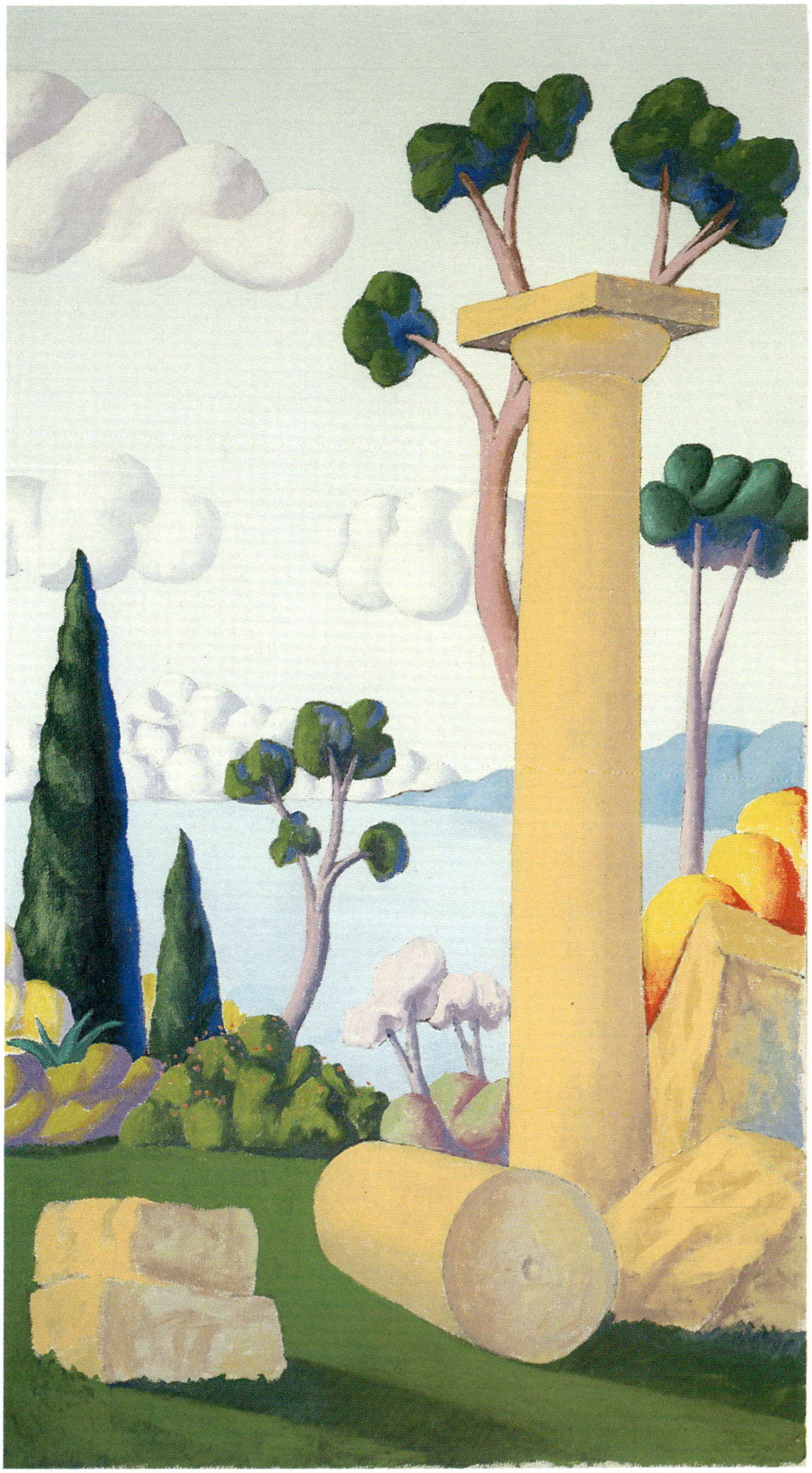

35 Salvo, *Untitled* 1984

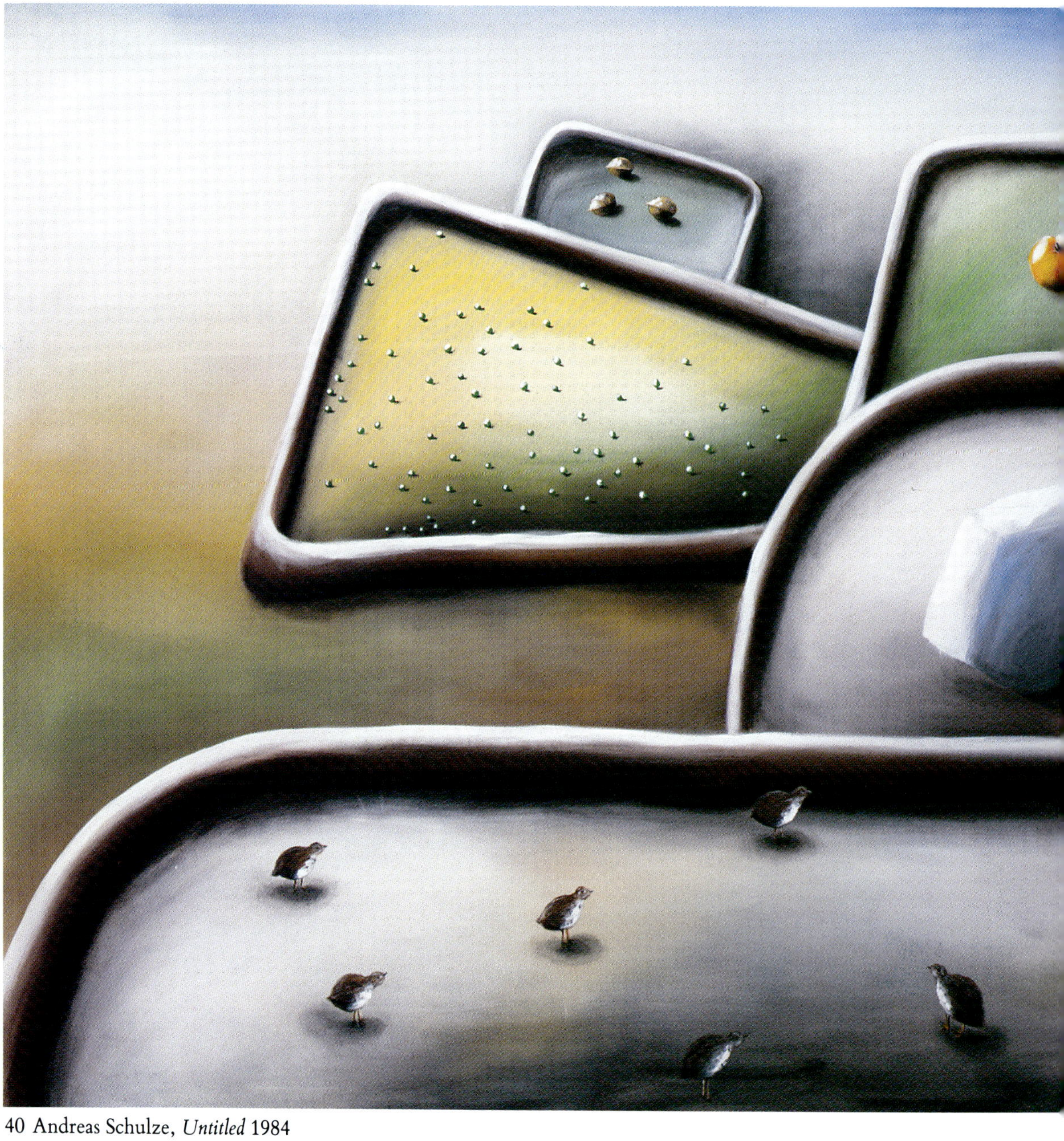

40 Andreas Schulze, *Untitled* 1984

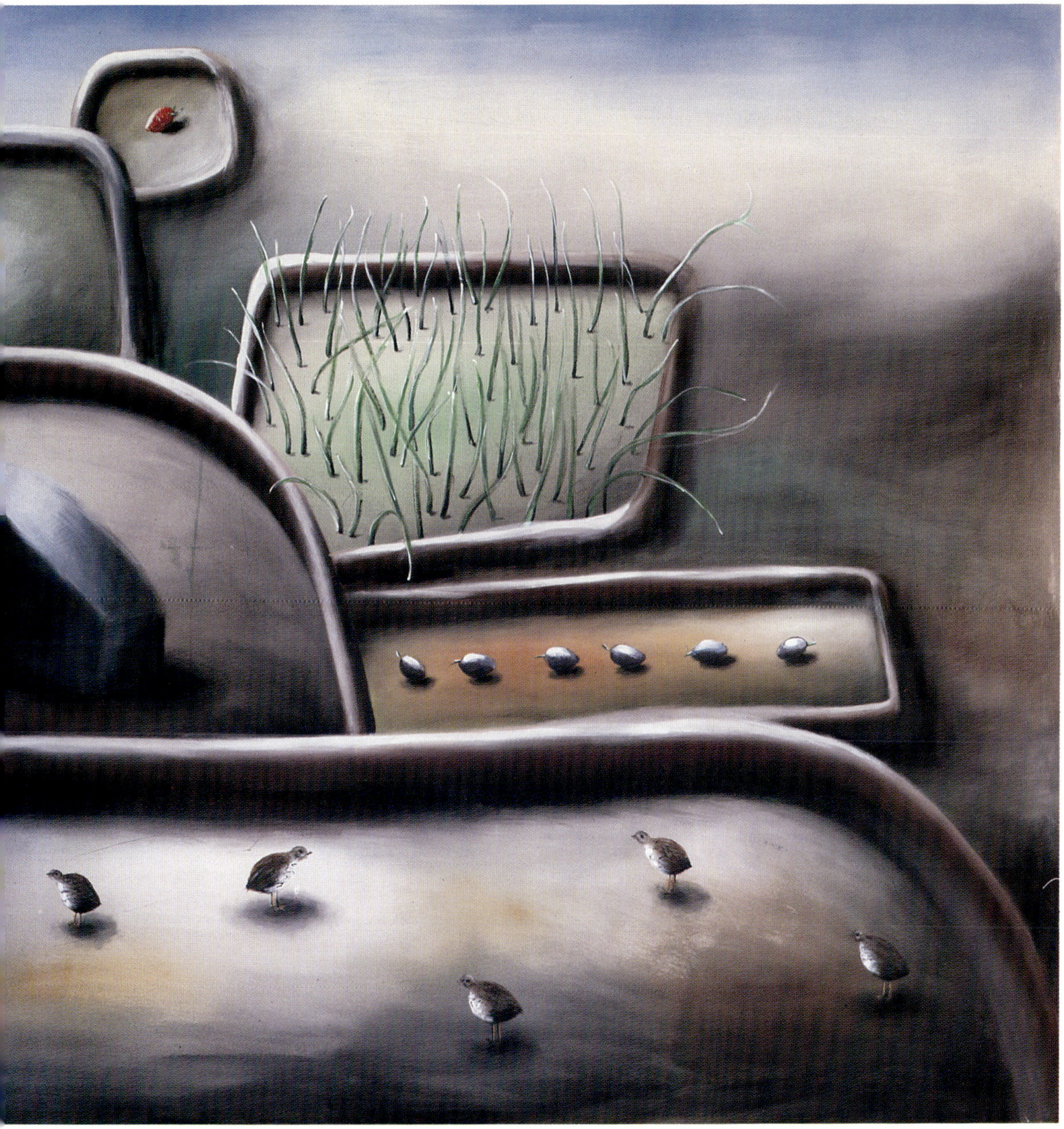

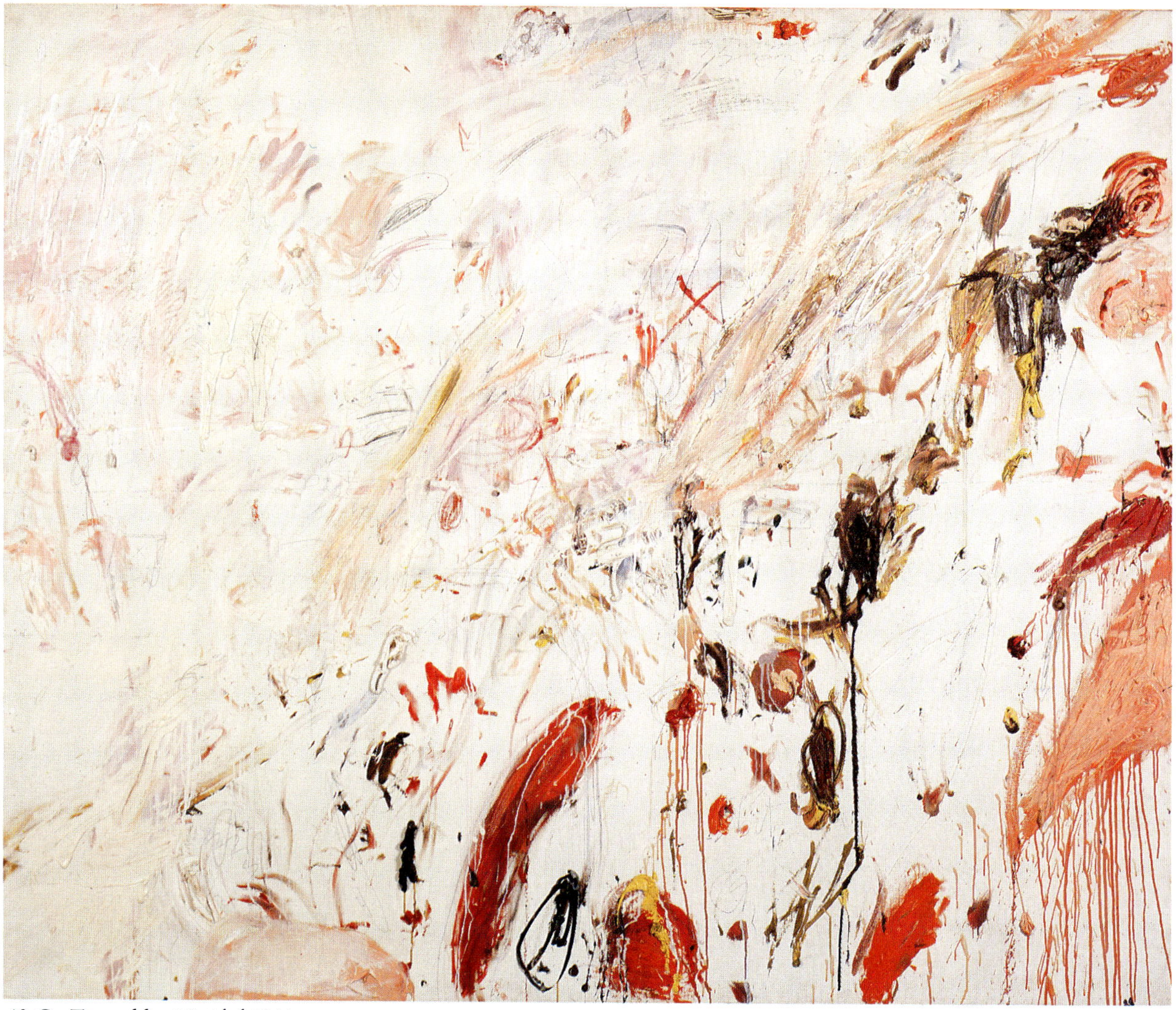

43 Cy Twombly, *Untitled* 1961

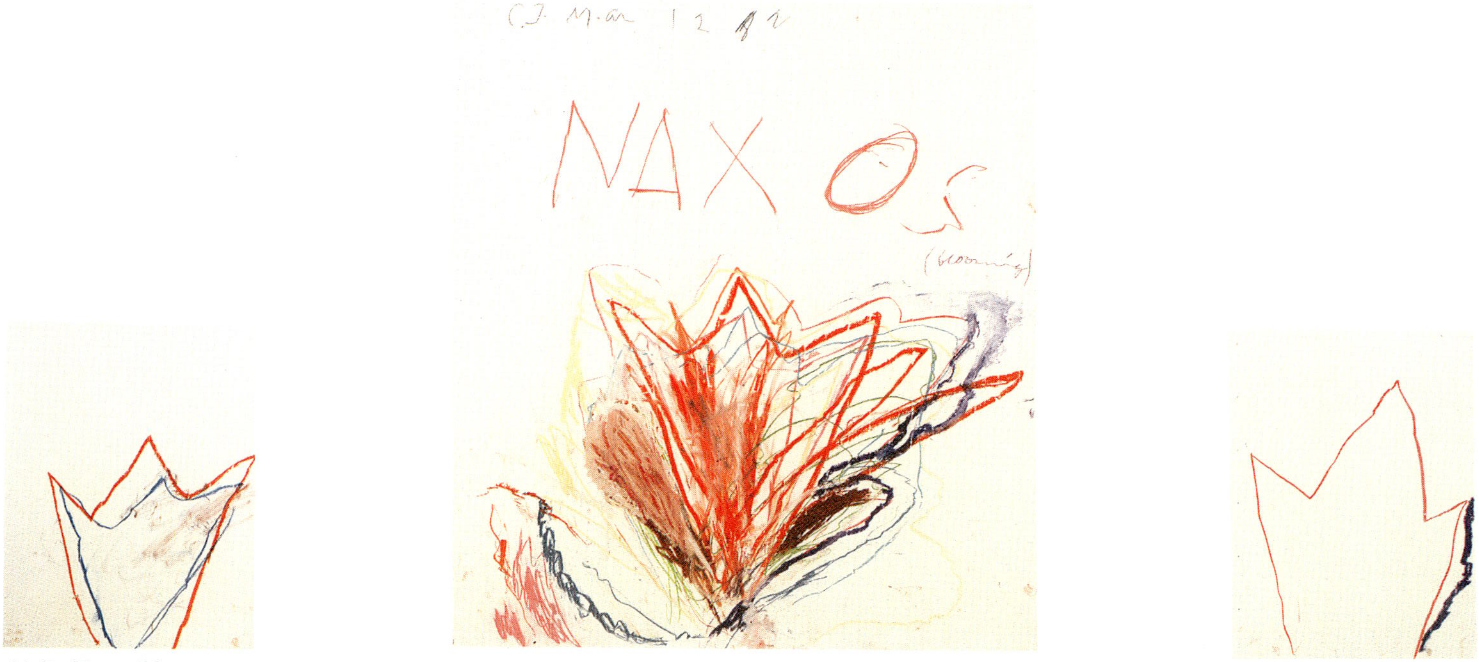

46 Cy Twombly, *Naxos* 1982

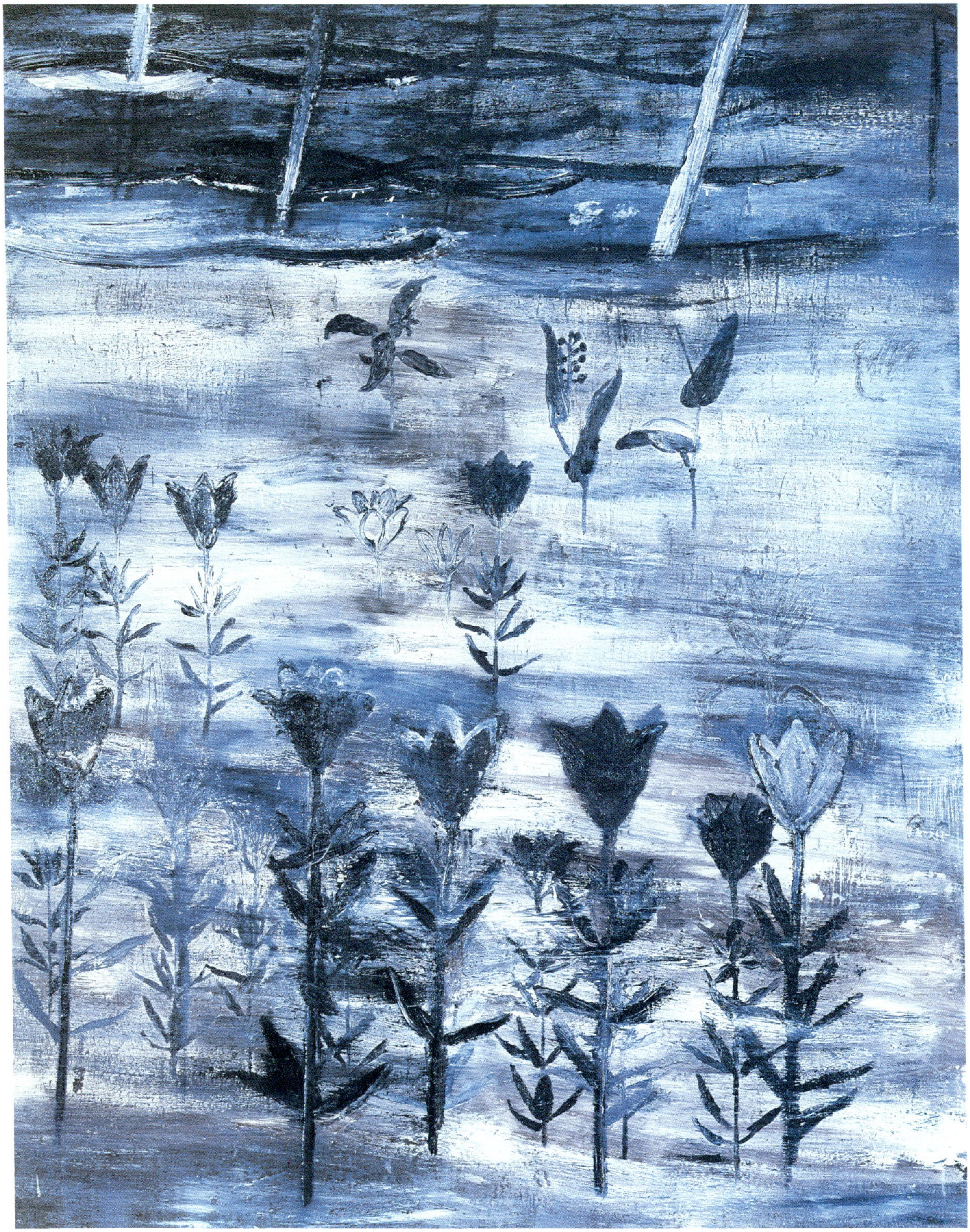

53 Terry Winters, *Theophrastus Garden I* 1982

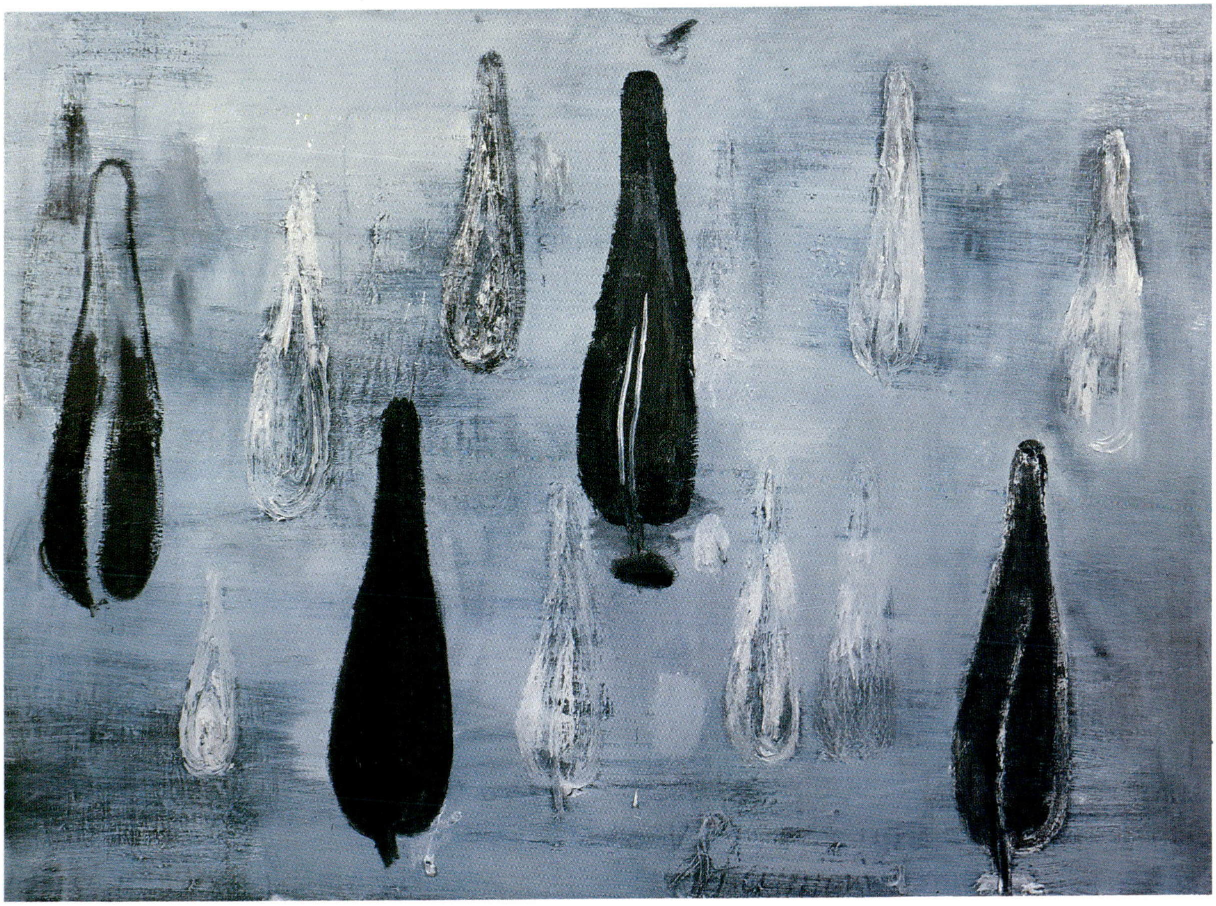

54 Terry Winters, *Stamina II* 1982

Isolde Wawrin, *Object* 1986 with *Untitled Drawing* 1987 ▷
(47: detail)

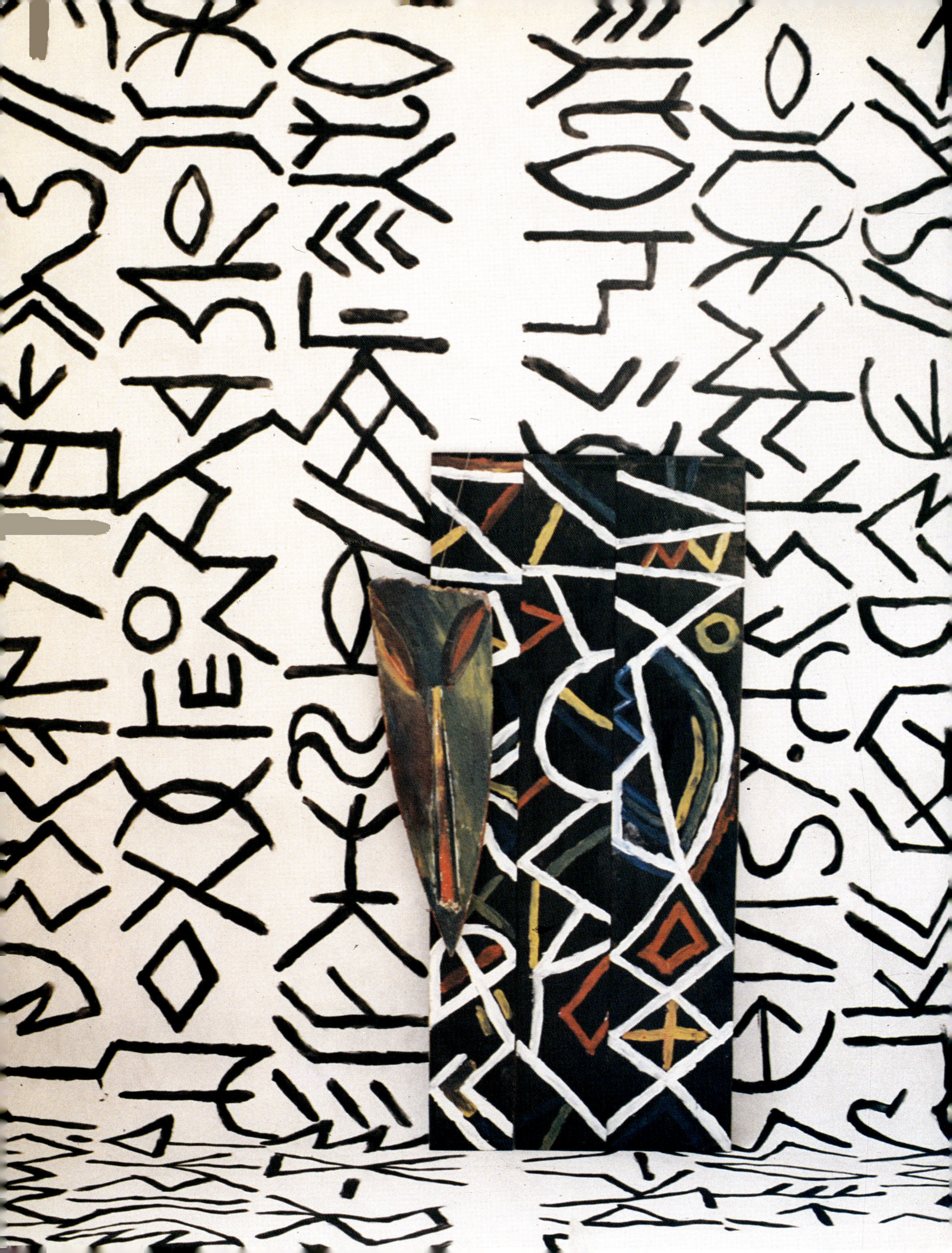

Dear Michael Compton

Lets use the Giant Black
Figure for Edinburgh.
Please contact michael
for that.

yrs JLByars

MARY BOONE
GALLERY 417 WEST BROADWAY
NYC NY 10012 431-1818

JAMES LEE BYARS

Beauty goes Avant-garde

A solitary spirit, James Lee Byars wanders freely in the domains of art and philosophy, heedless of the boundaries that are meant to separate one from the other. He rejects the limits of both: as an artist he experiences inwardly the ability to decipher the tension of a gesture, of the sign-signal, an ability that is denied the philosopher; as a philosopher he has the ability to work out concepts by elevating them to ultimate symbols that can render the intuitive process visible. His is an intuition that defies time and, by affirming all the implications it is capable of containing, this intuition affirms all the expressive tension that art alone, and in this case its archetypal-spiritual aspect, is capable of calling forth.

It is not given to the philosopher to experience inwardly the tension of the artistic creative process except as the tensions operating between the diverse motivations lying at the root of the work. And this is why he will never be able to distinguish the fragility of expression of a mere artistic endeavour from the vigour of a genuine work of art. It is not given to the philosopher to peer into the heavens and to discern among the clouds the outlines of the countenance of some benevolent spirit; he can merely read, comprehend and interpret its thoughts along lines that are credible.

To be an artist, however, subsumes the ability to be a visionary. To be an artist includes for Byars the ability to philosophise about his own gestures, to conceive of time within the context of a given era, with all that this implies. And more than ever, in this case, being in time is equivalent to being out of time, to standing outside contemporary fashions and passions.

For the Dadaists art and life were one in the same way that the idea and the work of art were one; for the Surrealists—in a happy but not very realistic definition by Dali—art was "a colour snapshot of concrete irrationality". In other words, it took its inspiration from the realities of the dreamworld. Byars is far removed from the spirit of Dadaism and of Surrealism, bearing as they do too strongly the stamp of their own time. In fact, Byars is the negation of both these movements. But if from Dadaism he has absorbed the equation, art is life, by adding it to the spiritual element inherent in the work of artists such as Malevich, Kandinsky and Klee, from Surrealism he has taken the ability to give voice by the principle of automatism to the depths of the unconscious. Both Dadaism and Surrealism, insofar as they were movements inspired by ideas, go beyond the artists who were the means of expressing these ideas in their works. Like Duchamp, Byars limits himself to living out his own aesthetic nature; like Ernst he throws his energy into expanding the confines of his expressivity by charging with suggestive tension the objects he touches.

But, unlike Duchamp, Byars does not affirm an aesthetics of visual indifference, the total anaesthesia of the eye; his is an aesthetics of beauty as visual participation in the perfection of the object, rich in the myriad implications it is capable of containing, implications that are not only aesthetic but much more: Newton as scientist demonstrated how mathematics, alchemy and theology are the single compendium of a unified body of research; Malevich as artist confirms that science and art have no boundaries because what is known has no limit. And moreover, unlike Ernst, Byars does not believe that in order to arrive at poetic objectivity in the work it is necessary to separate reason, taste and conscious will from the creative process.

In support of the thesis that the philosophy of our century is one single unit, countless examples could be cited of affinity between artists of differing extraction and tendency. Byars' affinity to Magritte has already been mentioned despite their being artists who are profoundly different yet linked by their common fascination with mystery. For Magritte this mystery is to be found in "images of things familiar, brought together and transformed in such a way that they cease to accord with our ingenuous ideas and knowledge of them". This is a statement that calls to mind the art of Byars and that yet fails to posit a similarity between the images of Magritte and those of Byars in works that, though differing in their formal expression, do bear witness to how different images and tendencies can conceal similar passions.

Beauty is never *neo*-classical. Being an archetype, it is a property common to all times and as such can only be classical, that is, beyond the bounds of temporal connotation. For James Lee Byars art is a unity capable of gathering into itself the Cosmic All, as one page among the pages of the Great Book in which each page contains all the others. For him, art is an esoteric message, a probable indicator of possible paths, of converging routes that bring the out-there and the in-here, East and West, closer together. He sees it as a journey of initiation into consciousness and Knowledge, given expression in work in gold and black. Within the pot appear all the colours the artist can draw upon: black, white, yellow, red. In Jung's view yellow disappears and gives way to the sequence black-white-red, thus confirming Byars' tendency to send out messages and then conceal them. He inscribes in golden yellow on a red background, knowing that yellow is the colour that disappears, absorbed within the folds of the red, and taking with it the secret of the work. Red and yellow are interchangeable and to inscribe yellow on red is the same as inscribing yellow on yellow or red on red. An artist-shaman, Byars shares with Joseph Beuys the idea of art as an instrument of individual and collective liberation, an ethical system that aims at recomposing the fragments within one single body. But whereas Beuys saw himself as a *central* figure, as a catalyst, in this process, Byars sees himself as a figure on the sidelines: Beuys is apparent, Byars is not: a work of art, an exhibition, as too a thought that affirms the potential inherent within an object, are for him by all means manifestations of the power of being, but they are first and foremost deliberately ephemeral signals, for those few who would in any case have happened upon them more or less by accident.

Demetrio Paparoni

Edited version, translated by Irene S. Jack, of Demetrio Paparoni,
Beauty goes Avant-garde, published in *Tema Celeste*, no. 12,
June-September 1987, Syracuse, by permission.

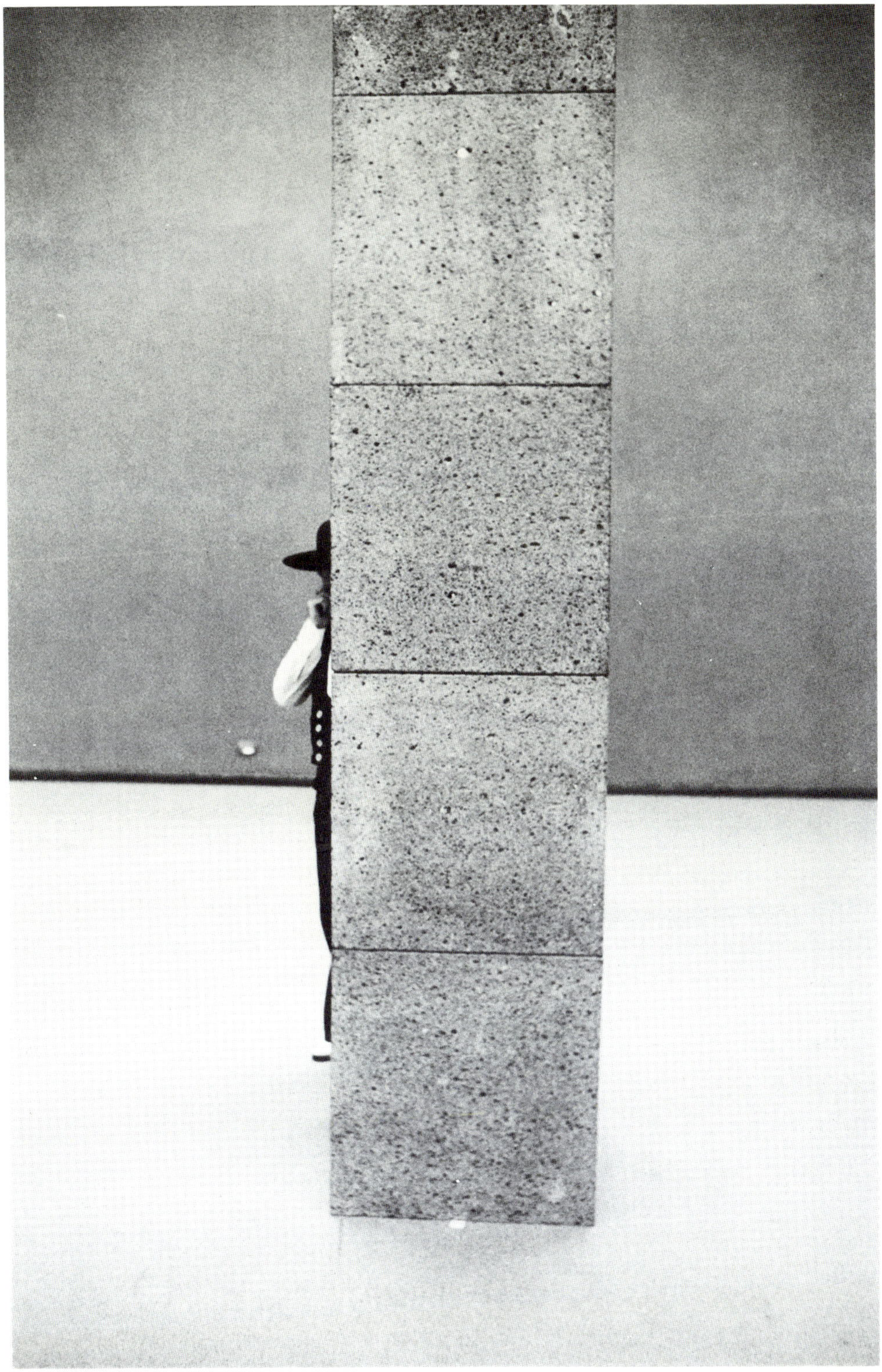

James Lee Byars, installation of *Figure of Death*
at *The Philosophical Palace,* Städtische Kunsthalle, Düsseldorf (1986)

TONY CRAGG

Pre-Conditions

Late at night I left the house to buy cigarettes from a nearby dispenser. It was mid-winter and cold, the asphalt crunched frozen under foot, suddenly from the nearby Wuppertal zoo the wolves starting to howl, a dramatic device well known from films but the sound erased the fences between us and changed the sleeping town into a dangerous, almost primeval landscape—it was my first encounter with wolves. Perhaps the wolves will be gone one day, surviving only as mythological creatures in literature and saga, relegated to the same existence as dragons and dinosaurs, but still occupying an indestructible place in the genetic memory.

All the creatures which have been, and many more which could have been—lost in the lottery of genetics and survival, and all the extinct landscapes channelled into, and made subject to the needs and comfort of one over-animal.

Well defined by his powers to change the physical world, building systems of change through language and technology, and exploiting all that is given by nature to the survival of himself and other groups to which he feels related and will give him mutual support. An ever accelerating process since the time the last large glaciers melted and released him from the burden of searching for food and mean survival. Changing the geography, the geology, the vegetation, the animal-kingdom, the water-flow, and the atmosphere. Using language, technique, politics and built-in criticism if it serves the purpose of his progress. And, one has to suppose that as long as we want to survive—and those who don't, don't—it will continue in the same way depending on certain physical limits which may, or may not be in sight.

But at the centre of all these changes is the perpetrator himself, he hasn't changed physically very much over the last ten thousand years and one could say the same for his basic spiritual condition. The few ideas he has had about his essential self usually get converted to useful practical formations—church, social structures, political structures, commerce, culture. Sometime in this apparent chaotic struggle one must allow oneself the luxury of believing that something is really going to change to make things better, the idea that we are going somewhere, but where? Perhaps to a place where survival is assured: a place where we can peacefully make other kinds of progress. Are the gates of Eden still open? No! I find the possibility of such an utopia absurdly unlikely and even frightening. The vision of hell on earth and a few struggling into outer-space seems equally absurd but marginally more probable.

All individuals have to make a picture of the world and their existence in it.

Most have the faculties for reflective activity and one can assume that many great thoughts have been thought without being expressed, many expressed unclearly (understandable considering the immensity of the subject) and many more forgotten, overshadowed by higher valued practical thoughts and actions. Even then, there remains a discernible ragged line through history of thoughts and actions which illuminate a little of the true nature of the human animal and the situation he finds himself in. The identifiable individuals are philosophers—people who think reflectively, poets who use words—the building bricks of thought?—to breathe meaning and expression into landscapes, objects, human experiences and thirdly, artists.

The fundamental difference between the former two and the latter lies in the fact that one way of, not defining, but at least marking-out the boundaries of philosophy is language and with language is meant, words. The poet enriches the world he describes and simultaneously the word he uses. The artist of course, knows words are there and may even use them, but the main act is the reorganisation (sometimes only proposed) of material into images and forms, which offer themselves as complex symbols for new experiences, insights and freedoms.

Naturally occurring formations, materials, phenomena and objects, are part of the original inventory of the universe and as such provide us with a vocabulary of qualities which also has become the language for describing human activities and their results. Descriptions of colour, shape, form, motion, etc. which can be relatively objective or extremely subjective. It is futile to be critical about nature because of its original quality which human beings in the process of evolution have learned to accept, or had to accept, as conditions for existence. But, human intervention and modifications of nature are always accompanied by very sophisticated methods of critical questioning. Painting and sculpture are two activities which are distinct for their reflective qualities and the creation of new images and objects in space, taking on the responsibility of changing a part of the physical world. Trying to cope with the appearance of, description of, memory of, feeling of, expression of. . . .

My initial interest in making images and objects was, and still remains, the creation of objects that don't exist in the natural or in the functional world, which can reflect and transmit information and feelings about the world and my own existence. They are not intended as dogmatic statements but as propositions, for me an essential distinction. The impulse comes directly from my observations and experiences in the world around me and rarely results out of literature or cultural history. But, I acknowledge positively the fact of, and influence of living at a particular moment in time.

The materials, because of their physical characteristics and the emotions and ideas they bring with them, play an essential role in the forming of the work. A pre-condition for working with man-made materials is that they are equally worthy of carrying significant meanings as natural materials. Many new materials originated for economic reasons, as substitutes for natural materials and as such have automatically been valued as inferior. And, many others as parts of practical constructions and industrial systems have assumed an everyday, banal function. This banality provides a hurdle that is essential to overcome in order to start a dialogue with the work. Otherwise, a Beuys' sculpture still remains a bit of fat on a chair and a work from Dan Flavin is just a fluorescent light tube. To be defeated by banality is to be confounded by ignorance and that is a problem for us all.

The forests, the oceans, the mineral deposits and the rocks themselves are used to provide the building bricks of these materials and objects. The wonder of these substances begins on a molecular level with relates directly to the physical properties and appearance of a material. For

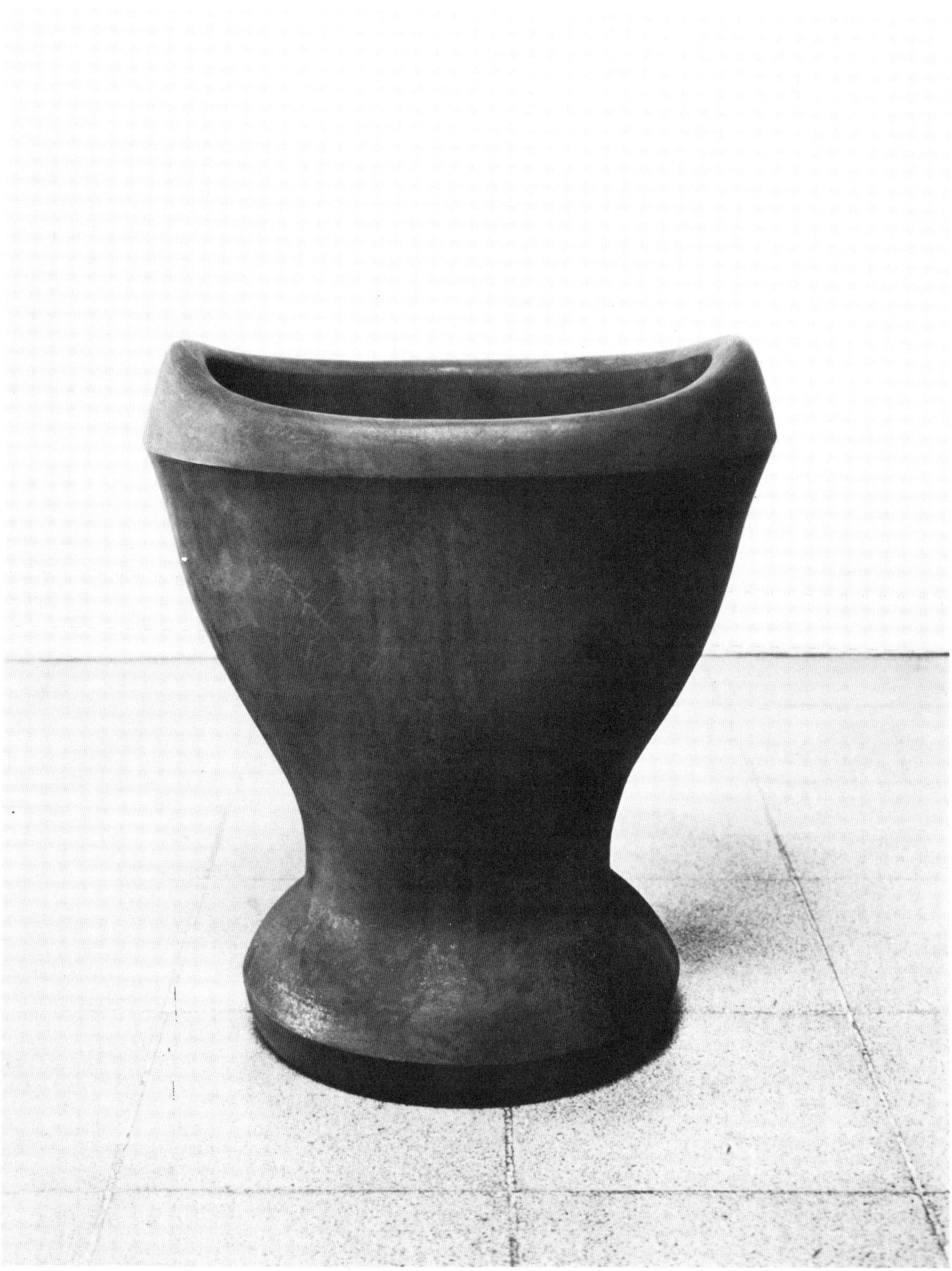
2 Tony Cragg, *Eye Bath* 1986

example, the six strongly bonded atoms of carbon in graphite are arranged into a flat hexagon to form a surface which can reflect; the material has a gloss. These plates of molecules slip friction-free over one another; the material has a slippery feeling. The plates, face on face, compact to form a mass with high definition, the strong molecular bonds cause brittleness and a characteristic almost metallic ring. For every material a new list of specific qualities, providing a rich vocabulary in the language of objects. The materials I use are man-made or at least man-modified and as such belong to a huge category of materials/objects which are integral to the physical, intellectual and emotional lives of men. Though, in fact, one has to emphasise the physical relationship, which is parallel to the already mentioned notion of progress; a progress almost entirely of a materialistic nature. And we have such a bad physical relationship to the objects and materials we produce that it is almost embarrassing to consider the metaphysical, the poetical, the mythological.

The development of and eventual choice of images and forms often is related to subjects which seem to suffer the same kind of dangerous devaluation, and enslavement to functionalism as the materials themselves. People, objects, buildings and landscapes.

The landscape is changing under the direction of strong survivors who seem always to know what they want, and I believe that the sometimes unclear, unsecured by science and logic, almost alchemist activities of artists offer vital and essential clues to alternative attitudes.

Tony Cragg

Reprinted from *Tony Cragg—Sculpture,*
published by the Kestner-Gesellschaft, Hanover (1986), by permission.

Tony Cragg, installation of *Spiral*
at Galerie Bernd Klüser, Munich (1982) ▷

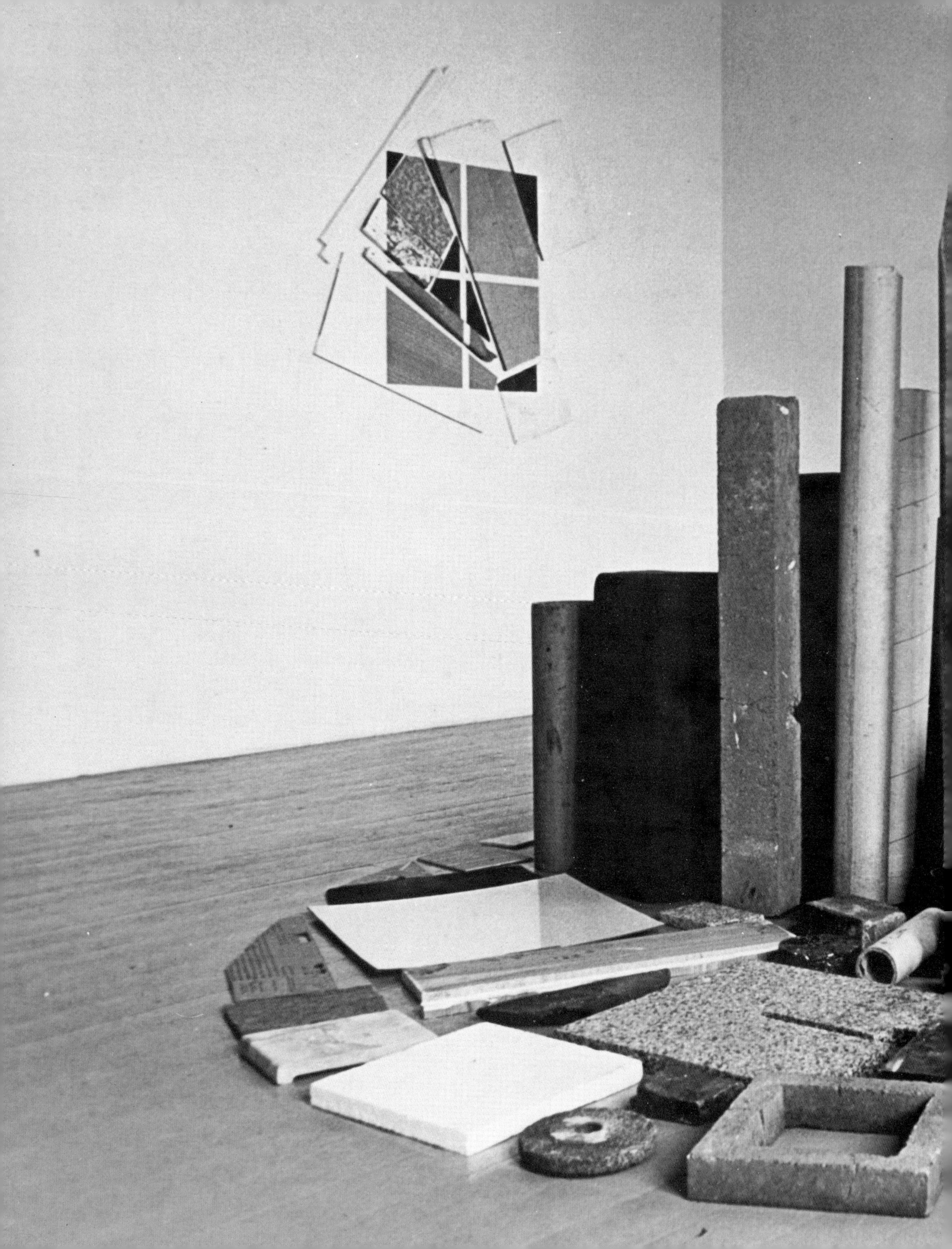

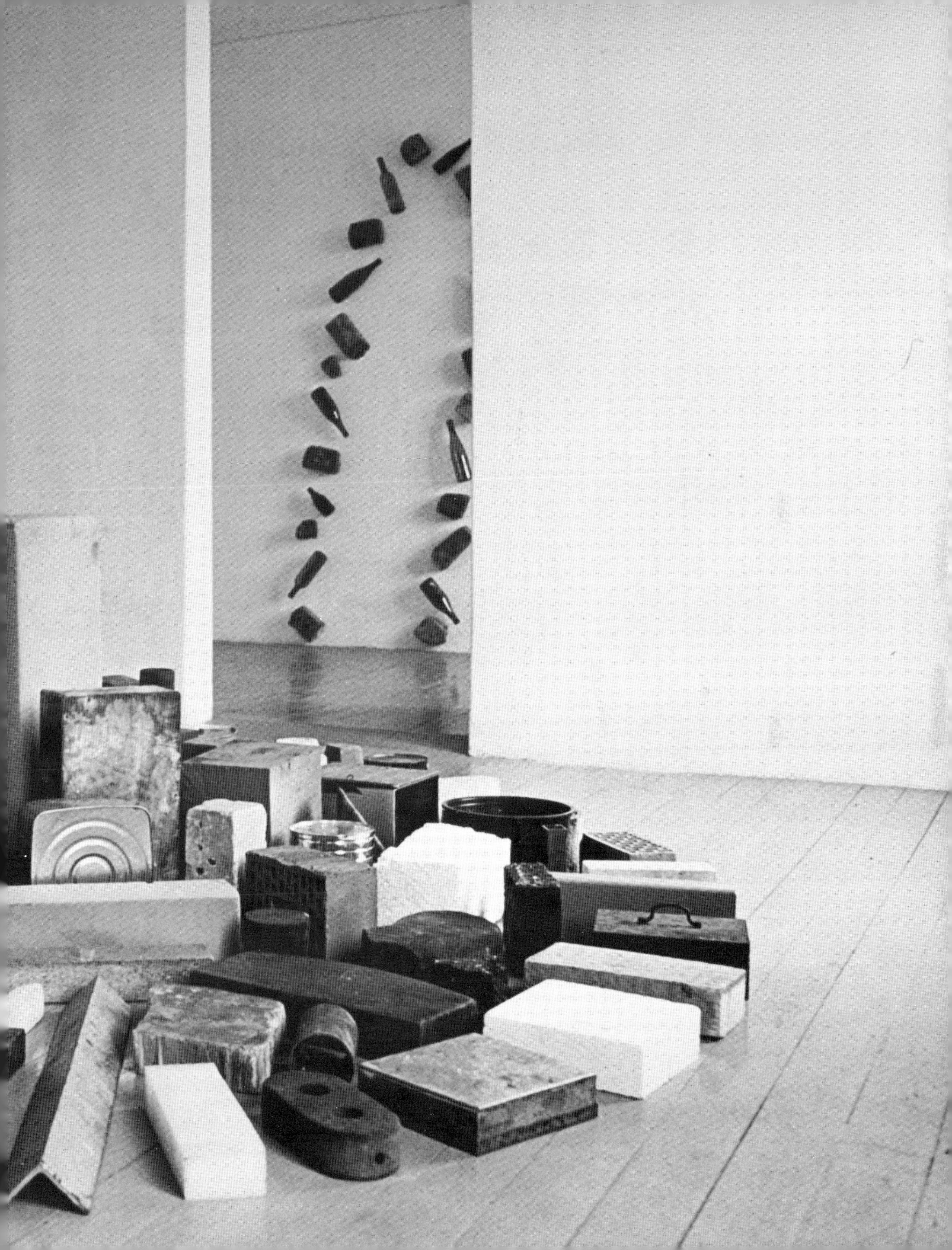

RICHARD DEACON

A Sonnet to Orpheus

A god can do it. But how, tell me, shall
a man follow him through the narrow lyre?
His mind is cleavage. At the crossing of two
heartways stands no temple for Apollo.

Song, as you teach it, is not desire,
not suing for something yet in the end attained;
song is existence. Easy for the god.
But when do we exist? *And when does he*

spend the earth and stars upon our being?
Youth, this is not it, your loving, even
if then your voice thrusts your mouth open,—learn

to forget your sudden song. That will run out.
Real singing is a different breath.
A breath for nothing. A wafting in the god. A wind.

Rainer Maria Rilke

From Rainer Maria Rilke, *Sonnets to Orpheus,* First Part No. 3, translated by M. D. Herter Norton and published by W. W. Norton & Co., New York (1942), by permission.

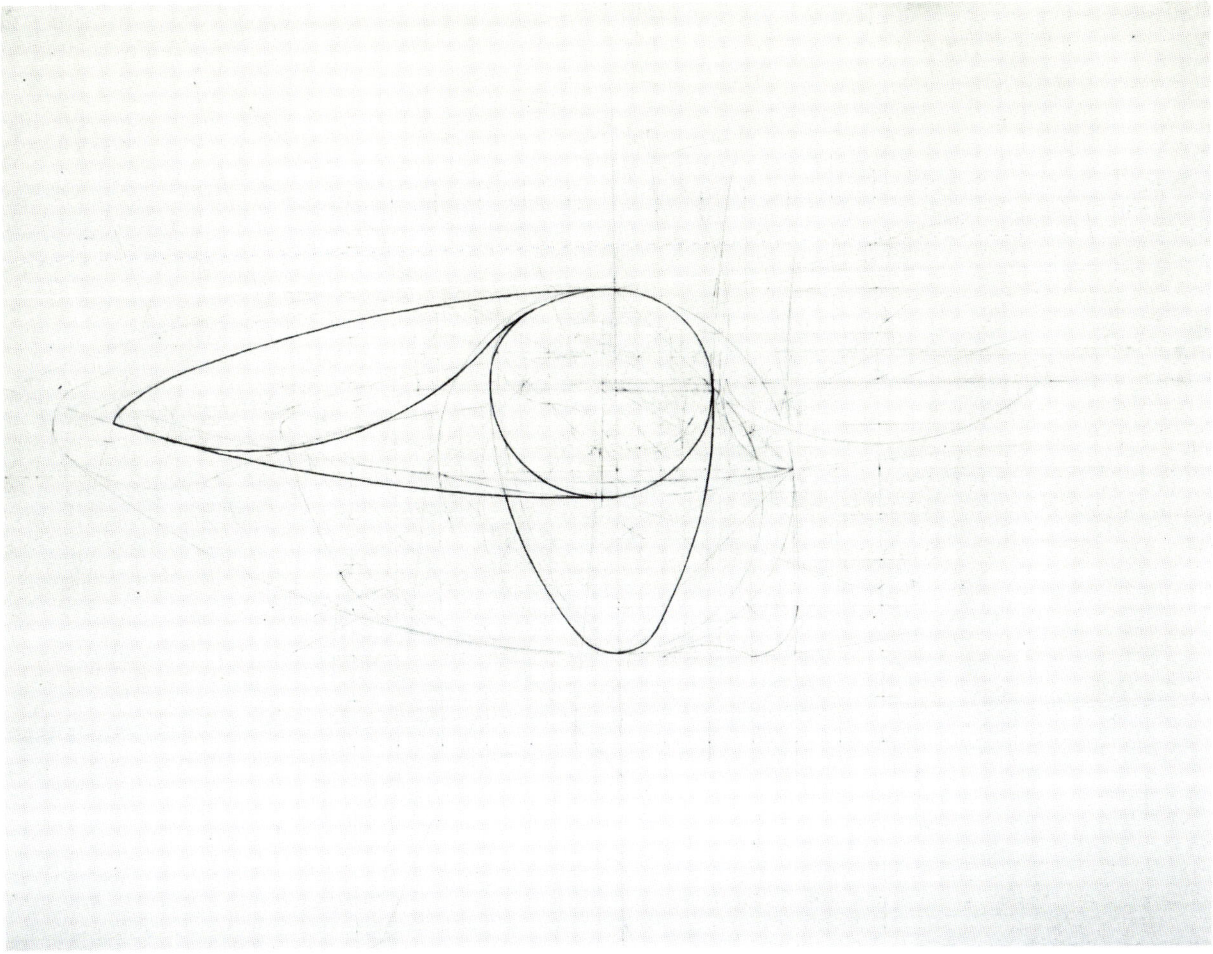

7 Richard Deacon, *It's Orpheus When There's Singing No. 4* 1979

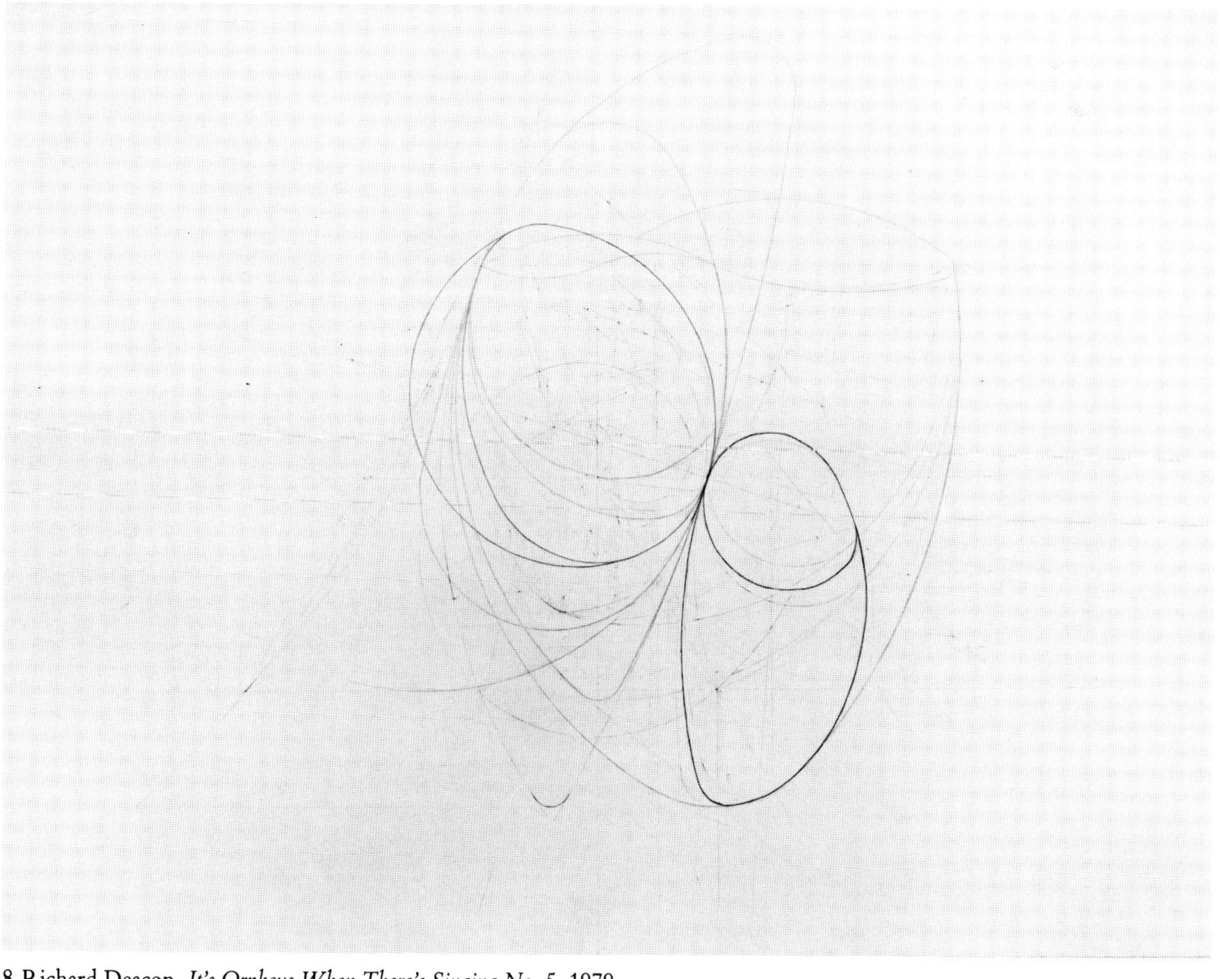

8 Richard Deacon, *It's Orpheus When There's Singing No. 5* 1979

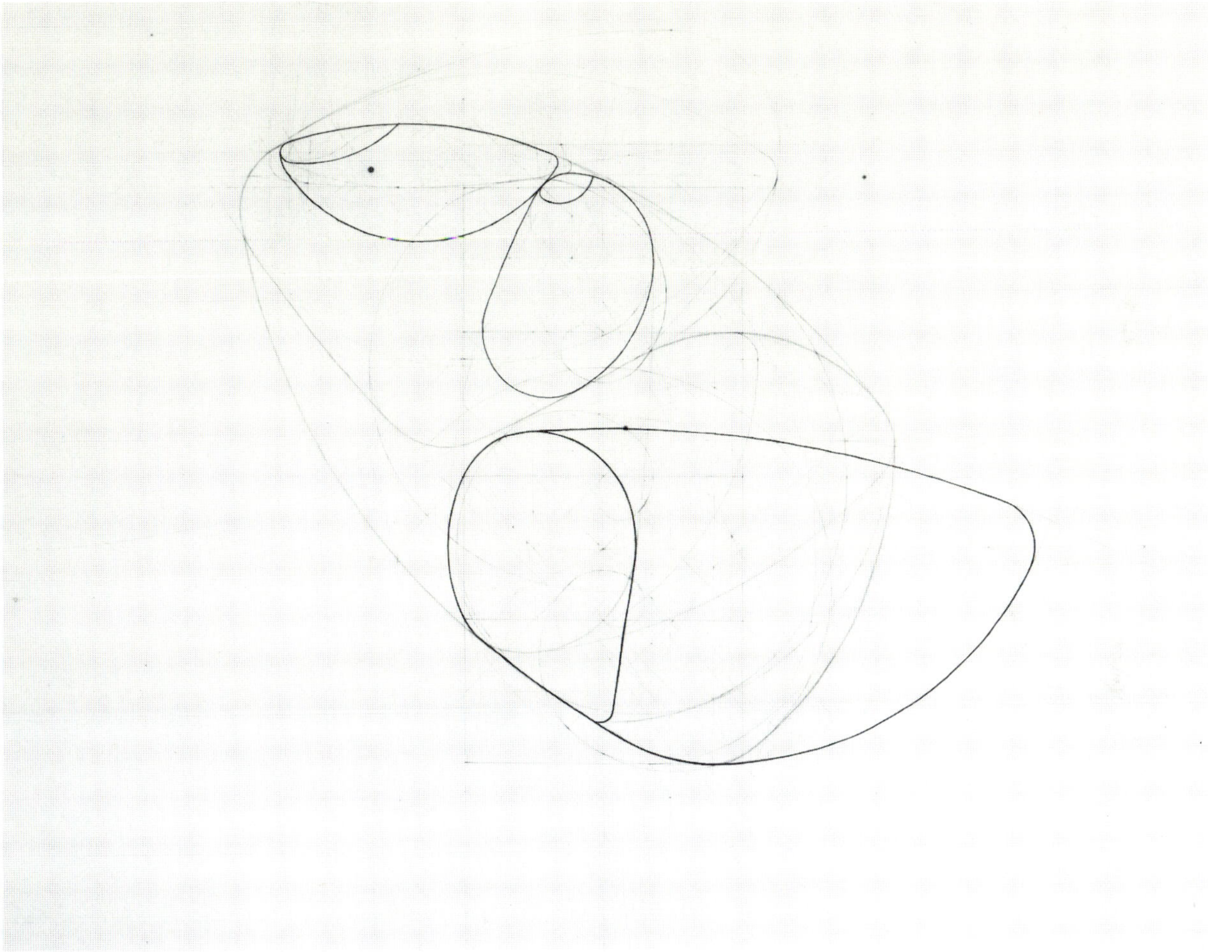

9 Richard Deacon, *It's Orpheus When There's Singing No. 6* 1979

IAN HAMILTON FINLAY

Aphrodite of The Terror

The Venus de' Medici, so called because it held pride of place in the Medici collection in Florence from the Renaissance onwards, is one of the small group of antique sculptures which have served as the touchstones of the classical style. This significance has outlived the attack on the canons of classical taste from the later eighteenth century onwards. Even William Blake, concerned to find earlier models for the visual arts in the mythical achievements of Asia, conceded that such works as the Venus de' Medici and the Apollo Belvedere were 'copies' of the original images of the Cherubim that he could glimpse by visionary means. Admittedly the Venus de' Medici has suffered a special kind of onslaught in the present century through being herself copied and diffused in innumerable casts, many of them reduced from the actual size. But a kind of belated justice has recently been done to her by the Italian artist Paolini, who places two life-sized casts opposite one another, mutually absorbed in contemplation, under a light-drenched cupola in Hans Hollein's Museum at Mönchengladbach.

Ian Hamilton Finlay assumes the generic quality of this type of ideal beauty. But he does not abandon the Medici Venus in Paolini's self-reflexive circle. Utilising the strategy which Lucius Burckhardt has termed the 'minimal intervention', he adds a single, decisive detail to the classical cast. Because the Venus is already separated from us by an irreducible distance—existing as a type and a concept prior to any material realisation—it provides the sharpest possible contrast to the minimal element which has been added: nothing but a red silk thread.

Yet the red thread evokes an entire historical dimension. After the fall of Robespierre, and the end of the revolutionary Terror in 1794, French women took to wearing threads of red silk round their necks in commemoration of relatives who had died by the guillotine. In a society which had brusquely reverted to the pursuit of pleasure, these slight reminiscences of the cutting blade must have had a galvanising effect. In choosing to bring out this historical reference, Finlay is adding to the already considerable number of works which he has devoted in the last few years to the thematic of the French Revolution. *A View to The Temple*, his contribution to the 1987 Documenta exhibition at Kassel, gave an epic grandeur to a sequence of guillotines with texts inscribed on the bronze blades, framing the prospect which led to an eighteenth century garden temple. This *Aphrodite of The Terror* strikes a more intimate note, evoking the softer themes of grief and suffering as a counterpoint to the demands of revolutionary virtue.

This is, however, not simply an evocation of the French Revolution through the acknowledged symbolism of the classical tradition. Finlay detects a Terror which rages in the modern world no less violently than the Terror of the revolution. A secular Terror rages against the Ideal, and if its weapons are not as specific as those of the revolutionary period, its effects are all the more uniform and pervasive, since they have entered the very texture of contemporary thinking. The *Aphrodite of The Terror* is in mourning for the Death of the Gods, her own relatives. Thus the type of classical beauty is utilised to deplore the contemporary mentality which impoverishes tradition, and cuts art off from its sustaining roots in religion and myth.

Stephen Bann

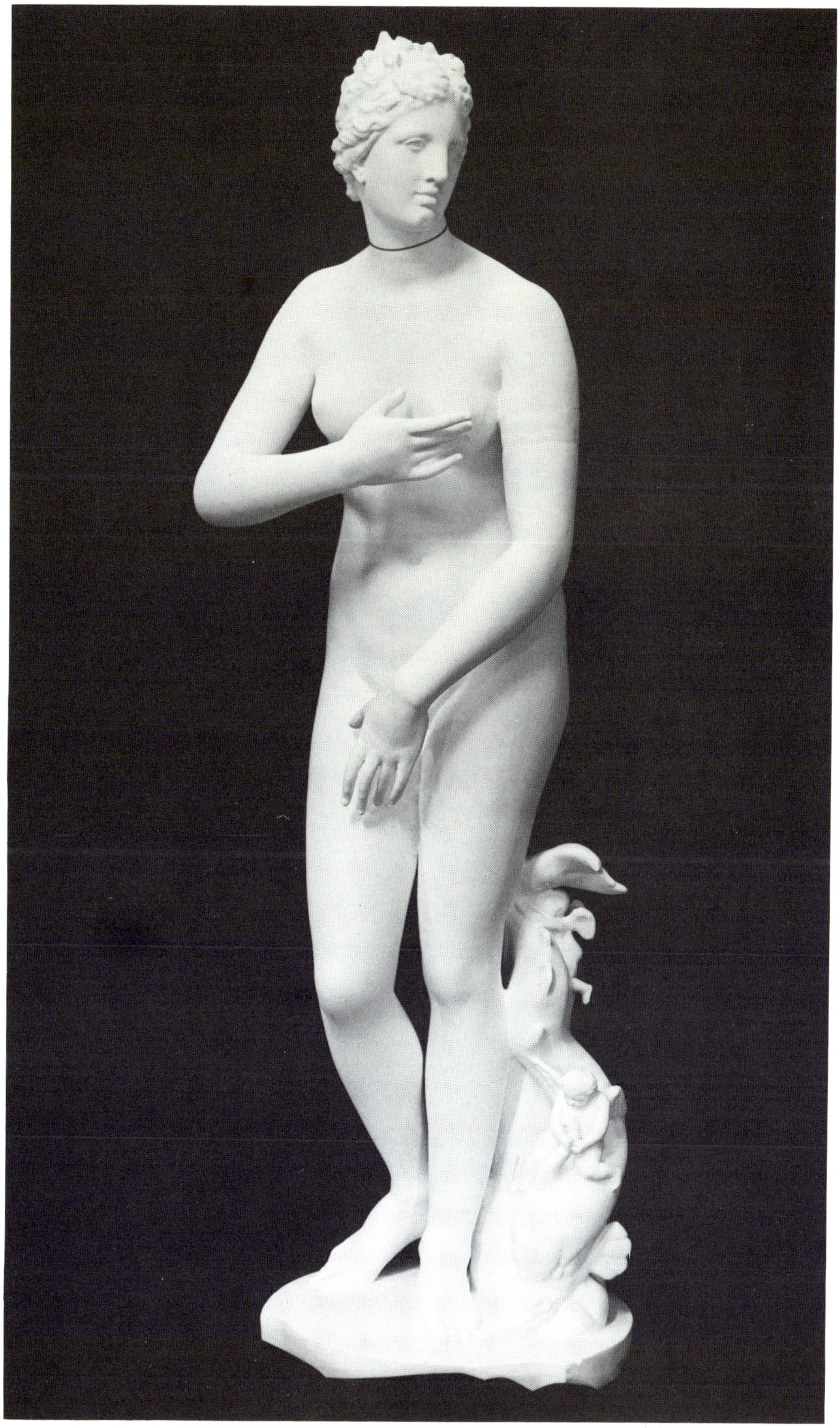

10 Ian Hamilton Finlay, *Aphrodite of The Terror* 1987

Aphrodite of The Terror

Consider the *Aphrodite of The Terror* from this other point of view: consider her as Didactic on the question of the function of the plaster-cast. We can see that the plaster-cast, in cultural history, has been set various tasks: it has been charged to Record, to Decorate and to Teach. Twice it has been called upon to suffer—firstly as a martyr of marble, and then in the stocks of Modernism, where it bore the crude insults of art-students with overcoming dignity. Above all these functions, the plaster-cast fairly *strides* as the propaganda arm of neo-classicism. In this capacity it can disseminate Antique Law even to the Americas, and can take Thorvaldsen from Rome to Copenhagen, and thence, believe it, to Greenock. Consider the plaster-cast as prescient of a Liberating Force.

What Trojans these plaster-casts are! Now Finlay has shown us, in this *Aphrodite of The Terror*, the character of the latest labour incumbent upon the plaster-cast. Here is an Aphrodite who, above telling us of proportion, and scale, and composition, and formal attitude, will tell us of Virtue and mourning. She will shame us into Sentiment, drive us to a frenzy of remorse over our mindless mutilations of the past, cause us to invoke the names of Revolutionaries, breach for us the fence around the Halls of Secularism.

In art theory the interpolative part of this work would be termed 'minimal intervention', which is a proper term. Yet our perception of the 'call' of this work should be so intense as to lead us towards viewing, as a similar act of 'minimal intervention', the Storming of the Bastille. Art theory must learn that, in neo-classicism, nothing is done for argument's sake.

Alexander Stoddart

Aphrodite of The Terror

This is a minimalist work, in contrast to the maximalist presence of the guillotines in *A View to The Temple*, exhibited at Documenta. The reference is again to the French Revolution, during which the relatives of people beheaded on the guillotine wore just such a thread to commemorate the manner of their dying. The goddess is thus in mourning. One may perhaps imagine her mourning the death of the gods through the Iconoclastic Revolution, in spite of its well-known predilection for neo-classicism. But then one recalls that the gods of ancient Greece have no reason to envy the convulsions of the Revolution, a fact acknowledged by Anatole France, who entitled his novel on The Terror, *The Gods Are Athirst*. The classical and modern are thus parallel moments; the moment of death which the statue commemorates can equally be a classical moment of strife in the heavens, or a moment of modern revolution. Death was already on Mount Olympus—just as iconographic tradition has long recognised its presence in Arcadia, by way of the *Et In Arcadia Ego* tag, whose impact Finlay has done so much to renew.

One should moreover not be taken in by the common view of eighteenth century history, which regards The Terror as an aberration in a century of enlightenment. The Robespierrists, with whom the neo-classical painter David was associated, insisted on a Rousseauistic sentiment of religious reverence. Their rule was cut short and they were executed soon after the Festival of the Supreme Being, David himself only just escaping the guillotine. The Enlightenment had set out to replace religious sentiment with the rule of reason, that modern secular goddess. The history of the last two centuries has, however, repeatedly undermined what faith we may have had in her. For Finlay, the gods for whom *Aphrodite of The Terror* is mourning are the victims of modern secular terror, their demise celebrated by the *jeunesse dorée*, whose spiritual impoverishment the artist sees reborn in current attitudes toward the arts.

Ian Hamilton Finlay's repeated returns to the classical moment in art stress our distance from origins, both by highlighting questions of rhetorical continuity and by dramatising the death of sacred antiquity. At the same time, however, his perpetual inventiveness re-ties the broken threads of tradition. The gesture thus accomplished is never a matter of nostalgic reconstruction. By revealing anew the irreducible presence of death within the Apollonian splendour of classical Greece, Finlay unequivocally presents it as an internal limit with which any serious commitment to form must come to terms. If he is a neo-classical artist, it is to the extent that neo-classicism formulated a response to just such a predicament, which is, at bottom, that of the human condition, but by which the carrion crows of contemporary irony are so obviously enervated.

Yves Abrioux

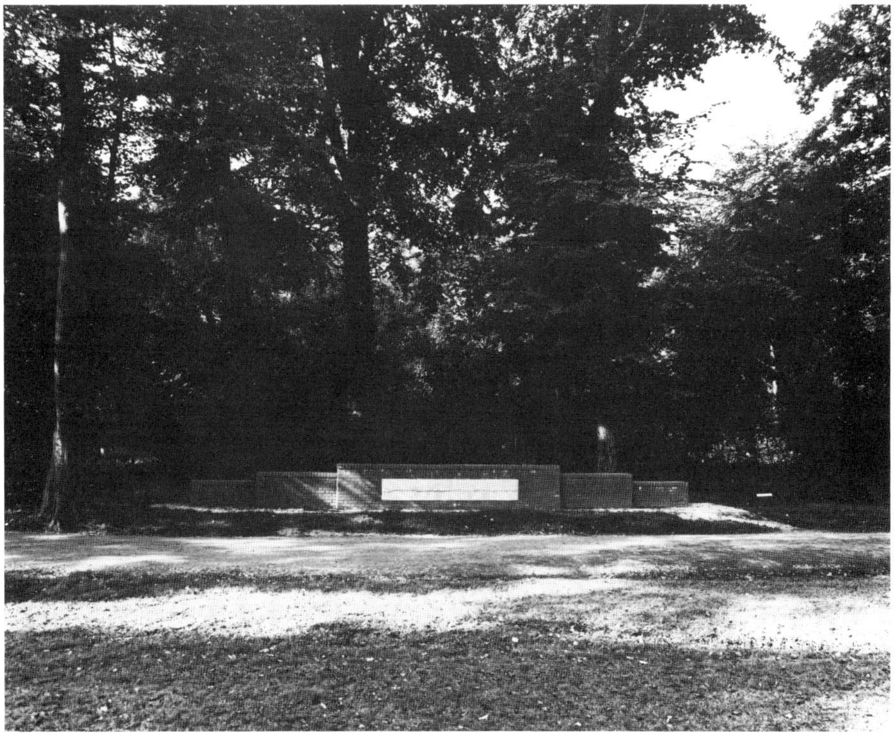

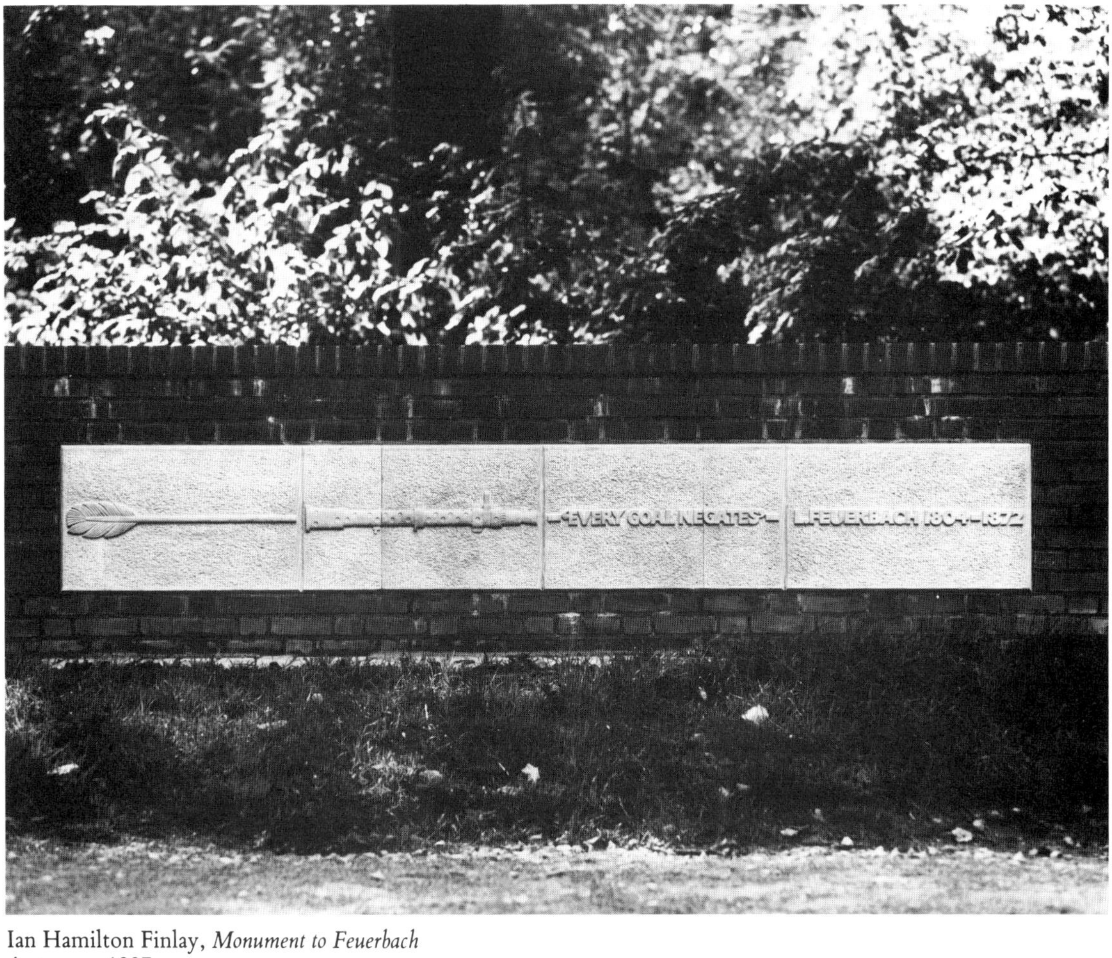

Ian Hamilton Finlay, *Monument to Feuerbach*
Antwerp, 1987

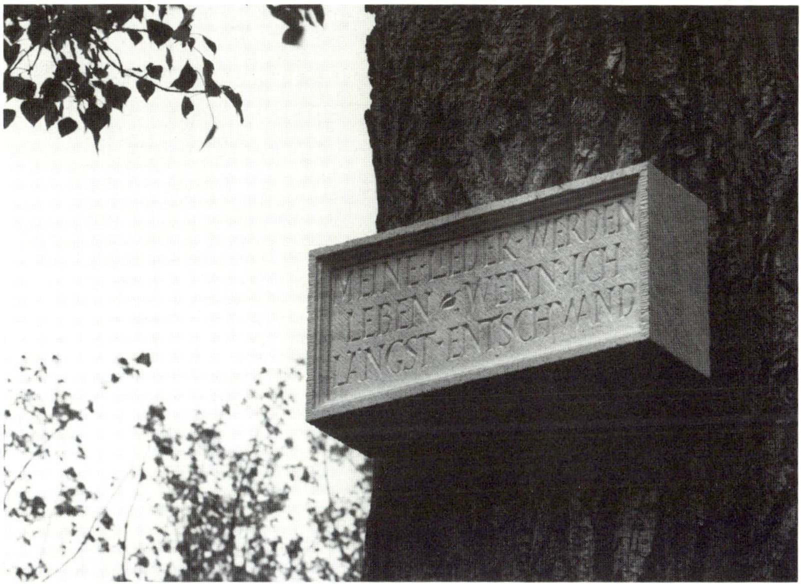

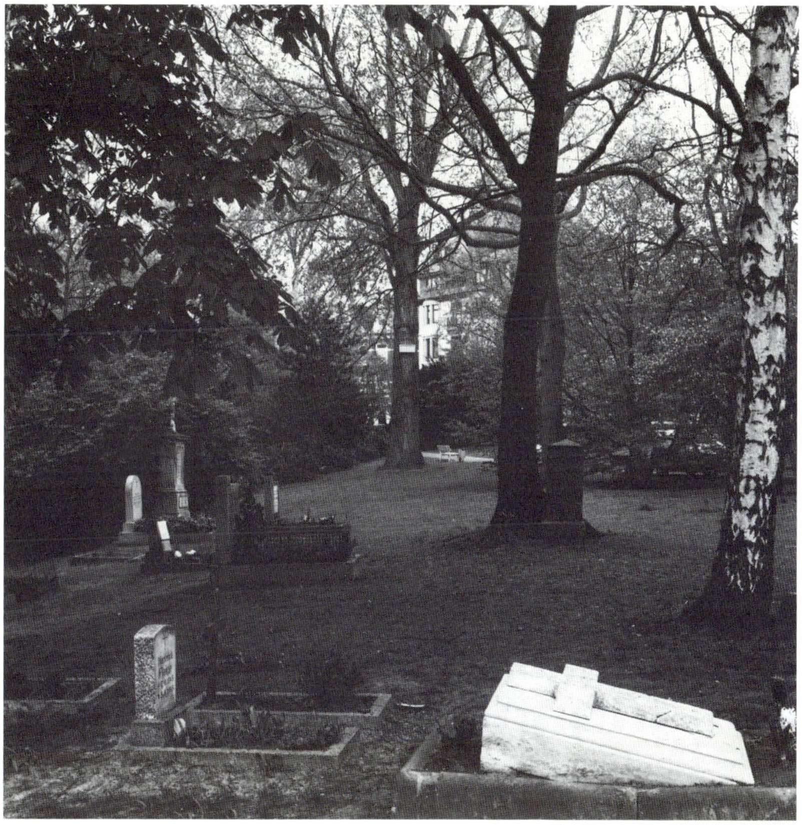

Ian Hamilton Finlay, *A Remembrance of Annette*
(Annette von Droste-Hülshoff, 1797–1848)
Münster, 1987

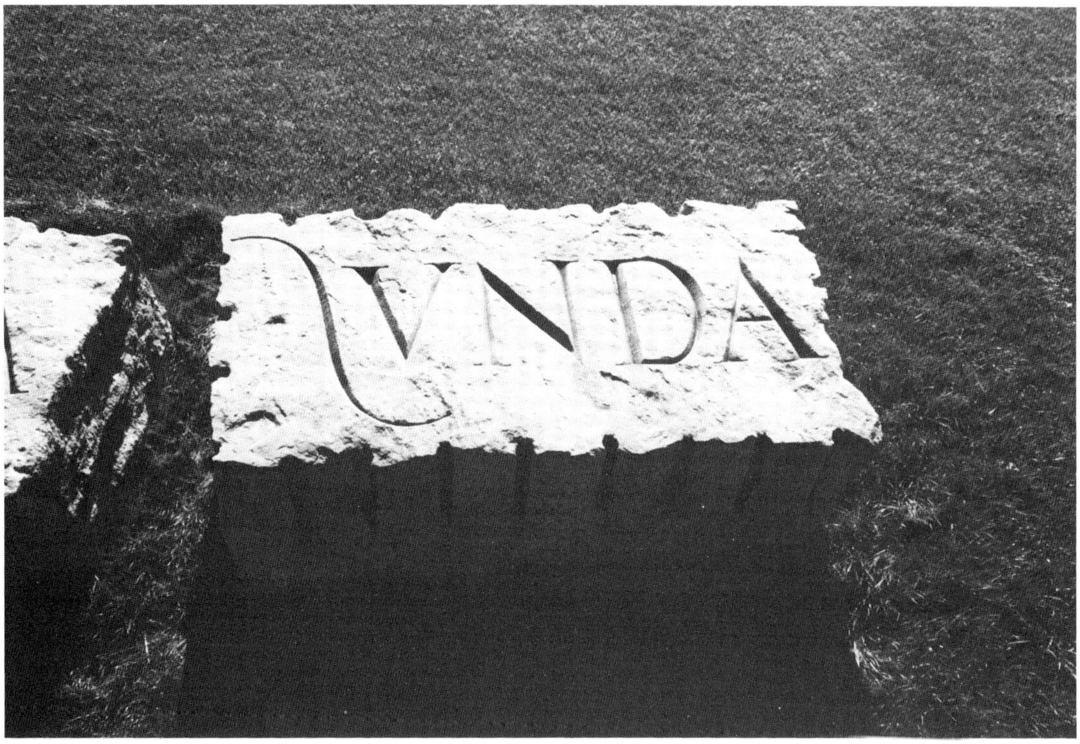

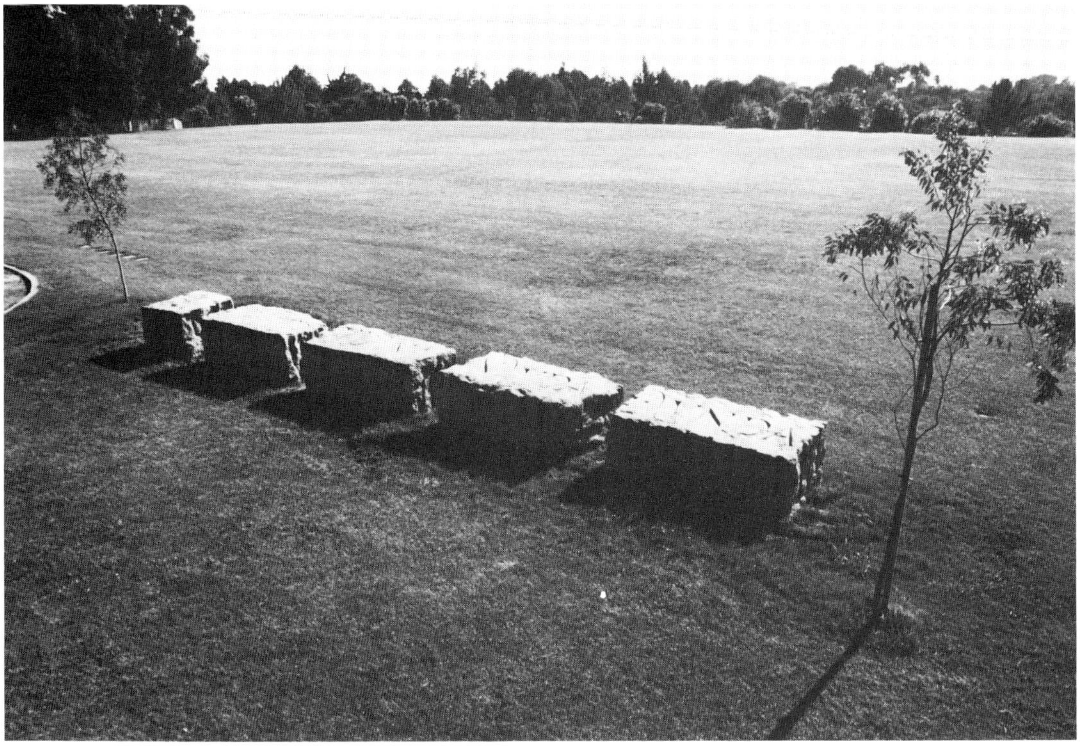

Ian Hamilton Finlay, *Unda* (wave)
Campus of the University of California at San Diego, 1987

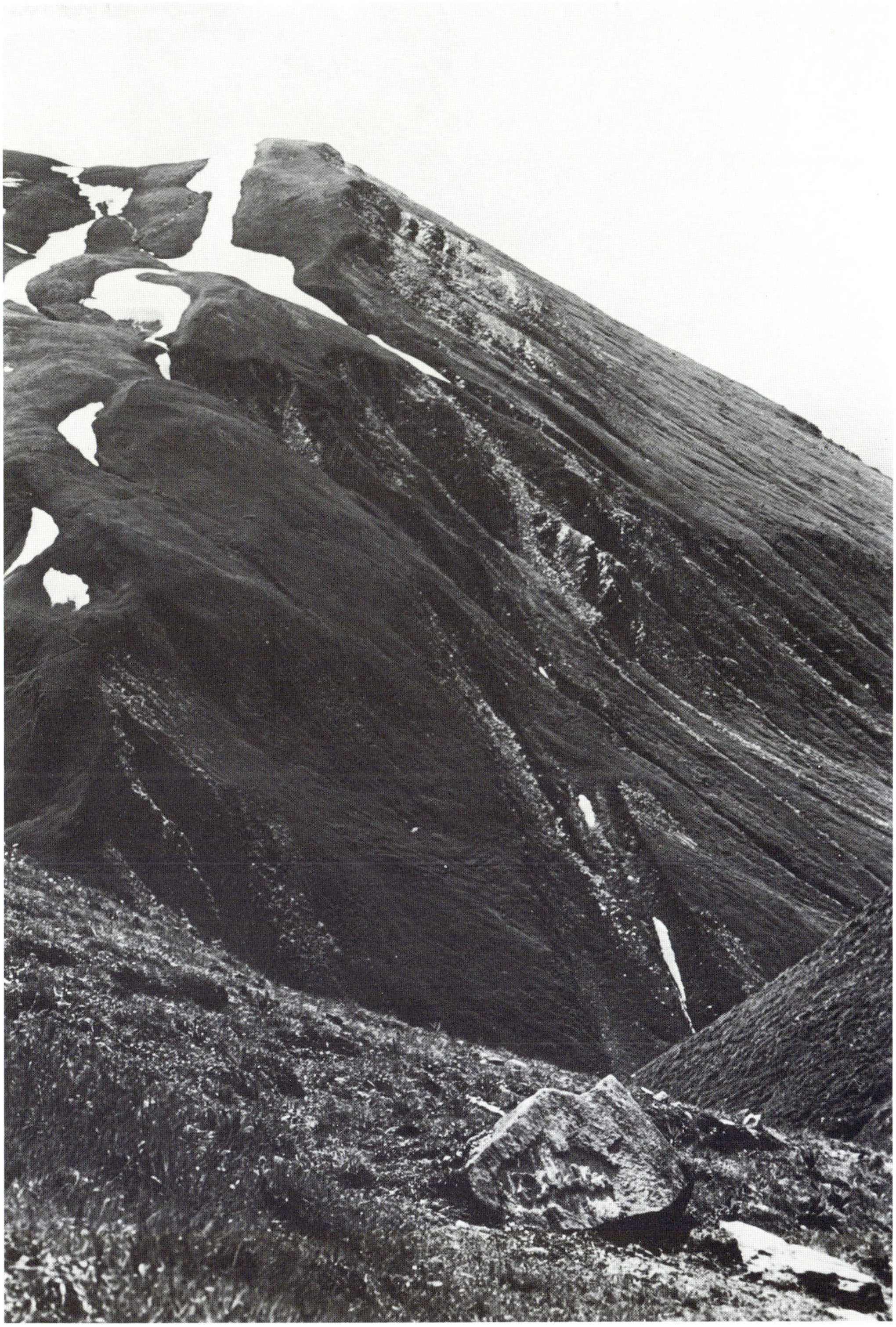

Ian Hamilton Finlay, a project for the Furka Pass, Switzerland.
(The Swiss artist Hodler's signature inscribed on a rock.)
Furka, 1987

GÉRARD GAROUSTE

The Silent Heart

Gérard Garouste is one of a generation of contemporary painters who are conscious of the history of painting. Having been categorised as a conceptual artist for part of the nineteen seventies, he returned to painting with a wider awareness of the ideas that have traditionally confronted the painter. A concern for content, expression, colour and composition brought about Garouste's conscious decision to be a painter, allowing him to explore the classical ideas that have been of interest to artists for centuries.

Looking at his paintings, particularly of the period from 1982 to 1984, I am aware of the classical idea expressed in Horace's phrase *Ut pictura poesis* ("as in poetry so in painting"), which gave both the arts the same aim, albeit through different means. The aim was to instruct as well as please through the depiction of noble acts. This concept was revitalised during the Renaissance and then again it had a strong influence on French poets and painters in the sixteenth century. Criticism in those centuries focused on the painters' ability to provide nobility of content and to be able to adhere to the accepted rules, which allowed for little, if any of the artist's personal expression. This classical approach has some affinity with the ideas which were prevalent in the early nineteen seventies, when minimal and conceptual art established similar rules which gained international acceptance. Conceptual art provided a strong link between the visual arts and the written word.

Garouste's association and familiarity with the major influences and ideas of the seventies provided him with an awareness of the artist's ability to place his work in a predetermined context. Garouste's paintings exist within a context of questioning the contemporary values of modernity, and show a strong awareness of the historical relationship between painting and literature.

By the eighteenth century the idea of painting and poetry being interlinked was interpreted more freely, and by the nineteenth century the French Romantics, though rejecting the Classical tradition, still supported the idea of the close relationship between literature and art. Within the French tradition Diderot expressed a unity between the arts that was more flexible than that of the Classicists while focusing on the mutual benefit they gave each other.

> "One recognises poets in painters and painters in poets. The sight of paintings of the great masters is as useful to an author as the reading of great books is to the artist".[1]

For much of the twentieth century the relationship of literature to the visual arts has been overshadowed by the development of cinema and television. Literature has served these other media to such an extent that the silent art of painting became devoid of content other than its own formal values. Cinema and especially television have stressed the narrative aspects of literature's relationship to the visual world, while ideas of the *poetic* have been relegated to far fewer aspects of the literary and visual imagination.

Garouste's paintings deal with the artist's concern for the poetic, and the dialogue between artist and writer. The fact that such paintings as *Lucrèce* (1982) and *St Thérèse d'Avila* (1983) by Garouste are from historic and literary sources of the past can be interpreted as evidence of a desire on the part of the artist to be concerned with the classic traditional problems of style and technique free from a modernist context. Through his choice of subject matter, Garouste reveals a literary imagination which is working and revising concepts of the artist's function as a painter and his relationship with his work.

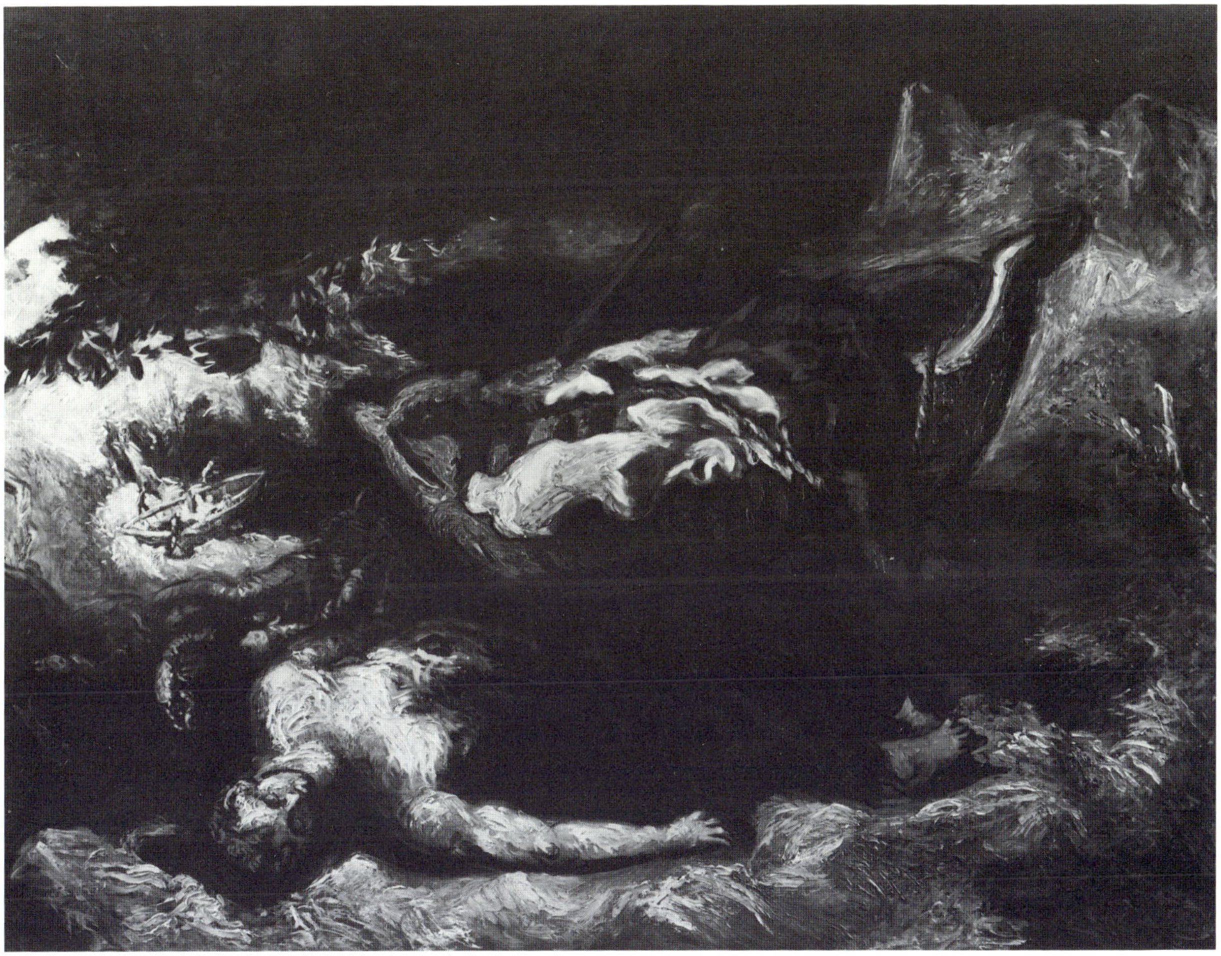

Gérard Garouste, *La Barque et le Pecheur—Le Pantalon Rouge* 1984
Private Collection courtesy Liliane & Michel Durand-Dessert, Paris

His painting *St Thérèse d'Avila* was originally painted in response to a commission from the Church. It shows his interest in the possibility of a contemporary painter making a religious painting. In this picture Garouste develops the idea of the subject matter reflecting on the role of the contemporary artist. It is not just the subject matter that refers back to older traditions but also the idea of the painter as one who responds to a traditional role in which the artist works within rules established by others. Within these rules the artist is free to develop his own expression and imagination, although they may not reflect his own beliefs, while the subject matter provides a link between the imagination of the artist and the values of the past. The relationship between the artist and his work is often confused as being a statement of belief and could in some circumstances lead to the idea that a religious painting by Caravaggio is a lesser masterpiece because the artist may not have been a religious believer.

Painting can be seen to be as much a part of a fictional world as literature itself. Garouste's paintings have a quality which through their content and style open up a world in which even the paintings themselves could appear to the spectator as being the work of an artist who himself was a character from fiction.

The knowledge we might have of the artist as a person does not inform us about the paintings. With Garouste it is more the case that the paintings evoke the idea of a fictional painter. Garouste's paintings could even be seen as the work of a character from a Balzac novel. Although the spectator can see the hand of the artist, through the brush strokes upon the canvas, they cannot be located within a contemporary context. Garouste's style and painterly technique, quotes from Watteau and Delacroix rather than from a more recent painterly tradition. Paintings such as *La Barque et le Pecheur—Le Pantalon Rouge* (1984) and *Le Secret* (1982) although not referring directly to a known narrative still refer the spectator to the idea of a literary meaning of what is depicted. The figures depicted in these paintings exist as characters that have grown from the artist's imagination and placed upon the canvas like an author places impressions of people and relationships before the reader's eye in a poem or novel.

Garouste's work has its roots in past French literary and artistic traditions introducing a Romantic element into contemporary European painting. His paintings highlight the artist as a myth maker, using the skills of the painter to evoke a poetic awareness. His work is closer to a Romantic tradition than it is to a Classical one, in the way that his paintings include, as part of their content the expression of the artist. The expressive elements in Garouste's work paint a literary portrait of the artist rather than a factual one, in the same way that an author can give the reader experiences through the changing perceptions of the narrator within a novel. Garouste is the narrator who has worked out his own techniques for combining art and fiction.

Barry Barker

[1]Denis Diderot, ''Pensées detachées sur la Peinture'',
in *Diderot Oeuvres Esthétiques,* ed. Paul Vernière, Paris, Garnier (1959), p.749

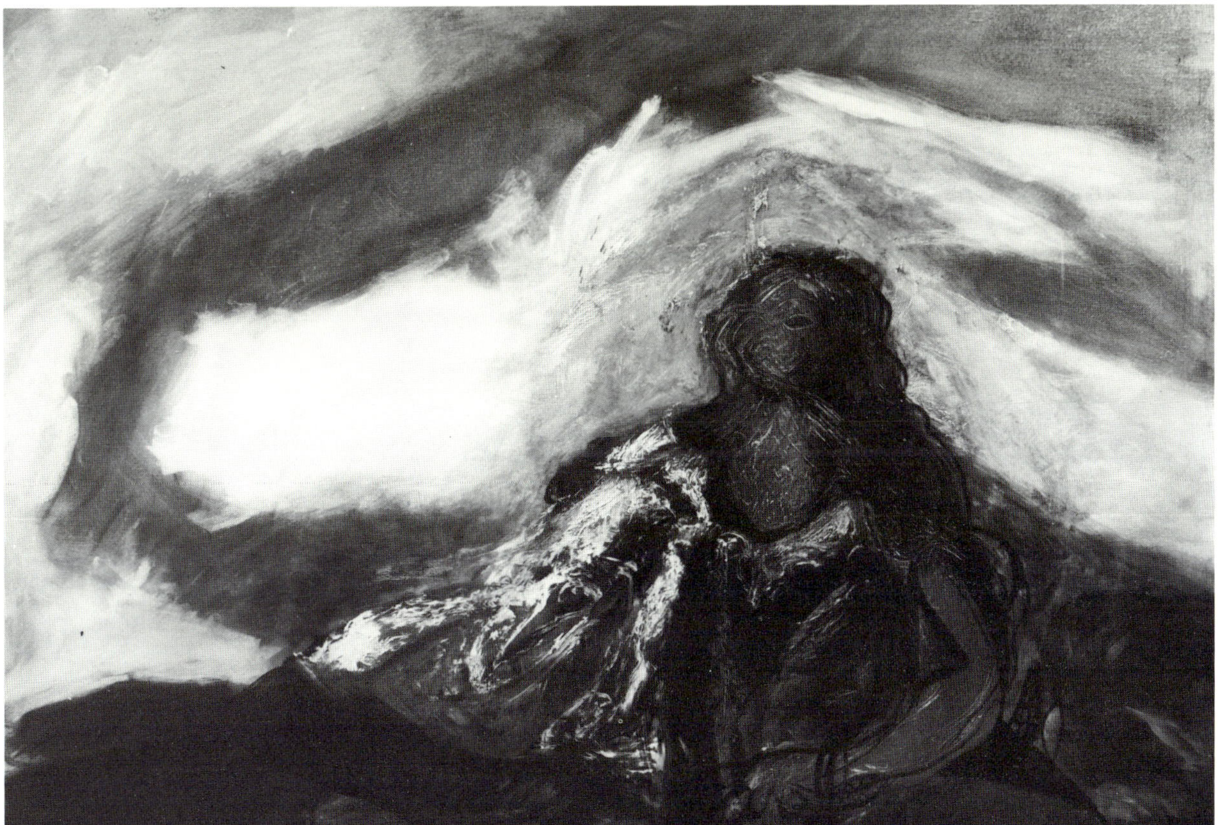

Gérard Garouste, *Untitled* 1986–87
Courtesy Liliane & Michel Durand-Dessert, Paris

REBECCA HORN

Gentle Transference

In recent years Rebecca Horn has been able to show large scale exhibitions and installations, such as at ARC in Paris (1986) and at the sculpture exhibition *Skulptur Projekte* in Münster, West Germany (1987). Each of these events revealed with great clarity one of the most characteristic qualities of both her sculptures and films: the viewer feels at the mercy of subliminal processes which trigger off gentle effects, finely orchestrated transference reactions he cannot ignore. Anyone who contemplates one of Rebecca Horn's installations or sculptures subjects himself to subtle processes which are somehow mirrored in the central nervous system. In much the same way as we feel on seeing an eyeball slit open in a movie, Rebecca Horn causes us to respond with intense, though not quite so drastic feelings of empathy.

An egg held between two needle points, a small steel hammer beating against a sheet of iron, a paint brush soaked in watercolour and slapped against a wall: these are, first and foremost, live happenings devised by an artist who orientates her aesthetics by the perceptual models explored in the Performance Art of the seventies.

In those days when the spectator, no longer able to rely on the corset of conventionality, submitted almost unconditionally to a particular happening, Rebecca Horn investigated the extent to which the imaginative powers of an artist could influence an individual or collective 'audience'. In some performances selected participants were induced to put on body-extending devices, aerials or 'overalls' made of hosepipes, feathers or bandages (as in *Cornucopia*, 1970, *Unicorn*, 1971, *Feathery Instrument*, 1972, *Overflowing Blood Machine*, 1970). This appeal to our perceptual ability and our readiness to yield to a time sequence beyond familiar models of expectation turned the audience into actors.

With these earlier works, Rebecca Horn attained the artistic capability of compressing and filling time sequences.

She began employing time in a fruitful way in order to represent the intensity of experience simultaneously with its analytical dissection. Her machines record time sequences which generate tension similar to that of her films. The persistence and immutability of the tension stems from the fact that one finds oneself at the centre of events—until the repetition begins to reproduce itself as an image reflected *ad infinitum* in self-reflecting mirrors.

In just the same way, the large quantities of mercury, coal and sulphur which appear in her work, in tubs or on the ground in the form of conical heaps, are signs of states either shortly after or before something happens. Their 'charge' is indicative of a contact which has either already occurred or is awaited. Such contacts always bring about passionate consequences, if one goes on the assumption that the physical element in these works is equivalent to the spiritual.

In this sense, the viewer occasionally experiences touch on a spiritual level. An instance of this was a medieval keep used as a prison by the Nazis, which was chosen by Rebecca Horn for her installation at the sculpture exhibition, *Skulptur Projekte Münster* this summer. It was another clear demonstration of how the artist manages to appropriate a particular space and use it to develop intense time sequences.

By employing subtle, simple means, the passage through the staccato concert of thin hammer blows became a passage through the collective memory, seizing the viewers with extremely physical, though undefined inner sensations and threatening them with naked, unmitigated inevitability.

Although Rebecca Horn seems to love using materials and objects heavy with symbolism, the disarming candor with which she applies it to her repertoire of motifs subverts an all-too-straightforward literary interpretation. It is as if they were traps for an intellect seeking facile explanations for sensations which defy explanation. The artist wants to stir the emotions without telling superfluous stories, while also allowing the stuff of life to have its full sensual impact. Even the 'story' of the films *Der Eintänzer* (1978) and *La Ferdinanda* (1981) is obviously only a pretext for weaving together events on a more elementary level of experience.

The 'stories' in these films are like protective vessels within which persons and machines play their ironically sensitive game—a veritable ballet of sensibility and self-protective vulnerability. Irony springs from the distanced stance of the artist, aided by her invention of communicative constructions. She pulls the strings from her position as a detached observer in the background, well aware of being able to trigger off in the viewer those accurately aimed transference reactions described above. It is as if the binoculars which have figured so often in her recent installations were constantly being passed back and forth between her hands and ours so that we are vicariously moved by events without actually having to take part in them. This may explain the fascination of the mirrors; duplication creates a cushioning distance from brutal reality.

The transitions in Rebecca Horn's world are a state of flux between pretence and reality, spirituality and surface appearance, seeming and being, between live event and fiction. And everything appears to be sustained by the calming sense of control exercised by the rituals in which humans and machines are caught up. In their gentle compulsion they are reminiscent of Buster Keaton to whom Rebecca Horn has devoted her next film.

Bice Curiger

Reprinted from *Parkett* No. 13, Zurich (1987), by permission.

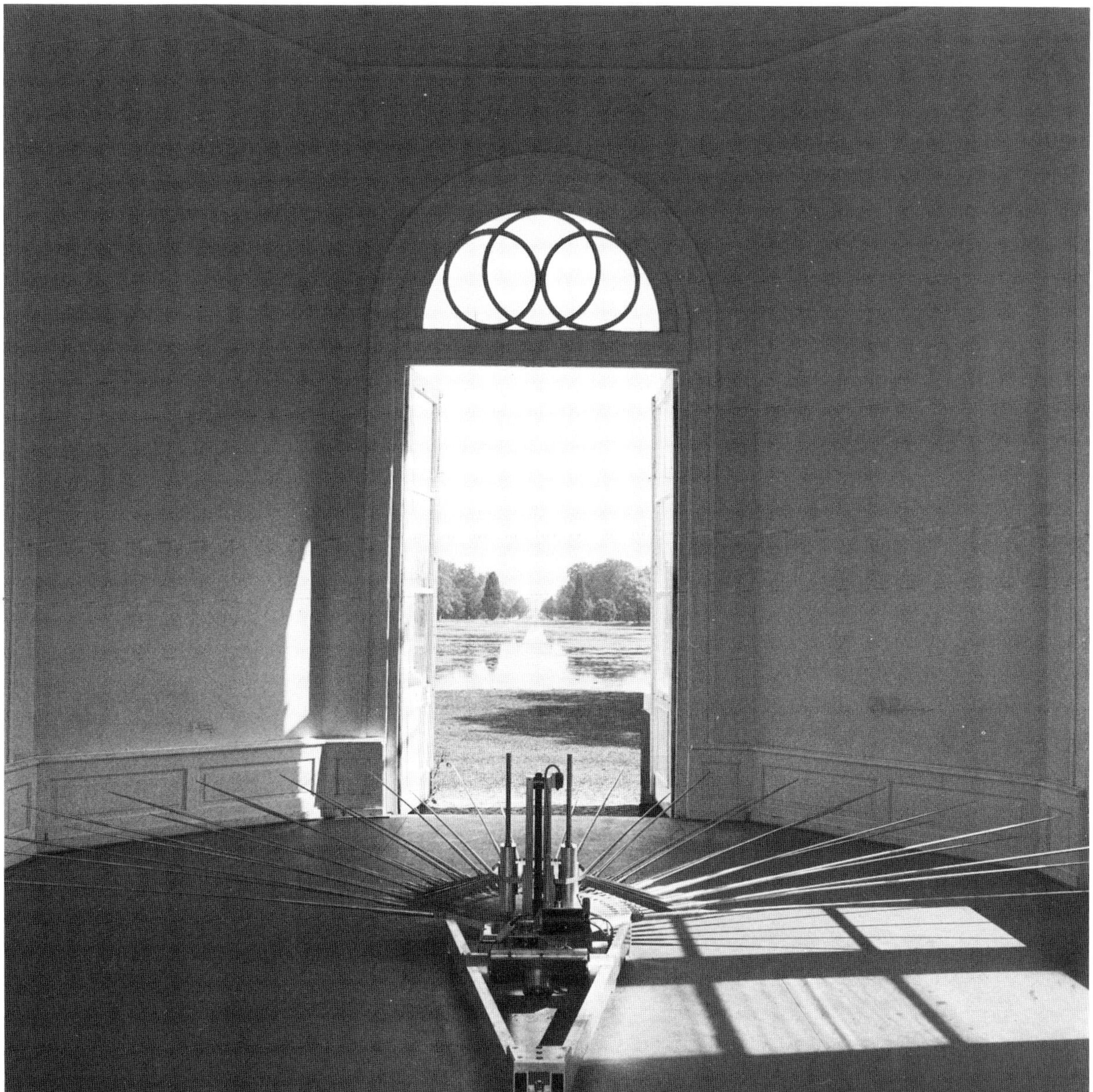

Rebecca Horn, installation of *Peacock Machine* at Documenta 7, Kassel (1982)

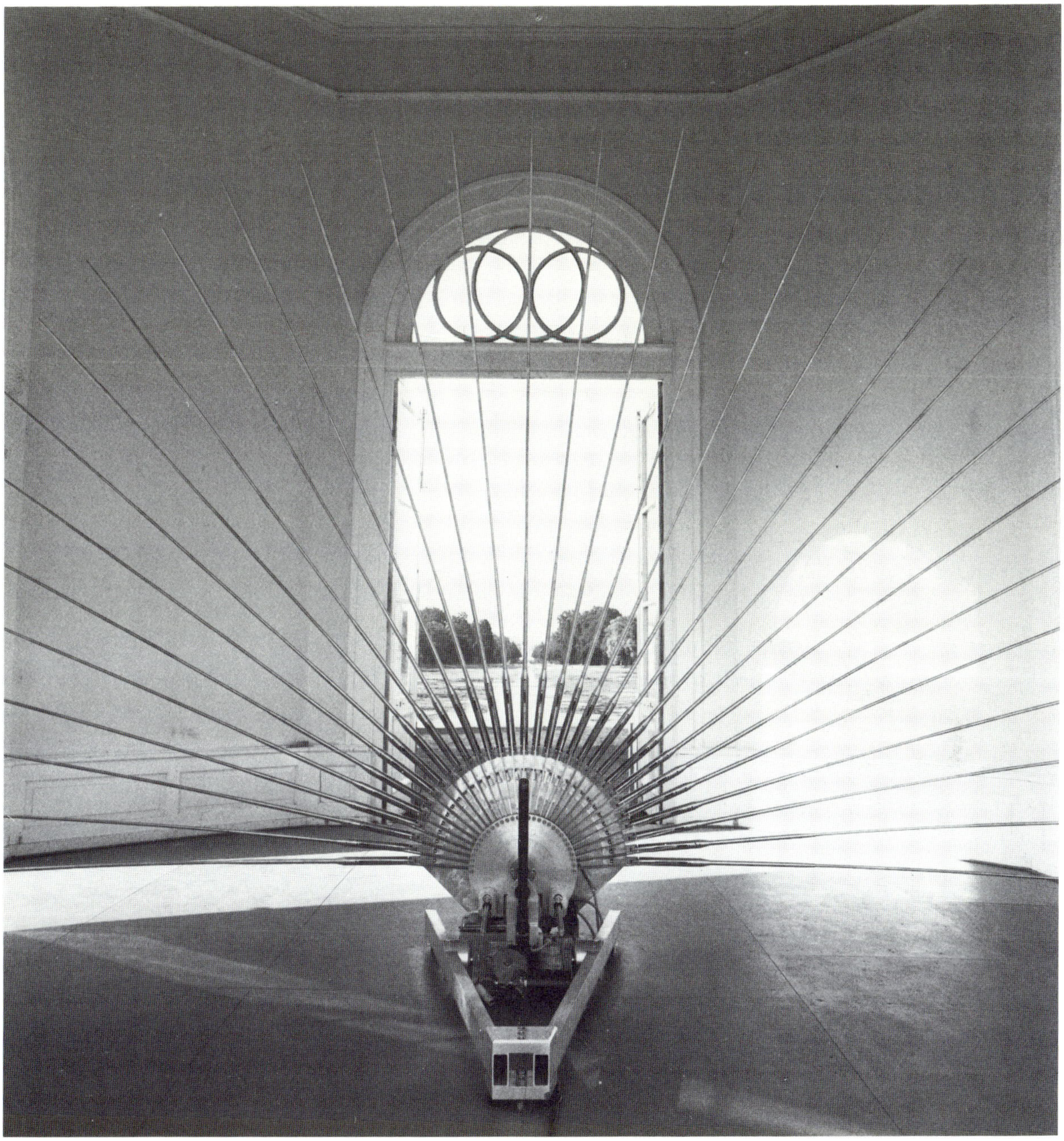

STEPHAN HUBER

This Business of Living (from the Diaries of Cesare Pavese)

12 December 1939

To take the mystery to pieces in order to use it 'cold' in one's work (without the agony of creation) is the impulse behind the whole history of the spirit. Herein lies the dignity of man, but also his temptation.

23 January 1939

. . . One must foster instinct, seek it out, recognise it, rely on it, without dulling it by reflection. But thought is needed, too, to act in accordance with it and take its place in moments when we are deaf to it.

18 February 1940

Once the fervour of a monomania has lapsed, it has no central idea that might give significance to random moments of inner reflection. In short, the more the spirit is absorbed by a dominating mood, the richer and more varied is one's inner breadth of vision.

One must look for one thing only, to find many.

29 January 1939

The most banal thing, discovered in ourselves, becomes intensely interesting. It is no longer an abstract banality, but an amazing co-ordination between reality and our own individuality.

7 May 1949

In any other business or profession one can live according to the clichés *of that particular job, 'playing the part'. Writers and artists, no. They would be* bohemians, *blockheads, intolerable bores. Why? Because painting or writing is not a business or profession. At least, not in these days.*

Reprinted from *This Business of Living: Diaries 1935–1950* by Cesare Pavese, translated by A E Murch with Jeanne Molli, and published by Quartet Books, London (1980), by permission.

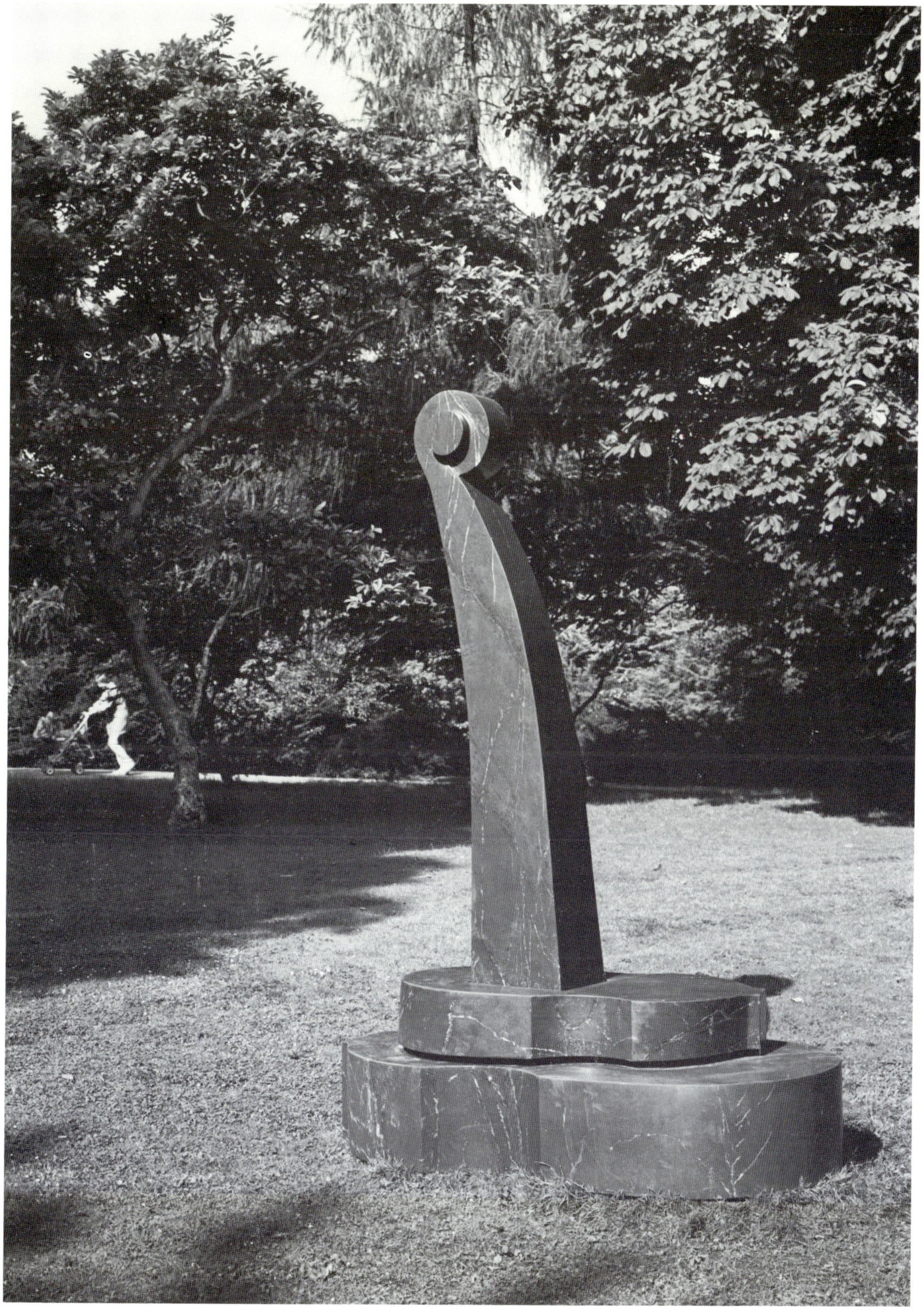

Stephan Huber, *Cello* 1987, Stadtpark, Essen

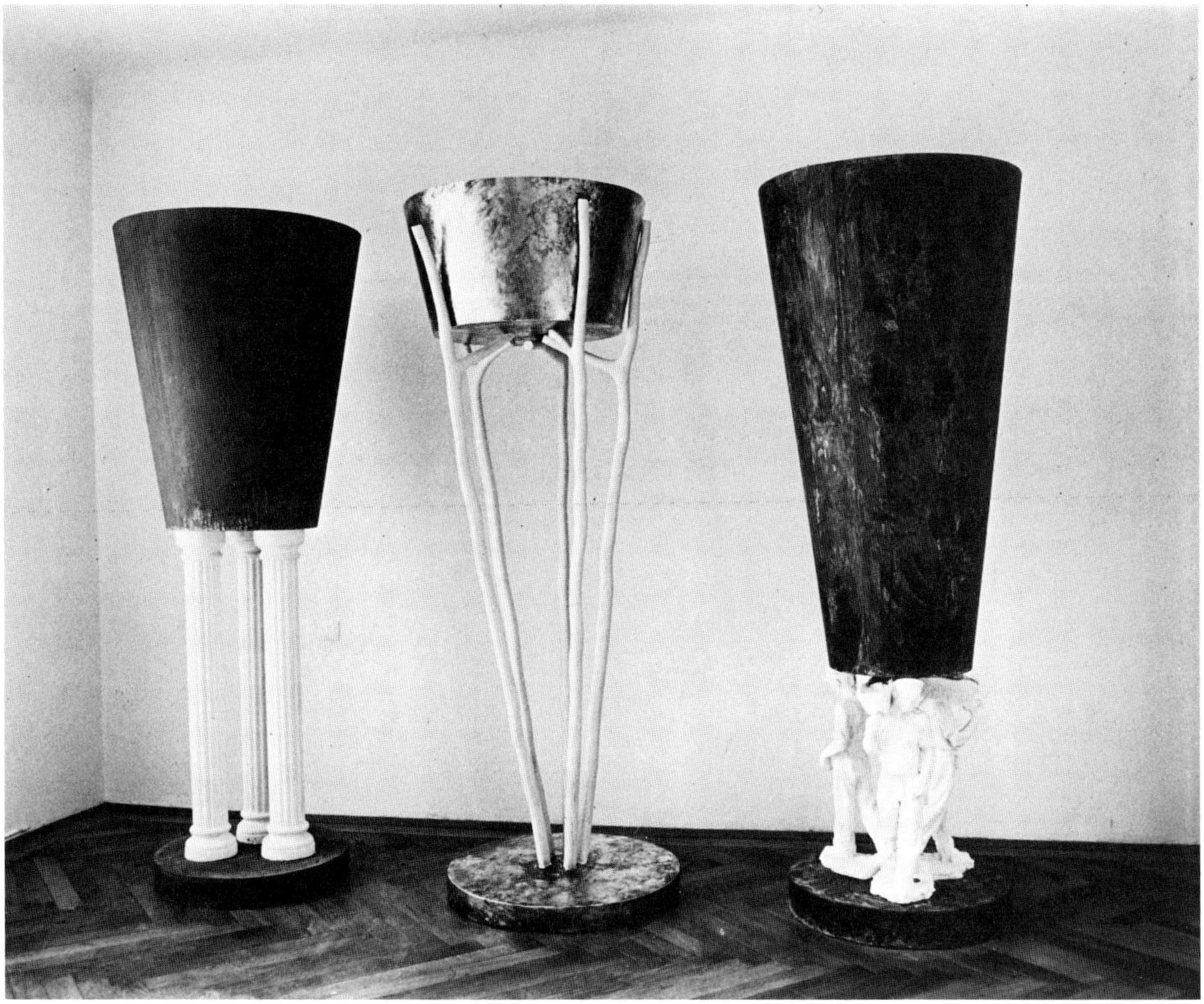

Stephan Huber, *Die Macht, Das Glück, Das Geld* 1986
Private Collection

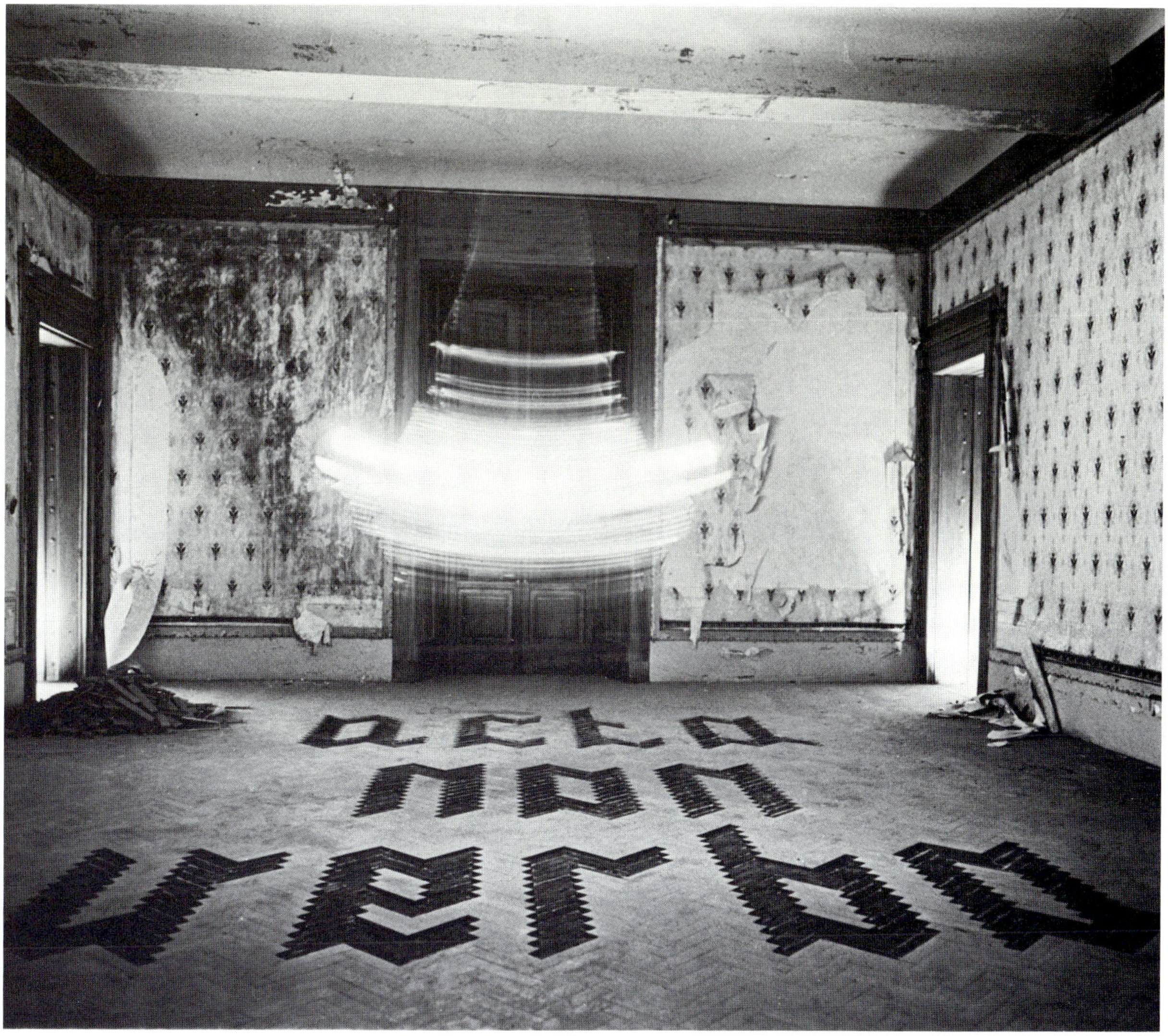

Stephan Huber, installation of *Acta non Verba* at the Villa Demidoff, Florence (1986)

AXEL KASSEBÖHMER

Of Memory

A tower made of iron rods is set up and on the top is attached a closed wooden box for camera and camera-man. Two men climb up the tower. Crows, which should be observed, fly up to it from the trees. After a while one of the men leaves the tower; only then do the crows return to their roosts in the trees.

The ability to retain a sense of danger in one's memory, even if it is no longer discernable, is considered by behaviourists as an astounding feat—though it does not seemingly stretch to crows in any appreciable way.

We could remember similar experiences decades later. Could it not be that what distinguishes the human being most notably from all other living creatures is the effectiveness of his memory?

Ought we not really to be bundles of nerves, unable to live because of fear? Human beings have developed several ways of avoiding that danger. Indeed, people even try to objectify what they remember and to make it available to the community.

Art belongs in this category. It is part of our memory, and it is—among other things—an attempt to overcome fear. But what use is art which refuses to face up to its history?

Axel Kasseböhmer

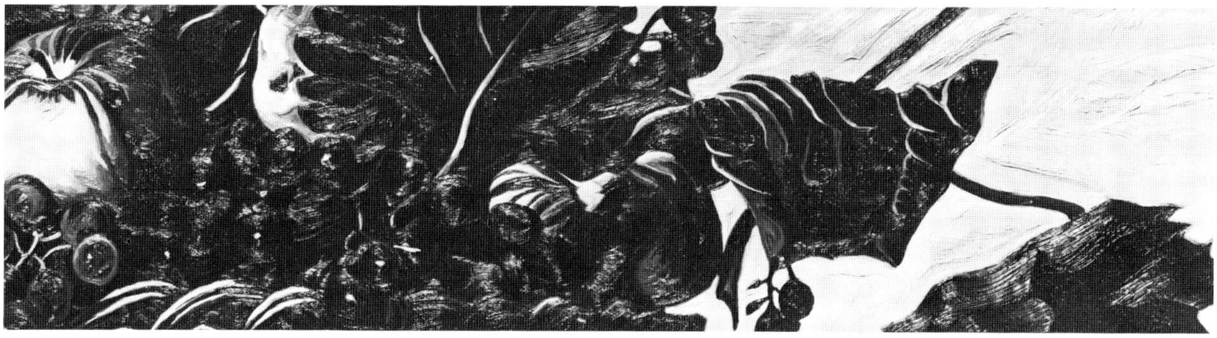

17 Axel Kasseböhmer, *Still Life IV* 1984

The Means of Meaning: Axel Kasseböhmer in Quotation Masks

An *Internationale* of pastiche has demonstrated during the last few years, how difficult it has become for younger artists to survive—not economically but in terms of trade and craft. Who could be more aware of this crisis than a painter who experienced Gerhard Richter's teaching, as Axel Kasseböhmer did some ten years ago.

If Sartre and Camus defined existentialism for everyman, it was Richter who defined it for the contemporary painter. But in contrast to those writers he does not offer the slightest hope or enthusiasm. His teaching can hold good only for those strong enough to find their own way. For Kasseböhmer it was a way back to the social roots of painting. While Richter destroys the means of painting by quoting them *not exactly,* Kasseböhmer reconstructs them carefully and with patience, as if some forgotten knowledge could reveal itself unexpectedly to the devotee. But neither mannerism nor historicism are his passwords, although he crosses unembarrassedly the borderline that modernism once established between the contemporary and the obsolete. Whoever poached beyond that border knows you can find your game there and eat it on this side light-heartedly enough, if you can keep your head. Painting is a trade that cannot survive without tradition, but as a modern artist you can have your choice.

Kasseböhmer, however, is not an eclectic. He does not go for this style or another. He is looking for the very core of them all. If he revitalises the historical means of painting, it is in order to save their meaning—not to tell a story already often told, but to paint a modern picture, i.e. deliver the solution and leave the riddle to be guessed.

Kasseböhmer's reinsuranced modernism is not the fashionable attitude of *Paint it again, Sam!,* with which a Mike Bidlo or other postmodernist defeatists squander their loot. Kasseböhmer takes his task very seriously; he is not interested in another provocation of the spectator but in the evocation of content. Though modern art remains a riddle for him, too, he is not going to ridicule it. One of his favourite riddles is, whether painting can regain a general meaning and understanding instead of continuing to produce eccentric forms. A short text he wrote is dedicated to this question (*Vom Allgemeinen*). From its very beginning modern art's radical changes of form were counterbalanced by efforts to secure a broad understanding and a direct access to its meaning; efforts, however, that turned out to be utopian if not vague. According to an analysis that Claude Lévi-Strauss gave of the development of modern art, primitivism was one of these efforts to 'return to a collective function of art', after impressionism had suspended academicism and cubism rediscovered the object and its semantic challenges. The failure of primitivism in this respect was that it aroused even more hostility against modern art instead of giving it a common meaning. Since the constructivist variant of this utopian plan failed too, the central dilemma of modern art has not been solved, the dilemma that concerns 'not only the artistic forms, but their place within society'. Although the dilemma is as old as modern art itself, the circumstances under which it has to be considered have changed radically. If—as Lévi-Strauss suggests—the variety of styles and their eligibility for use at the discretion of the artist were the *results* of this dilemma, today they are *preliminaries,* so much the more so as modern art has established itself as a new academicism—more influential, more shining and probably even more successful than its nineteenth-century predecessor. Like any academicism it does not appear as the petrification of a historical process, but as a dogma by habit, be it even the habit of 'anything goes'.

For Kasseböhmer, modernity has to be judged by the results and not by the promises and suggestions it made. The loss of a general understanding is not the only result that makes him wonder if modern painting was wrong from the start. In a second text, written a few months ago and printed here, Kasseböhmer sees art as a major agent of *memoria* and wonders how modern art could abandon this origin by adopting the idea of progress (*Vom Gedächtnis*).

Those are the problems that inspire Kasseböhmer's painting, and he is far from answering the questions that his pictures pose. As results of his investigation they are fragments, hints, essays, interferences or pastiches; he does not celebrate the end of modernism, but still marvels at its very beginning. Will we ever be able to look at modernism without being prey to its propaganda and illusions? Does the border really exist, that modernism established to separate the old from the new? The more often you cross it from both sides, the less you believe it, says Kasseböhmer, still on this side.

Walter Grasskamp

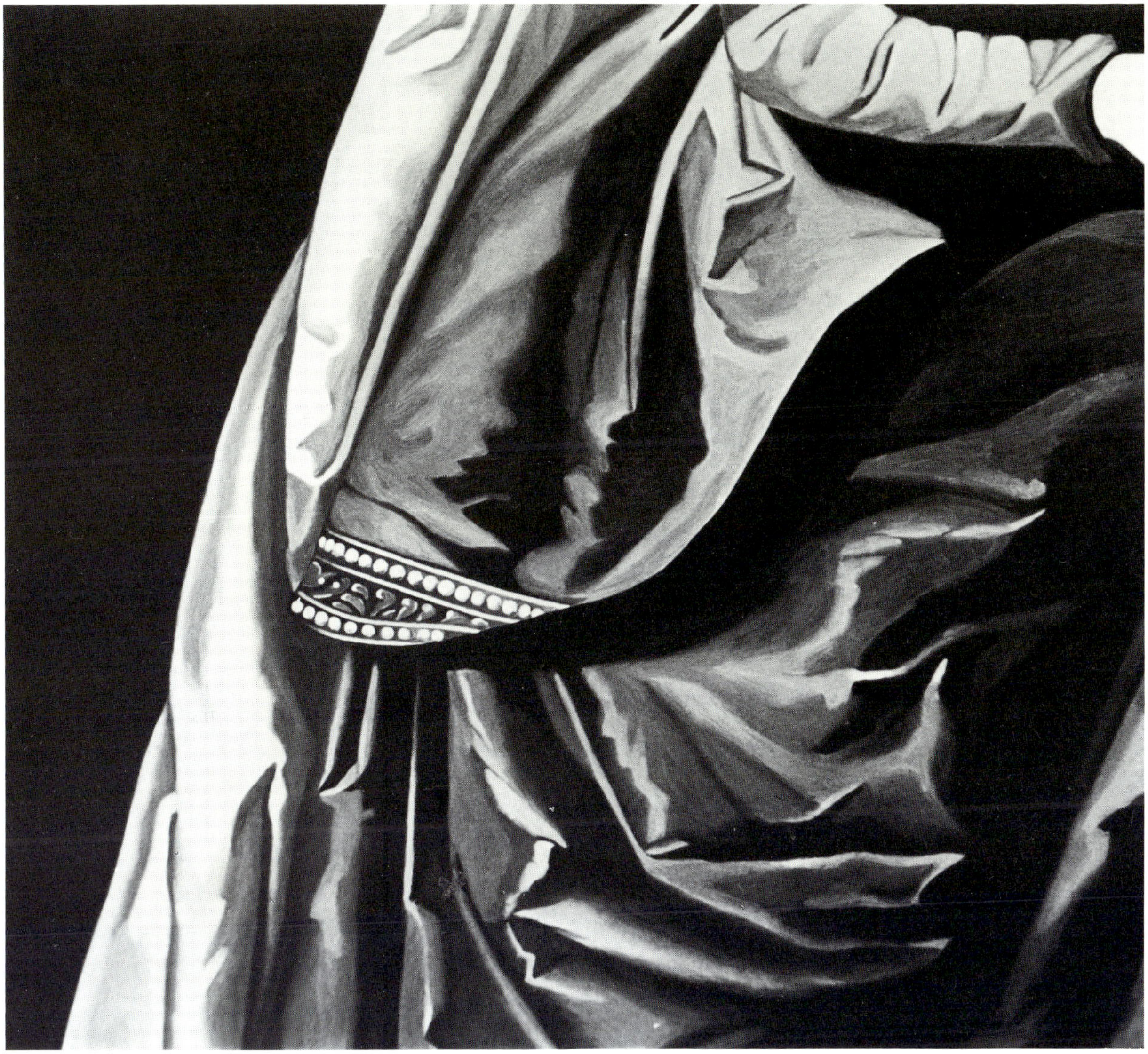

15 Axel Kasseböhmer, *Drapery* 1981

SOL LEWITT

The Words and the Drawings

'A given system of signs must make it possible to analyse things right down to their simplest elements; it must be able to unravel things back to their origin. But it must also show how the combinations of those elements become possible and how the complexity of things has sprung from one idea.'

Michel Foucault in *Les Mots et les Choses,* 1966

The wall drawings of Sol LeWitt differ in many respects from the forms and functions of drawings as we know them from the work of other artists. They stand apart, for example, through their articulation in two phases; they are first expressed in language—in the form of a definition that lays down the properties which the drawing is to have, and at the same time acts as a descriptive title—and on the basis of this instruction they can then be executed using traditional drawing techniques. The final form in which the drawing manifests itself on the wall is therefore no more and no less than a shadow projection (as Plato might have put it) of the artist's Idea, and in no way constitutes the essence of his work. For, as Sol LeWitt says, his art is not concerned with formal innovation and cannot therefore be understood in terms of a formal approach.

The two forms of articulation of the wall drawing are in fact concerned with the distinction between artistic invention and execution. In itself that distinction is nothing new. Even Vasari and his contemporaries used different terms for the conception and the realisation of their art: underlying the *Disegno* (literally the design, but then already used in the sense of drawing) there was always the *Idea* being the pure form in which the work of art initially reveals itself in the mind of the artist. But in those days the *Idea* still came from God, and the *Disegno* still served within the hierarchy of the arts the higher purpose of painting, sculpture or architecture.

Sol LeWitt gives new and radical shape to the traditional distinction between invention and execution. He uncouples the Idea from the material realisation by conceptualising it in another medium (language) which differs essentially from that used for its embodiment in a drawing. Drawings have the character of sketches or outlines, and in the creative process they are therefore usually situated in the preparatory phase of the work. In Sol LeWitt's method of working the act of drawing acquires a different momentum; it takes place only at the end of the creative process, so that the ultimate wall drawing becomes a kind of *a posteriori* sketch which cannot manifest itself until the Idea underlying it has found its own form and content in language. In this way LeWitt evidently makes the execution of a work of art subordinate to its conceptualisation.

Drawings are also characterised by the personal uniqueness which they derive from the hand of the artist. The concept of a wall drawing is formulated by Sol LeWitt in such a manner that the drawing itself can in principle be done by anyone in a variety of circumstances, without losing quality or authenticity. We thus are dealing with a form of drawing which, remarkably enough, seems to be capable of repetition. One thinks immediately of a comparison with reproductions.

In itself the reproduction of art is again nothing new. Walter Benjamin remarked that the phenomenon is probably as old as art itself because anything made by man can also be imitated by man. But the reproductions to which he refers—whether they are copies of a painting, done by an apprentice on the instructions of his master, or a photographic reproduction—are always derived from an original with a material character.

This materialistic attitude to art therefore brings him to the conclusion that 'the uniqueness and material permanence in the original are just as closely interwoven as the fugitiveness and repeatability in the reproduction'. The repeatability of Sol LeWitt's wall drawings is of a different nature. Sol LeWitt's view of art is not materialistic but conceptual. If one can speak of an original in his case—let us assume for a moment that this role is in a sense fulfilled by the formulation of the concept on the basis of which the drawing is executed—then that original has by no means a material character, and indeed it is not factual in nature but linguistic, because it can only be recorded in language. For that reason it stands apart from space and time, and in principle it can be visualised by anyone anywhere, always provided that the local conditions allow the implementation of all instructions. By definition, however, those conditions will always be different. Depending on such differences, every realisation will always have a specific character. If we compare in the work of Sol LeWitt the wall drawing in the form in which it ultimately appears on the wall with one of the many possible reproductions of an original, then it is precisely the 'reproduction' that is here materially permanent and unique, even without the support of the artist's own 'handwriting'.

It appears from the foregoing that Sol LeWitt's method of working makes variations of form possible in which the Idea retains its validity under all circumstances. In other words, his concept for a wall drawing is equivalently present in every good embodiment of that concept. This imposes certain demands on the formulation of the concept. The manner in which the concept formulates the Idea must make it possible by draughtmanship to produce a number of tangible images, which are interchangeable relative to the concept. The sum of all possible embodiments of one and the same concept is consequently a collection of homologous pictorial representations. The concept therefore has to function as a generic name indentifying all common elements of which a particular genus of images is composed and at the same time regulating their mutual structure. That is the content of the concept, and also the substance of Sol LeWitt's art: he treats the organisational structure of simple pictorial elements in a conceptual manner. By using language as a system of notation for the Idea, and through the well-considered construction of the concept, Sol LeWitt develops an aesthetic message which is rich enough in information to convey the essence of his work under all circumstances—even when he himself does not apply the drawing to the wall—but which is at the same time so openly constructed that anyone implementing the concept is left with enough freedom of choice and interpretations to stimulate his creative capacity. LeWitt seeks and also makes possible a dialogue with the user of his art.

He does that in a manner which renders superfluous the cult of the 'objet d'art' and the fascination for the ritual of spontaneous expression, without lapsing into the integral rationalisation or indifference of the scientific construction. The rich variety and pictorial splendour of his wall drawings speak for themselves.

Jan Debbaut

Reprinted from *Sol LeWitt Wall Drawings 1968–84,*
published by the Stedelyk Museum, Amsterdam (1984), by permission.

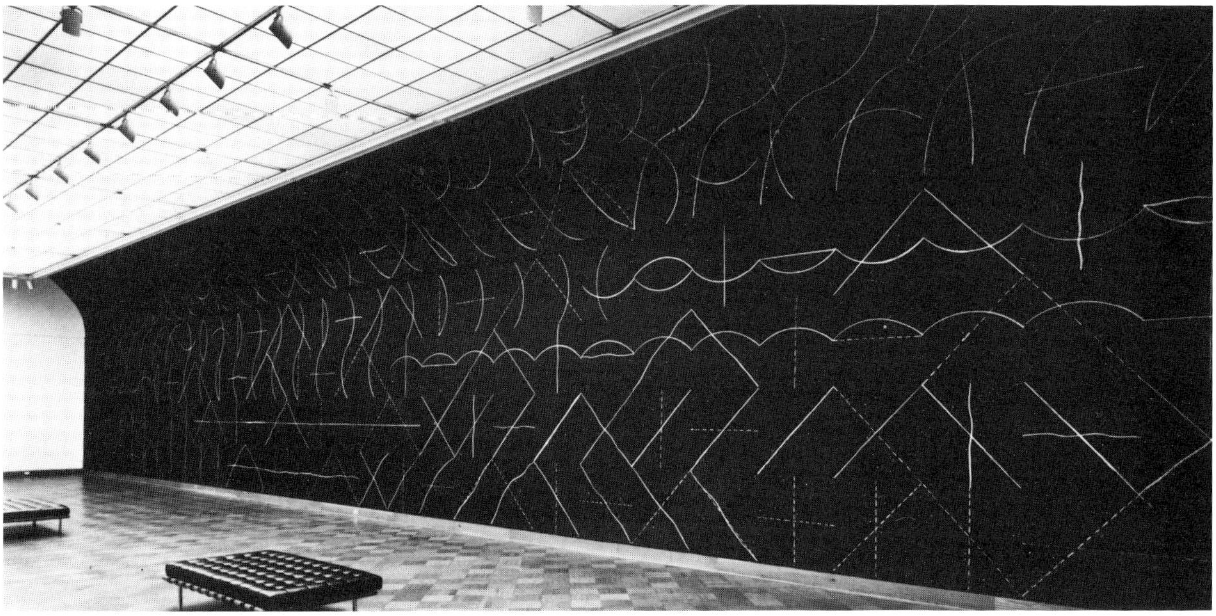

Sol LeWitt, *Wall Drawing* # 260
on black walls, all two-part combinations of white areas from corners and sides, and white straight, not straight and broken lines
First installation: San Francisco, Museum of Art, June 1975
Collection of the Museum of Modern Art, New York

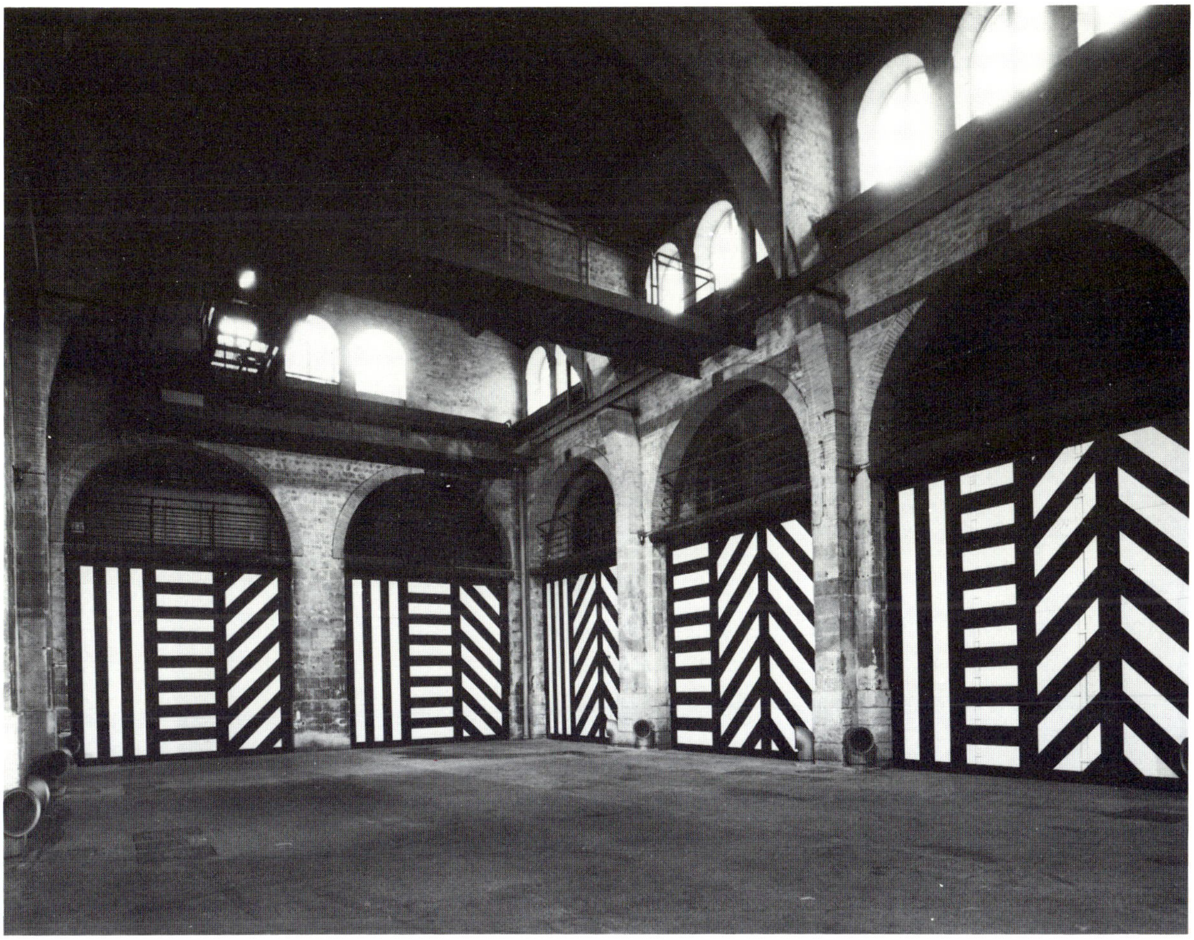

Sol LeWitt, *Wall Drawing* # 390
16-part drawing: all one-, two-, three- and four-part combinations of 12″ (30 cm) parallel bands of lines in four directions drawn in India ink
First installation: Musée d'Art Contemporain, Bordeaux

ANN McCOY

Alchemy is not a lost art but is alive and well in the dreams of modern man

It is hard to be an artist in America with its thrust toward mechanical expansion, extroversion, and materialism. In an art world which favours media appropriated imagery, an artist involved with psychic interiority feels isolated. I have never owned a television. Growing up in the Southwest I was greatly impressed by the Pueblo Indians who still believed in the importance of dreams, visions, and the inner life. The images in my works are not appropriated in the usual post-modern sense. I am not interested in simulation, or in 'plundering the past' for nostalgic reasons. The images in my works come from dreams, the collective unconscious, the psychic reservoir of human experience which is transpersonal. For me the artist stands between two worlds, an outer world which makes us understand everything as the effect of physical and physiological forces, and an inner world which shows us everything as the effect of spiritual agencies.

The images in the works are obtained through a process known as 'incubation' in the classical world. Incubation is a 'sleeping in' to obtain dreams for therapeutic and prophetic ends. Like Nietzsche, Cassirer, and Jung, I feel dreams represent a philogenetically older mode of thought, which although displaced by our modern scientific culture still exists. Through a study of dreams and myths, something may be learned of the unrecognized laws of existence our rational and scientific ways of thought are unable to penetrate. For me our 'rational' commonsense view of reality is not the whole picture, a new mythologem is rising in our midst from the depths of the collective unconscious. The unconscious is no mere repository of the past, but contains the seeds of future psychic situations.

The drawings are the end product of a longer process. For the past twenty years I have catalogued my dreams and visions. Those which are reoccurring or are of special relevance are catalogued, and traced down in the world's iconography. I also pay attention to synchronistic, acausal events which I feel are related to the images in the dreams.

The Temple of Isis

The events which led to the making of *The Temple of Isis* came from a dream fragment. In a dream I was handed an ancient instrument by an unknown woman. The next day as I was looking up a word in my dictionary, I saw a picture of a sistrum, the ancient instrument from my dream. The synchronicity of the events was underscored the following afternoon when I found a brochure from an Egyptologist in the street. I entered his shop and saw a sistrum in the case. When I told him about my dream, he sold me the sistrum at a greatly reduced price, and informed me it was the first he had ever had. The sistrum was thought to contain the magical properties of Isis, and when rattled was believed to make the Nile rise and fall. This votive rattle meant to keep the worshipper in a state of spiritual attentiveness.

In a second dream, I was with a group of archeologists restoring an ancient temple site. A child entered the temenos on a donkey. Unlike Christ, the child was a young radiant Goddess. The dream was for me an annunciation. We live in an historical period which is overly androlatrous. With the exception of the Virgin Mary, we have no feminine deity. For me the dream signaled not the return to a matriarchal monotheism, but an integration of the divine feminine into the psychic lives of both men and women. The Eros represented by the Aphrodite is sadly lacking in our culture dominated by Apollo, Ares, and sky gods. More than ever we need the goddess, the guardian of psychic interiority.

The night I began the drawing, I had a dream in which Isis appeared wearing a golden robe of silk. I touched the hem of her robe and awakened feeling changed by the numinious content of the dream. For me the dream began a meditation on Isis and her meaning for the modern world. A second dream in Venice followed: I was working on the excavation of a site containing huge clay cows. As we worked a friend read a text on a female figure who was resurrected. In Egypt the cow was associated with Hathor/Isis and the bull with Osiris/Apis.

Both dreams inspired me to take a pilgrimage to the Temple of Isis in Pompeii. I arrived in Pompeii in a thunderstorm, lightening bolts shooting through the black sky and off the rim of the volcano. The atmosphere was mysterious, and the place deserted of visitors. I climbed over a back wall and spent the day alone in the tiny temple.

Isis, like Demeter is an agricultural goddess whose mysteries many scholars feel had to do with rebirth in the underworld . . . as the seed beneath the soil was equated to a kind of psychological and spiritual renewal likened to the agricultural cycle of renewal. The goddess is the guardian of feeling, interiority, and the healing aspect of the feminine. Isis heals her husband Osiris and also symbolizes an agricultural renewal needed by our environmentally devasted world.

When the Temple of Isis in Pompeii was first excavated, they found eggs perfectly preserved on the altar. The egg is not just a cosmogonic symbol, it is also a philosophical symbol. As the philosophical egg of the medieval natural philosophers, it is the vessel from which the Anthropos, the spiritual, inner, and complete man emerges.

Coeur de Lion
My reoccurring childhood dream was of a king being dismembered and ground up with a mortar and pestle. Years later when I saw the drawing in the *Splendor Solis* (Solomon Trismosin, 1582) of the dismemberment of the king, I began to understand the relationship of my dreams to alchemical symbolism and analytical psychology. Around that time I also encountered the tale of the Alexandrian physicians who took the body of the king and ground it into a powder and placed it in a crucible. When I entered Jungian analysis, I began to understand the relationship of the *separatio* (dismemberment) to the alchemical process; C.G. Jung first made the connection between dreams and alchemical symbolism. The alchemical Great Work has to do with an inner transformation process, not the making of gold. Alchemy is not a lost art but is alive and well in the dreams of modern man. As in the *Splendor Solis* and the *Visions of Zosimos* the old man (the king) is dismembered and is reconstituted as the new (spiritual) man; Osiris is the prototype of this process. These phantasies of the early alchemists express symbolically occurrances on the deepest layers of the psyche, and provide a language for the steps in the inner transformation

process. The goal of the individuation process is the conscious realization of the Self. Alchemical processes, *mortificatio, solutio, coniunctio,* etc. have their parallel in the dream world and in the life of the psyche.

The scope of alchemical symbolism is too vast for a catalogue essay. Therefore, I will limit myself to a discussion of some of the symbols found in my work *Coeur de Lion*. A series of dreams beginning in childhood provided the material for this work.

The Red Mass is a stage of the alchemical Great Work. Seventeenth-century German engravings show Christ in the alchemical garden holding two chalices out to the sun and moon. Blood flows from his side wound into the Fountain of Life which feeds the later stages of the work. The sweating of the blood and wounding represent psychic advances in man which arise from the suffering of the soul.

The Christ in the Red Mass is a *soter cosmi* (preserver of the cosmos) who represents the still unconscious idea of the whole or complete man who will bring about the deliverance of the world. The blood which flows from the side of Christ into the Fountain of Life feeds the later stages of the work and is crowned by the figure of Mercurius, the divine child, whose birth is the outcome of the Great Work. The blood's essential quality is its power for redemption, its archetypal dynamism.

The author of the treatise *De Sulphure* says the soul ''is the vice-regent of God (*sui locum tenens seu vice Rex est*) and dwells in the life spirit of the pure blood''. (C.G. Jung)

The *Rubedo* the reddening process in alchemy is frequently compared to blood, and when it is a stone to the carbuncle *Gutheil.* Blood in alchemy is also linked to the blood of the lion, the rose, and the pelican (a Christian symbol) who was thought to feed her young with blood from her breast. In *Khunrath* the 'lion lured forth from the Saturnal mountain' had rose coloured blood. In the treatise the Son of the Great World is correlated with Christ, and his blood with the quintessence of the Red Tincture.

In the drawing *Coeur de Lion*, Christ has himself been transformed into a more complete image of God . . . Aion, the god of late Roman antiquity. The heart of the lion god finds its parallel in the *sacre coeur* of Christ. Aion encompasses both light and dark. A.E. (George Russell), the Irish writer, and C.G. Jung both discuss the importance of Aion in the visions of modern man. In the work both male and female lions are shown, the female in the form of the lion goddess Tanit. The two lions call to mind figure IV from *The Book of Lambspring*, ''Here you behold a great marvel—two lions are joined as one''.

The wolves (lower corner of *Coeur de Lion*) are from a dream I had in which a wolf tore off the sternum exposing my heart. In Michael Maier's *Scrutinum Chymicum* (1687), a wolf is shown devouring the king. In the background we see sublimation of the *prima materia* and rebirth of the king. The wolf is shown as the *prima materia* devouring the king.

My dreams are filled with dismemberment and the dissection of the body. The physician/alchemist Robert Fludd felt the body to be a reflection of God's cosmos in its organs.

Fludd's vision of the threefold man shows the light of God shining above three bodily realms. The heart is compared to the sun which Harvey would later call the capital of the body, and the sun is compared to God. The heart has special meaning for me, because like the Hopi, I feel it should once again become the centre of consciousness, Man must learn to think with his heart not his head. In India this idea is expressed in a return to the heart *chakra:*

> "Thus, the task of consciousness for the Coeur de Lion lies in recognizing the archetypal construct of its thought, that is actions, desires and ardent beliefs are all imaginations—creations of the himma—and that what it experiences as life, love, and world is its own enthymesis presented outside the macrocosm". *James Hillman*

The soul of the Philosopher's Stone is also found in its heart:

> "But as regards the fixation and permanence of the soul and spirit at the end of the sublimation, this takes place when the secret stone is added, which cannot be grasped by the senses, but only by the intellect, through inspiration or divine revelation, or through the teaching of an initiate. Alexander says there are two categories: seeing through the eye and understanding through the heart". *C.G. Jung*

This discourse ends on the heart and soul. It is these two elements which seem so lacking in the modern art world. As in alchemy, spirit must be wrenched from the dung, the new or spiritual man must replace the old man. The artist should retain his former role as carrier of spiritual ideas, and art should be returned to its transformative and transcendent function. For me the alchemical view has the greatest scope, and a study of alchemy can provide us with a helpful model. The transformation process described in alchemical symbolism is life's goal, and although an individual can never hope to experience the full range of alchemical symbolism, any experience of the process means an extension of man beyond himself.

Ann McCoy
25 July 1987
New York City

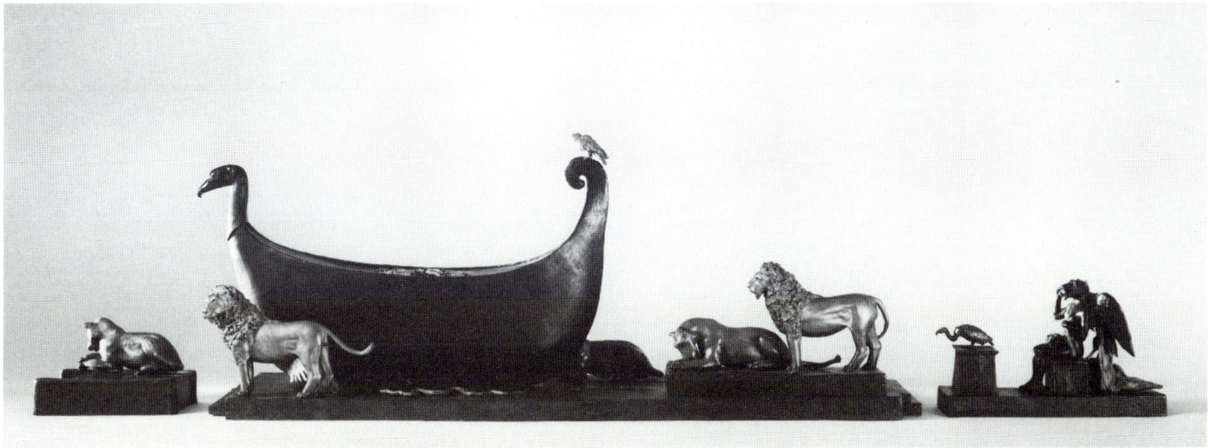

Ann McCoy, *Barque with Lion Goddess V* 1985
Private Collection

STEPHEN McKENNA

Synopsis for a Drama

Let us imagine a young man of good education and some aptitude of his own, arriving in the city and intent on making a name for himself. As part of his upbringing he had absorbed certain cultural values, developed instincts to guide his taste and learned to subject his acquired preconceptions to the occasional scrutiny of the intellect.

In spite of the depredations of war and the influx of new wealth, the city at that time still retained part of its old plan. The broad avenues, where the palaces had been largely replaced by commercial properties and museums, were crossed by smaller streets of eighteenth century residences fronted by trees.

In one of these lateral streets was a theatre of square facade, with large glazed doors opening to the foyer, once resplendent and now decently faded. The young man attended here regularly at the presentations of the standard repertoire of classical plays.

He sensed, at times, the weaknesses and distortions of the translations, regretting his incapacity to understand the original texts, and the gaps in his knowledge of mythology. The commentators, old and new, to whom he turned in an effort to deepen his understanding, seemed often to obscure with layers of scholarship or theory both the significance of the poetry and his enjoyment of the performance.

An interest in the theatre had been awakened early by looking at engravings, which either illustrated memorable scenes or represented some aspect of the technical and aesthetic history of theatrical productions. These engravings, frequently based on well-known paintings of the time, had some of the fresh, urgent, but slightly exaggerated qualities of the naive. The artists seemed undecided whether to portray the particularities of the actors, or to give generalised depictions of the roles in which they played.

Moving down one of the aisles converging on the stage, he would study the painted safety curtain while speculating on the depth of scenery behind it. His expectations were especially aroused if the evening's play were to be a tragedy. The inevitable progress of events towards an inescapable end stirred his sense of the cosmic, flattered also his views on the relationship of men to gods.

In painting, now the main occupation of his daylight hours, the tragic had no place, there being no dimension of time in which it could occur. Attempts at portraying the tragic were deflected into irony or bathos, or into an intangible atmosphere of romantic desperation. Such atmospheres, when they were not simply reflections of the artist's biography or an accumulation of picturesque detail, depended either on colour, with its nuances of exquisite taste and sensation, or on described or recorded gesture. His reflections on the possibility of a tragic geometry had led him to conclude that in an art which was fundamentally spatial there was always room for human optimism. The fascinating implacability of the interest in men's affairs taken by the gods, the proper subject of poetry, was replaced in painting by the more formal, more pleasurable, if less intoxicating arrangement of colours in space.

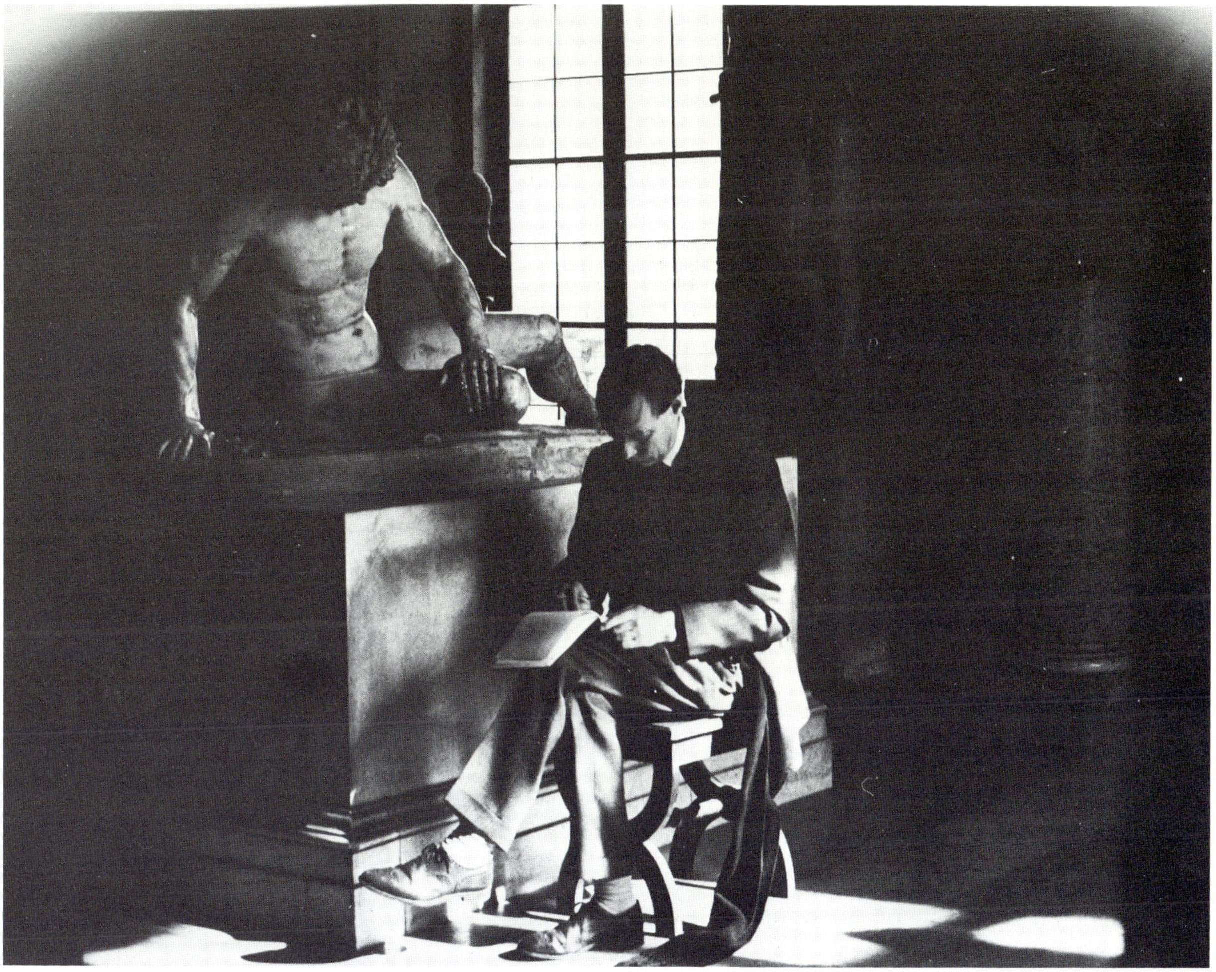

Stephen McKenna (Photo: Maria Gilissen)

The proscenium arch, or the boards, in the theatre had a function similar to the surface of the wall or canvas in painting: they invited the spectator to share in a ritual, the depth of participation being dependent on the extent of his knowledge of the conventions operating, and his understanding of their significance.

The theatrical performances contained endless possibilities of disappointment for both players and audience. The number of factors involved, from the traditional story through author, director, designer, actors and the response, often loud, of the audience made it almost inevitable that there would be errors of judgement or inadequacies of skill. The consensus needed to realise such a complex event made the influence of current taste and fashion unavoidable. But was this undesirable? Did not such communal performances thrive on the energy generated by a public appreciation and purpose?

Finding it more urgent to conserve his own energy, the young man preferred an activity with apparently fewer distracting participants. He had hoped, in painting, to find a more controllable language as effective as the theatre in recalling cultural memories and in giving those same memories a form on which the imagination could work. But the painter, confronted with the changing canvas, becomes involved in a dramatic dialogue with its appearance and meaning.

The energetic, if sometimes destructive adventurism of his immediate predecessors in the field had helped them with their problem of individual identity in a phase of cultural uncertainty. His concern was to recognise and preserve the trace of the configuration of culture in its entirety, to become aware of the present as an accumulation of the past. This was not the same as looking back through a temporal perspective which could be projected onto the future. The limits of the possible extend in both directions in time, and the ways in which they may be tested do not change essentially from one age to another.

His apparent singularity, not, in fact, dissimilar to that of many of his contemporaries, placed him in a position of romantic isolation antithetical to his pursuit of a cohesive, aerial view of culture. The very idea of resistance to a prevailing trend implied a dependence on it, and for a sophisticated, if shallow audience it was all too easy to see an attempt at the reformation of language as being only one more symptom of its decline.

The results of our young man's efforts, as he passed into middle-age, remained inconclusive. The work was continued by his followers. . . .

Stephen McKenna, 1987

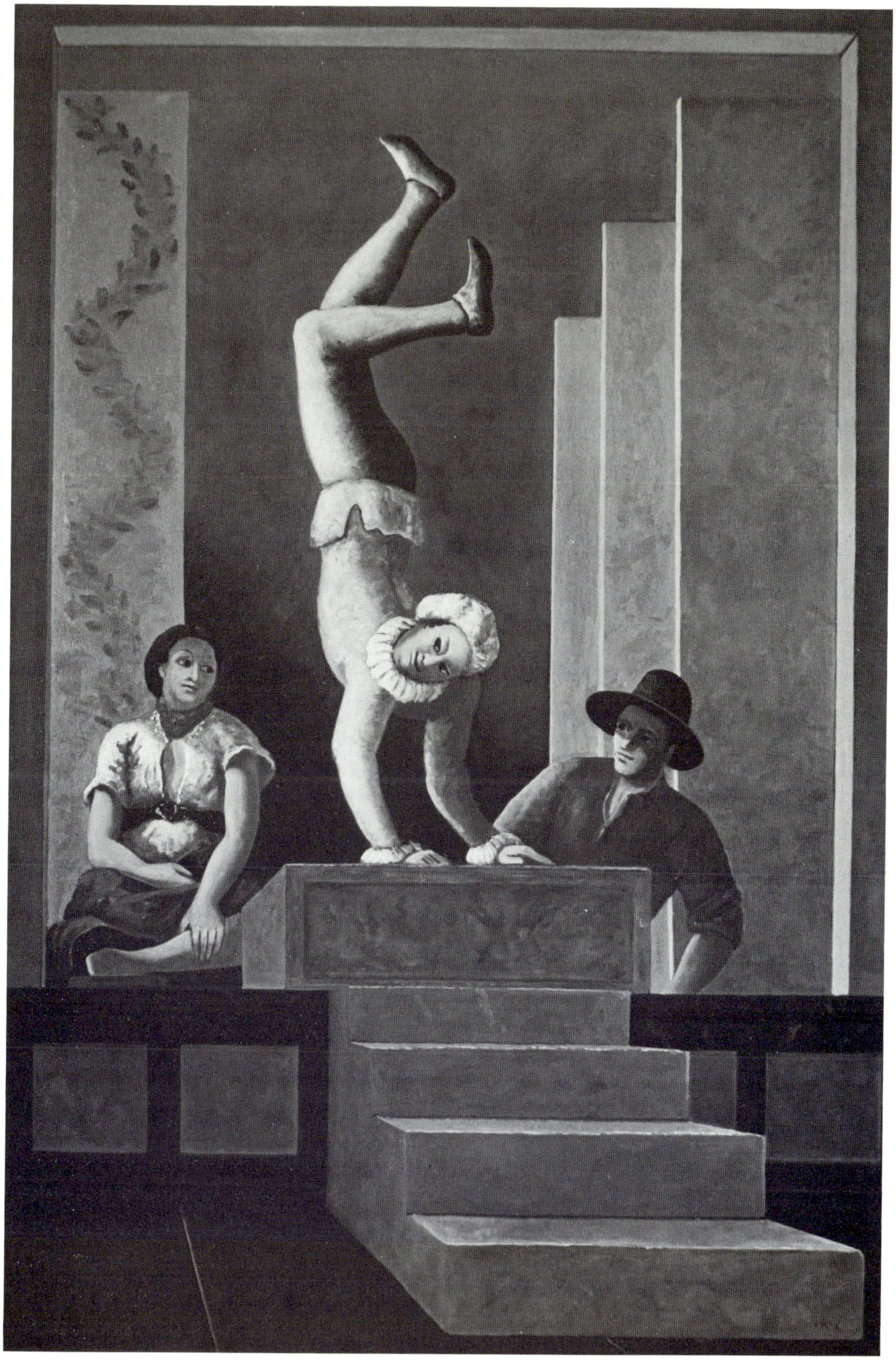

27 Stephen McKenna, *The Acrobat* 1987

Carlo Maria Mariani in interview with Carolyn Christov-Bakargiev

Carolyn Christov-Bakargiev: *Your work, together perhaps with that of Gino De Dominicis, opened up a whole new movement in Italian art, sometimes labelled Anachronism, New Romanticism, Pittura Colta or Hypermannerism. Although some of the artists involved had already had shows by 1979, this trend did not prevail over the Transavantgarde on the international art scene.*

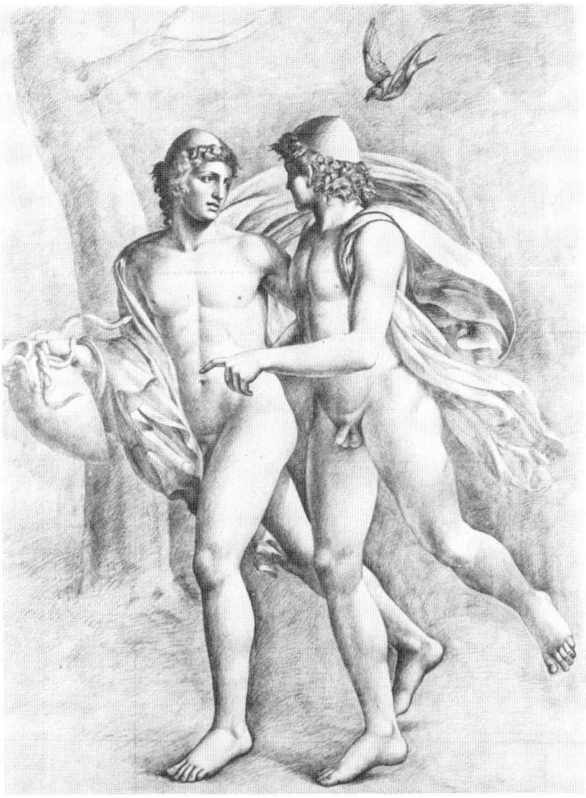

31 Carlo Maria Mariani, *Castor and Pollux* 1982

Carlo Maria Mariani: First of all, most of my followers haven't understood anything about my work and are simply straight revivalists. They are academic and scholastic painters with no conceptual identification with the past. I feel younger than ever today. I still have some tricks up my sleeve! I am an artist of the 1980s who looks to the past just as I could be an artist of the 1700s alive today, incapable of forgetting . . .

CC-B: *Forgetting what?*

CMM: Silence, calm, proportion, serenity—all these qualities of my works are a mirror image of what I would like to be as a man. What can I tell you? I was born in Rome, both my parents were Roman but my paternal grandfather came from Milan and some of my ancestors were German. My great uncle was a more or less unknown Nazarene Pre-Raphaelite painter. My first great loves were Tintoretto, then Titian. I studied at the Academy here in Rome (where I didn't learn anything I didn't already know) and my very first show (which I really shouldn't mention) was in 1966 or 1967 at Il Nuovo Carpine. My real introduction into the art world was thanks to Enzo Cannaviello who exhibited my work in 1975, and then, of course, came Sperone. People at that time used to say I was crazy because I still painted. I appreciated artists such as Burri and Fontana, but my work does not run parallel to the analytical reduction of modernism—it comes after that. Art had to start all over again, and in a radical, almost wild way.

When I have an idea for a painting, I usually start working straight away at the final format, with no preparatory sketches. I work alone, I could never have any helpers, and my sole companion is music, especially organ music. I work rather slowly (it took me a whole year to paint *La Constellazione del Leone*). . . . I've never taught art. About ten years ago, when I needed to earn a living, I tried to get a position teaching painting or drawing, but I was always refused a job because of being 'unfit'—can you believe it?

CC-B: *In the early 1970s art historians began to assess Neo-classicism in depth and several large exhibitions were held such as the great* The Age of Neoclassicism *show in 1972 in London. Your work went through an incredible blossoming during those years. Is there a connection?*

CMM: I did not see that show, but there may be an indirect connection. My interest for the late 1700s and early 1800s was not born in museums but rather in archives and libraries. I was at first interested by the aesthetics of the period, not by specific works of art. Until shortly before I had in fact, been looking more at the Cinquecento. But as a result of what I was reading I went to see the works of artists such as David, Mengs and Angelica Kauffmann. I understood, around 1973–74, that modern art was born with Neoclassicism. The relationship between art of the 1970s and that of Neoclassicists probably runs through Conceptualism. I realised that those artists, just like myself, worked primarily with their mind, not their hands. I also felt very closely their identification and competition with great art of the past, as well as their deep, latent melancholy at the thought of never being able to reach the splendour of the past; therefore I had the same attitude about renouncing originality. But while many of my colleaugues in the seventies reached a point of eliminating the visual, I felt there was a way to continue thinking through painting, and that was specifically concerned with the period in art history when the concept of autonomous art was born, together with those of sublimity, good taste, 'beauty' and 'elegance'. You know, today's society is craving to feel these things again, only it can't admit it.

CC-B: *Some critics have said that your work refers back to Neoclassicism through a 'negative ideology'. With abstraction and conceptualism, modern art reached the end of the line, so your adopting precisely the style of the birth of the modern cannot be but a nihilistic and ironic comment on the closing of an age.*

CMM: This is also true, just as speaking of irony in my work is correct. But it explains only one level.

CC-B: *Irony is fundamental in* La Costellazione del Leone *(1981), or in your recent portraits of Merz, Schnabel, Clemente and so on. Are they not reversals of Warhol's portraits where celebrities are incorporated into the flat, anonymous style of advertising? Are they not typically eighteenth century mock-heroic poems?*

CMM: Yes, of course. The subjects are presented outside of their actual time, in heroic poses. There is irony in other works as well, such as in the series on the *Artist* which I exhibited in 1984 in New York. The artist is crowned with laurels and portrayed neoclassically as a statuary figure, yet the situations in which he is placed are anything but heroic. I was actually intending to evoke 'the tragic' and I was referring to the feeling of folly and of impending tragedy in the eighties, or rather of art in the eighties. But to speak only of irony is simplistic.

CC-B: *Even when a painting of yours is 'straight neoclassical', such as in* Orpheus *(1978), there are intentions which create dual levels of meaning, especially in the relationship with the audience. A neoclassic artist may have wilfully chosen canons of Greek sculpture, but myth for him and his audience was still 'given' by tradition. When you use myth on the other hand, you are speaking a lost language, staging ancient myth as a postmodern myth of a lost, hermetic art. There is therefore not so much irony in the paintings themselves as in our interpretation of them. How does your use of content differ from the premodern and therefore from simple revivalism?*

CMM: In the sense that content doesn't really interest me; my work is actually abstract and not expressive. That is the big difference. I haven't used myth as a fundamental category of thought today (as perhaps Kiefer does), but rather as a pretext for painting. Further, when it is presented, it is often because my work stems from someone's remarks or thoughts on aesthetics. In the case of *Orpheus* which you mentioned, I was inspired by one of Bettina Brentano's letters to Goethe.

CC-B: *Is your attitude today still cynical as far as the possibility of finding new styles is concerned?*

CMM: First of all, my intentions during the seventies and early eighties were not exactly cynical. I was not sneaking around the edges of art but rather confronting great art head on, audaciously and openly. Secondly, a few years ago I discovered 'Mariani' himself and since then have never really identified with any specific artist of the past, even if I am naturally indebted to a specific period of art history. From this point of view, I guess I still feel modern!

CC-B: *Today's* Giant Heads *no longer confront the audience with exaggerated images of harmony and polished finish, perhaps because there are only faces and not entire bodies. They are basically serene and large abstractions where humanity and landscape meet.*

CMM: I have really only been interested in the human figure, which can become a landscape, architecture, anything. In my work up to very recently there was a sort of self-indulgence: I was working on the idea of disquieting morbidity, of a sensuality which could at the same time be noble. Today, I'm not really interested in that kind of image. I'm looking for a less sensual and less rich one, a more spiritual and abstract image.

CC-B: *These* Giant Heads *remind me of late Roman colossal sculpture. They also seem a development both of your* Giunone Ludovisi *(1979) and of the use of fragments of sculpture in your 'tragic' series on the artist, where the fragments were interchangeably ruins of colossal sculpture or parts of the body.*

CMM: These Heads stem from Winckelmann's definition of Beauty as that which is impossible to define. I was interested in the abstraction, and to have painted full-length figures would have been a distraction. These faces are fascinating and mute, they are semi-gods, astral rather than abstract. They could be the seven notes of the scale or the twelve months of the year, or many other things. Some are on paper while others are on canvas, but I try to maintain the same light effect of pastel and gouache even on the canvas. I'm not only thinking of Neoclassicism here but also of Picasso and Matisse.

Edited version of an interview published in *Flash Art* No.133 (April 1987), Milan, by permission.

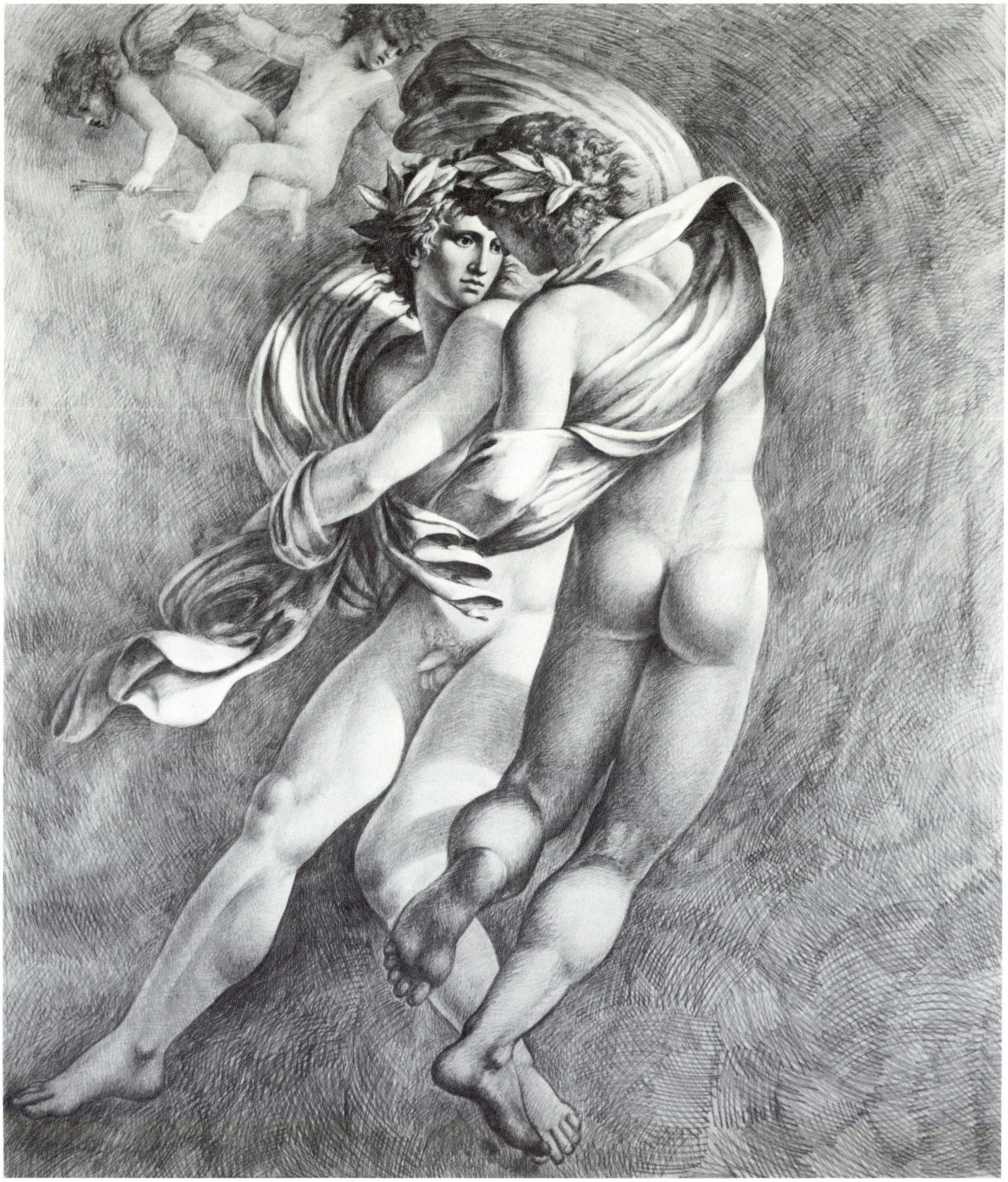

32 Carlo Maria Mariani, *To Look at Oneself in a Celestial Mirror* 1984

MICHELANGELO PISTOLETTO

The work of Pistoletto in this exhibition, *Venus of Rags*, made in 1968, is by a long way the earliest in date. It is however essential to the concerns of the exhibition. The use of classical sculpture in this way anticipated the somewhat later practice of a group of Italian artists, one that soon threatened to become a cliché. But the *Venus of Rags* was not nostalgic, neither did it look forward to a post-modernist deference to the authority of antiquity. It would be hard for an Italian artist to use such a sculpture without irony, given that, as Helmut Friedel points out below, the figures exists in Italy in such multiple and mass-produced form. *Venus of Rags* uses the antique figure as a rhetorical gesture in a more direct and full-blooded way than the sophisticated climate of post-modernism allows. Consider the change of political and social climates since 1968. The metaphor of contrasting sanctified authority and beauty (the Venus) with the rags representative of people at the margins of society, was sharply characteristic of 1968, year of protest and near revolution, and the beginning of a vastly increased consciousness in Western society of the dispossessed.

In the climate of the sixties the tide was still flowing strongly against such values as the classical Venus might be thought to stand for. In the present climate these opposing values are seen to pose a dilemma but can only be solved by withdrawal, a state of mind contributory to the growth of post-modernism.

Douglas Hall

Venus of Rags

For Germans travelling to Italy the first contact with the sculptures and gods which populate the towns and museums they are heading for frequently occurs half way there by the roadside, where every possible size of Michelangelo's David is on offer alongside Marzotto or cement statues of Venus for the garden. Venus, goddess and epitome of beauty, surrounded by rags! The naked woman before a pile of colourful articles of clothing becomes a symbol comprising the natural beauty of the human body and a heap of ragged clothes. This heap of clothes shrouds the front of the the Venus statue threatening to flow over her body and hide it. The surface of the Venus figure is coated with a fine glinting dust and consequently thousands of tiny reflections of her body are created, like small twinkling stars. They make it appear more valuable, radiant and 'beautiful'. "The female form, brought to life by deceitful magic . . . is covered with little stars and reflections which multiply the surface of her skin so as to please all the lovers who surround her. Changeability and irretrievability of expression seem to be a miracle of direct sensuous reproduction without anything mechanical creeping in. Is the mirror a metaphor for immediate knowledge, do the remnants of material stand for that ever-moving life associated with desire: signs and particles which bear longing?"[1]

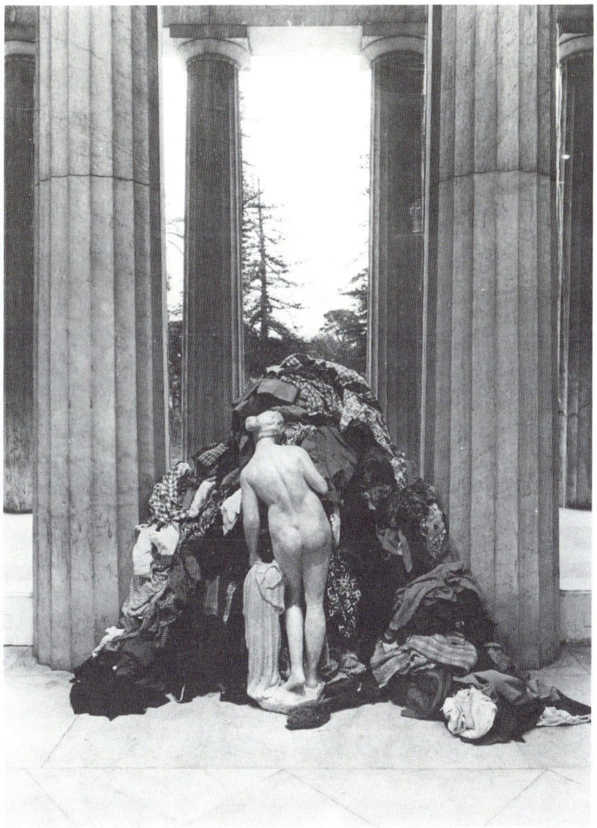

Michelangelo Pistoletto, *Venus of Rags* 1967
at the Museo Pignatelli d'Aragona, Naples (1977)

These rags, looking like the leftovers from a 'spectacular masquerade' (Celant), are reminiscent not so much of possible disguises which Venus might have worn, but, in their shabbiness, of the 'rags' of society, the outcasts who often are described as the scum of society. In some respects the terrible undressing of the victims of national socialist

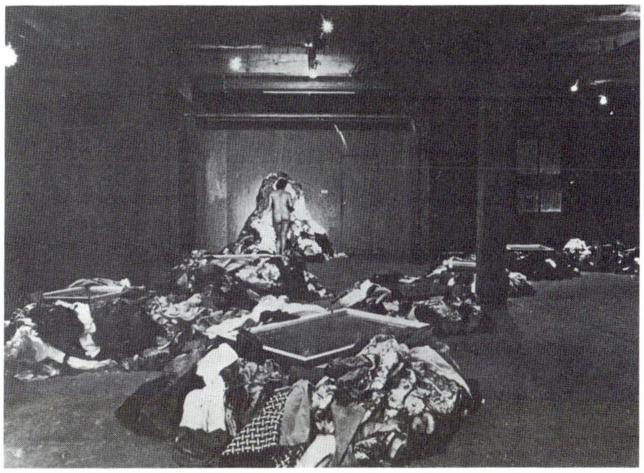

Venus 1980
Performance in 80 Laughton, San Francisco

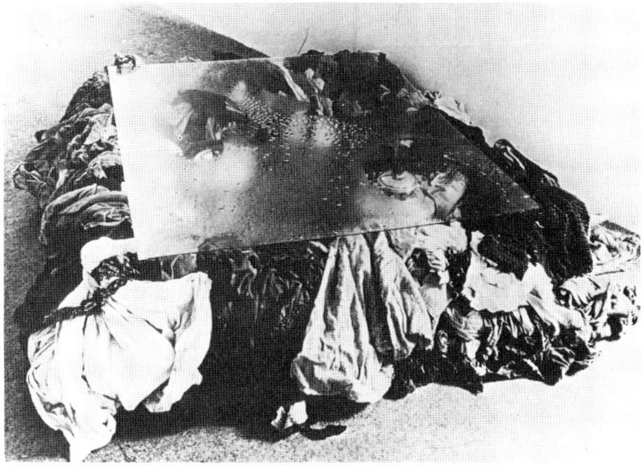

Michelangelo Pistoletto, *Orchestra of Rags* 1968

terror before they were put to death in the gas chambers and the heaps of stolen clothes and the wretched people stripped bare, as we know them from photographic and film documentaries, is recalled here. The shameful concealing of the naked woman who is turning away from us and just looking round hesitatingly could thus be seen as estrangement from the observer. In a performance in San Francisco in 1980 a model took over the role of the sculpture which made this aspect of the stealing of the clothes discussed here and also that of the sensual presence of the human body more clearly visible than does the twinkling Venus sculpture.

In the work *Orchestra of Rags*, 1968, a circle is formed out of old clothes and covered over with a glass top. Underneath the glass, hot water kettles bubble and whistle. A shrill situation arises in which one senses suppression and threatening explosion. In *The Great Arrow*, 1974–80,[2] the clothes which in the end represent people in ragged, tattered clothing, in other words wretched, poor people, are locked behind an arrow-shaped grille which thus allows for an even orientation of these rags. The pile of clothes is reflected back on itself again through the mirror which the arrow touches. In this way the rags surrounding the Venus figure, after at first sight seeming colourful and almost serene, begin to exert pressure which threatens to swamp the 'covetous beauty' of the woman. The shimmer on the goddess's skin then transforms this quickly from the great classical beauty into the shabby variety show beauty. The 'Venus in rags' becomes a 'Venus of rags', the neo-classical picture taken from an antique marble sculpture itself becomes a cheap disposable consumer product like the rags surrounding it. The piece of material which she holds in her hand stretches across into this pile of rubbish.[3] The heap of clothes forms a zone in front of the real wall marking the boundary of the room which the figure seems to be striding through and into which the Venus figure is already reaching.

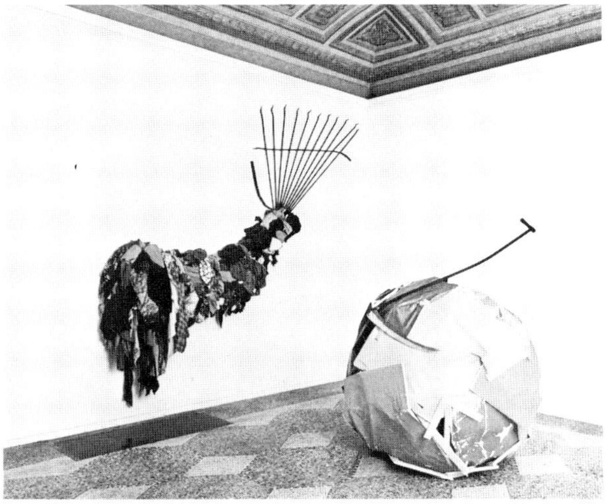

Michelangelo Pistoletto, *The Tail of Arte povera* and *The Scope of Canvas* 1980 at *Dietro-front,* Galleria Giorgio Persano, Turin (1980)

The Peacock, 1979, and *The Tail of Arte povera*, 1979–80, make use of articles of clothing which are moulded into meteoric waves and in the latter work a clear allusion to a *genre* of art can be seen, to which the use of simple everyday materials, even refuse for the realisation of sculptures, was of significance. In contrast to many other artists of *Arte povera,* the material with which Pistoletto worked was only important to him because of the semantics inherent in the material and never really became a 'stylistic device'. This applies as much to the rags as it does to the mirror, a second central means of expression for Pistoletto.[4]

Also in the context of the 'rag works' belongs finally *In the Sphere of the Canvas*, 1980, for which Michelangelo Pistoletto has made a ball of approximately one and a half metres in diameter out of painted canvases together with the stretchers. Here the canvas 'rags' become a colourful ball, above which the scythe stands as a symbol of the harvest and, by further interpretation, as an allegory of Time and Death. The artist's product, the painted canvas, is just as subject to the passage of time as is the clothing of people.

Helmut Friedel
translated by M. Ruth Melton

[1]Germano Celant, in the catalogue to the exhibition *Kunst Wird Material* at the Nationalgalerie, Berlin, 1982, p.84.
[2]A project conceived in 1974 and realised in 1980 in the Clock Tower, New York. See the catalogue to Pistoletto's one-man exhibition at the Palacio de Cristal del Retiro, Madrid, 1983, p.109.
[3]*Ibid,* p.190, in *Venere Cieca*, 1968–78, the figure of Venus is naked except for a piece of cloth held in front of her and wrapped around her head.
[4]Pistoletto has used mirrors in his work since the early 1960s, which, while in no way being a trademark of the artist, nonetheless links him to *Nouveau Réaliste* artists such as Spoerri, Tingely, Arman and César who have repeatedly employed one type of object in their installations. See Thomas Deecke in the catalogue to the artist's one-man exhibition at the Westfälischer Kunstverein, Münster, in 1983.

Edited version of Helmut Friedel, translated by M. Ruth Melton, *Innerhalb/Ausserhalb,* published in *Der Traum Des Orpheus,* Städtische Galerie im Lenbachhaus, Munich (1984), by permission.

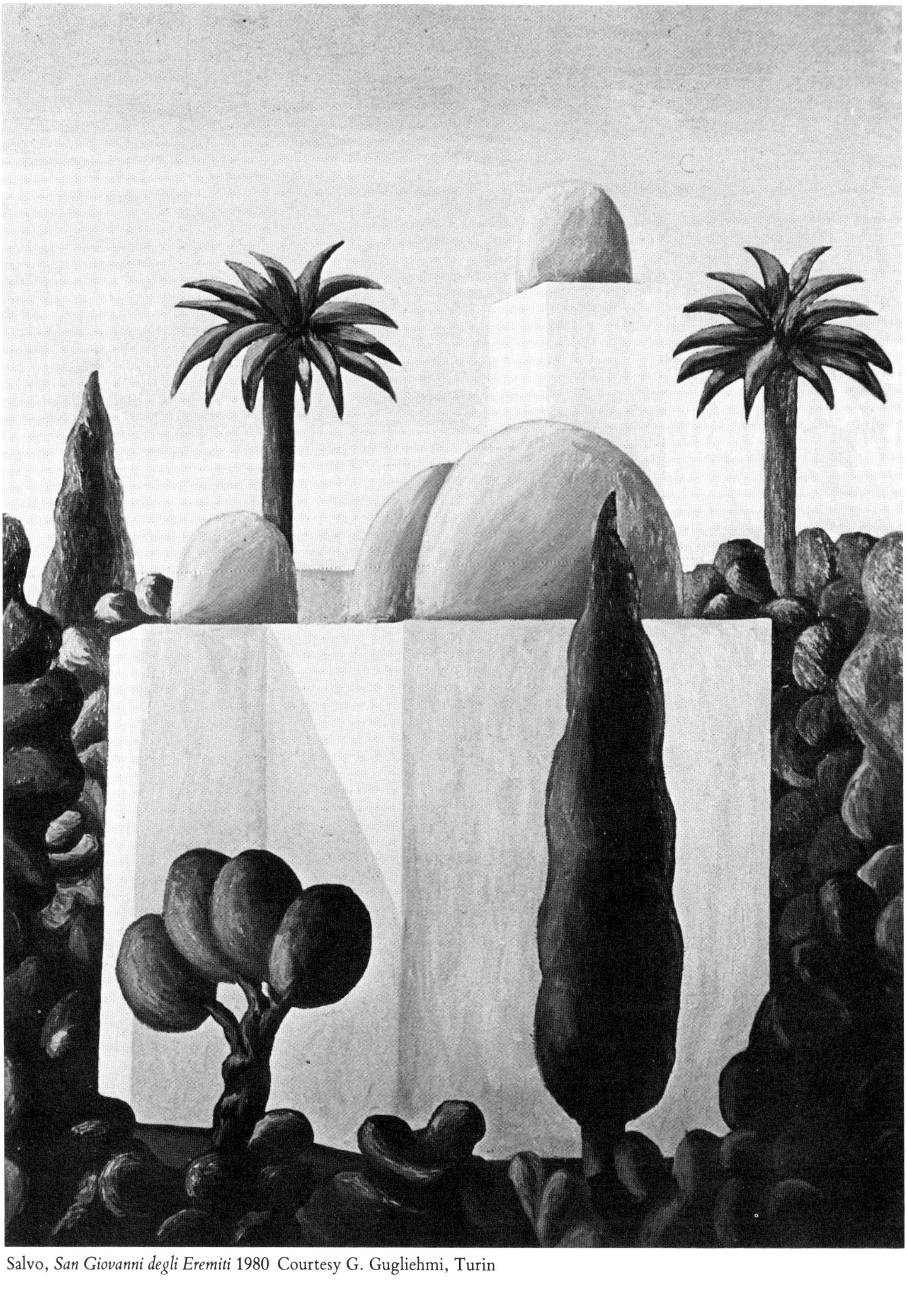

Salvo, *San Giovanni degli Eremiti* 1980 Courtesy G. Gugliehmi, Turin

SALVO

Concerning Painting

During the past fifteen years Salvo (born in 1947 in Léonforte, Sicily, as Salvatore Mangione) has built up a rich and varied oeuvre. In this way he expresses passionately his love for the art of painting, which he practises repeatedly, but each time differently. Almost every year his paintings show a different, unexpected image, from: *Ruins of Classical Temples,* 1977–78, through *Night Street-scenes with Tram*, 1980–81, to *Still Life with Books and Fruits*, 1982–83, and *Landscapes with Turkish Minarets,* 1985–86.

However appealing and attractive the different themes may be at first sight, they are of secondary importance. They are more like a facade. The proper sense and intention, i.e. the painting and the problems which arise, are hidden. Salvo focuses in particular on the exploration of possibilities of painting, by which he puts his imagination as a painter to the test with the help of continual new themes. Every painting is, so to speak, an exercise to gain more and more insight into and to grasp the art of painting. He systematically explores the range of painting in which the work is understood to be an aesthetic reality of colour, light and shape.

For Salvo, painting is a practical autonomous activity. Paintings are artistic constructions in which problems of painting will be analysed and solved if possible. Salvo does not believe in an art which is determined, in any way, by a theoretical doctrine. To him, theory as a basis for his artistic activity has lost all validity because it restricts too much the practice of painting. In the theses 127 and 128 of his book *On Painting* (published Paul Maenz and Gerd de Vries, Cologne, 1986) he formulates it as follows: "To me, man and nature give 'more space' than any other theory. A theory can become dogma, fanaticism and blindness". Paintings by Salvo aim only to be the expression of a pure artistic imagination, the point being the accuracy with which he is able to transform his vision into paint.

Above all, the choice of subject is an aesthetically formal one. The subject matter is not chosen because of its possible significance in content, but because of its shape and colour quality as well as allied artistic problems. Salvo reduces his subjects to a question of shape and colour. It is not the subject matter which determines the painting. The value of the theme is that it serves as a reason for him to paint. It is used as a guideline for painting. The subject matter guides the painting, for the subject requires a certain colour, shape and composition. Salvo preferably uses known compositions, like landscape, still life and portrait, the subjects of which are drawn directly from reality. Sometimes he stays close to the original example. More often he works on it in such a free manner that one can hardly discover any similarity. The paintings, therefore, always have a certain ambivalence. On the one hand they create the impression of being a product of fantasy while on the other hand they are so self-evident in tone and atmosphere that they could be a reproduction (although not naturalistic) of a tangible situation.

The concentration on shape is striking. The figurative elements are reduced to simple elementary forms which have lost much of their value in reality and which hardly raise any associations. Thereby the picture gains a strong abstract impression. Apart from this Salvo omits all known details which could make the painting recognisable and anecdotal. What remains is only a

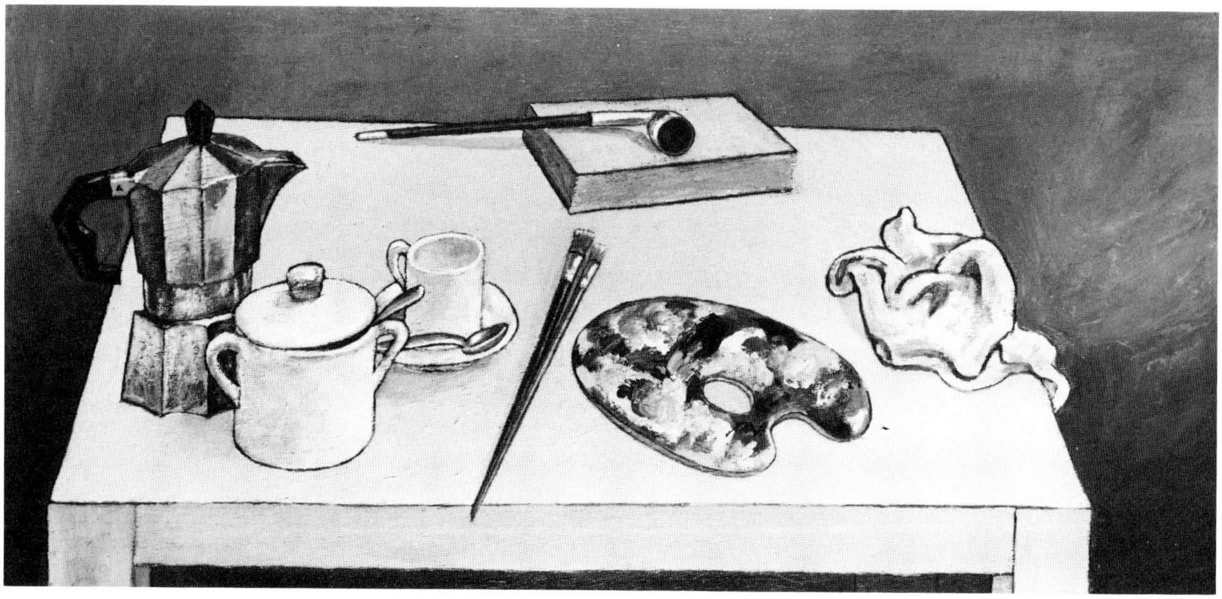

Salvo, *Still Life* 1978 Courtesy M. Remolino, Turin

'general' picture. Salvo takes possession of objects, so to speak, by the act of painting. By painting objects he separates them from their context and strips them of their possible meaning. The viewer does not become distracted by a familiar, narrative picture but will be able to focus his full attention on the real subject of the painting: the art itself. In general, Salvo works out every theme in a long cycle by which all kinds of variations are explored. Because he chooses again and again a different process, the repeated use of themes never evokes an impression of being an unending sequence of the same thing. He works through on a theme until it is completely exhausted. As he states in thesis 37 of *On Painting*: "As long as the model can be seen in a new way, as long as the definition is not completed, why should one interrupt the research? A logical motive is needed; for example, the 'definition' is finished, one cannot paint the 'model' in a new way anymore". With that sequential approach Salvo once more underlines that artistic research is central and that he wishes to avoid any semblance of anecdote.

Apart from that strong simplification and reduction in shape most of Salvo's paintings have another significant characteristic, namely, the all-dominating role of light. Light, as well as the sharp linear shadows, not only intensifies the constructive build-up of the painting, but also confirms the plasticity of the shapes and creates size. The unusual colouring, in a large range of vivid pastel-tones which are of the most unexpected colouration, gives the painting an intense radiation. The colours are not a true description of reality but, instead, are completely autonomous and self-sufficient. Although the expressive colour-tone is quite a contrast with the clear composition, Salvo never plays one off against the other. He carefully puts them in accordance with each other. The expression is always controlled by his intellectual discipline. This is the narrow margin in which emotion and intellect meet each other and attain an exciting balance.

Everything in Salvo reveals his personal relationship with the tradition of the Italian painting. He seems to have found a medium in the art of painting by which he can define once more his relationship with the Italian tradition. For example, Giotto is important to him for simplicity, painterly character and spatiality. Yet Salvo's strength lies in lifting his interpretation of the past above limitation. He arrives at a self-determined reflection of the past whereby he is able to form the conventional artistic values of painting into a new artistic reality.

Karel Schampers
translated by Theo van Asperen

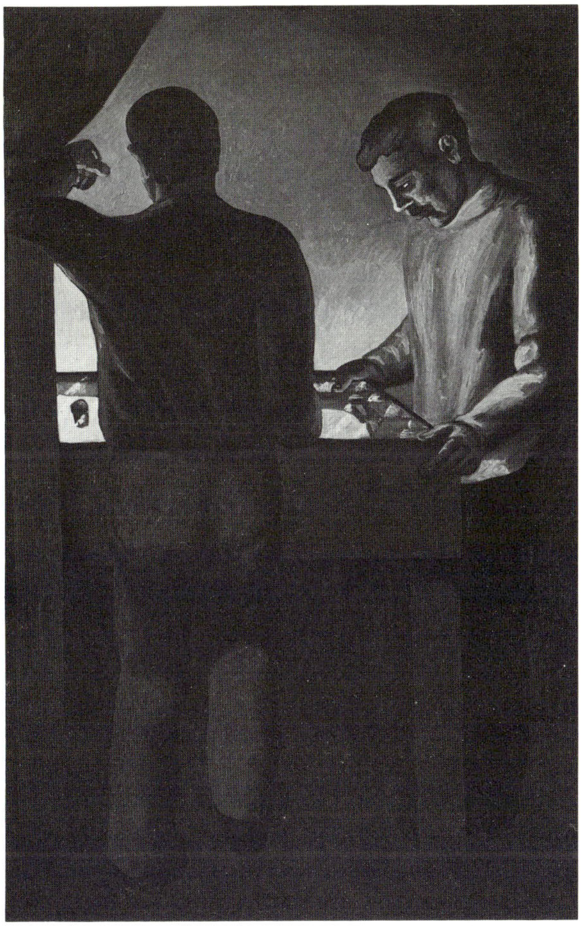

Salvo, *Flipper* 1982 Courtesy art and project, Amsterdam

ANDREAS SCHULZE

The Idiot of the Family: On the Aggressive Friendliness in Schulze's Pictures

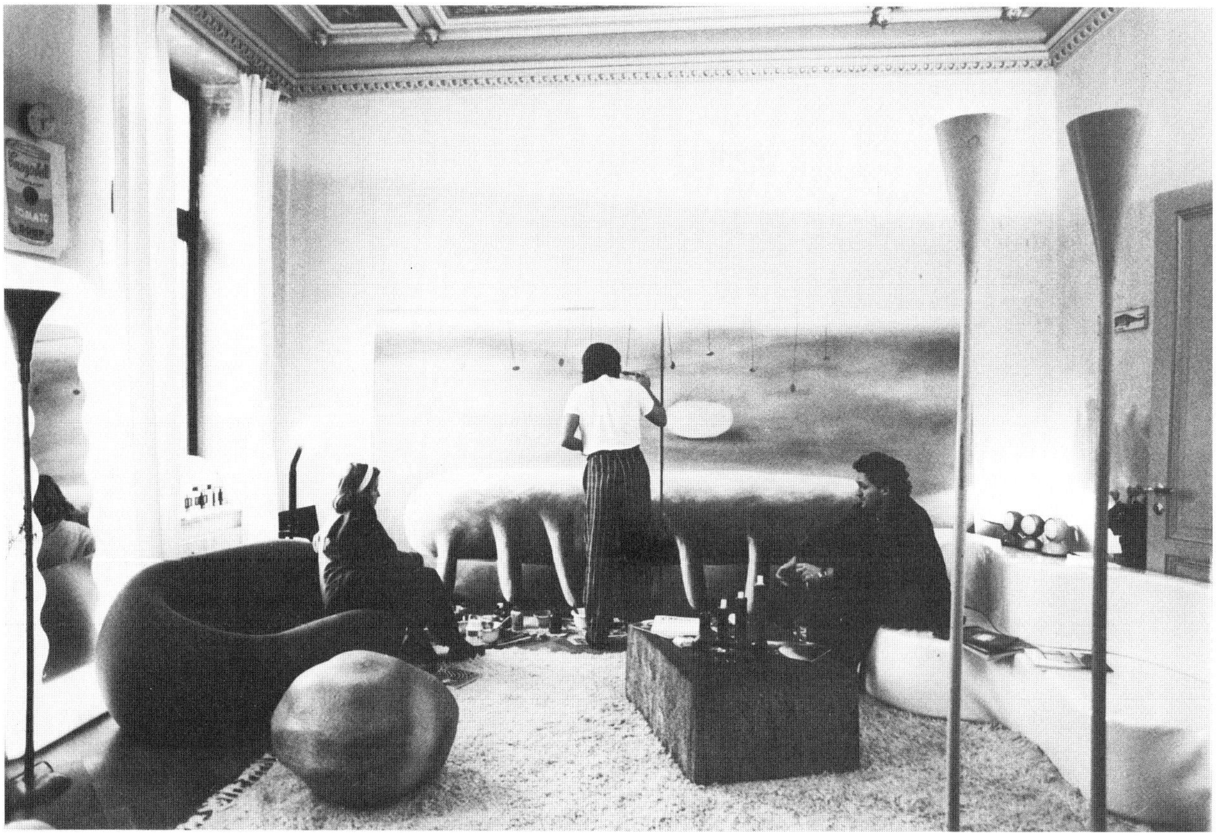

Andreas Schulze at work in his living room 1986 (Photo: Bernhard Schaub)

Strange biomorphical worm forms gather around a carpet and a Meissen china coffee pot for a picnic. Scattered peas and a few pieces of wood add to the scenery as a cosy party of things which, in this foggy, diffused landscape, seem completely derealised, even abstract. The objects which can be seen here are no objects. Their reference to an object of perception existing outside of the picture is highly precarious. They have lost almost all correlation to reality. They have become form, that is, a formal, aesthetic link in a painterly composition that moves towards the edge of 'abstraction'. And yet the abstract forms in this picture seem to be alive. Their inquisitive, interested attitude lends them a certain simple-mindedness and the lovable playfulness of sea lions. In a word, content is turned into form and constructive elements of form are loaded with allusions to content. The result is a curiously unreal scenery of forms with a wonderfully warm and comfortable atmosphere. The same mood prevails in the other pictures Andreas Schulze did in 1985. For example, he forms an abstract duck's head out of differently coloured surfaces in which he places fruit, vegetables and quails so that the surfaces look like individual garden plots. In another picture he paints two surfaces in such distorted perspective that they look like crazy pool tables shoved into each other with small coloured stones lying on them that turn out—on closer inspection—to be animal gumdrops. He always seems to be fading in and out between cutting the reference off from reality, thus disintegrating meaning and re-charging the purified forms with a positive, calming, intimate, even familar atmosphere. Footstools and internationally popular sweets invite us to spend a comfortable evening in front of a picture-filling TV screen in the style of the sixties, which looks out on to a serene blue sky where abstract birds are enjoying their dumb animal lives.

However, this has nothing to do with any so-called neo-surrealism. Neo-surrealism at least intended to refer to the reality of the unconscious or of dream images, in other words, to illuminate or explore the meaning of the real effect of imaginary things, but Andreas Schulze no longer bothers with meaning at all. With him, the objective neurosis *Zeitgeist* (spirit of the times) does not lead to a postmodern inflation of all interchangeable, emptied content beyond good and evil. On the contrary, he reacts to general popularity by initially withdrawing the pictures into a reduced, simple, formal principle.

Andreas Schulze brings the 'brilliant surface of nonsense' (J. Baudrillard) into play against the gamble of interpretation; he paints purified form that no longer feigns sense, but simply is what it is: sense-less, meaningful presence.

But neither does he bow to the currently fashionable nostalgia for Minimalism and Constructivism. He is concerned with a positive, modern actuality of painting which obviously cannot be explained by the presumed emptiness of pseudo-pure construction. He himself calls the aura which he would like to create in his pictures, 'aggressively mild friendliness'. There is something radically positive and intentionally naive about this. But naiveté in this case is not the inability to reflect; it is an artistic concept. 'The artist has to be dumber than the art trade permits', Andreas Schulze once said to me after we had talked half the night about commercialised art production in the institutionalised network of 'gallery-museum-collector-critic', which is subject to so much aesthetic blindness, simple-mindedness and stupidity that it defies the imagination. Is this a calculated stupidity as a strategy of quality? It certainly is, but the pictures transcend this intentional withdrawal. They continue to amaze by the sovereignty with which Schulze handles the unscrupulous vapidity of German petit-bourgeois Spitzweg-Romanticism—simple, flat, cosy, touching, friendly, harmonious—in the imaginary rectangle of the painted construction. Profane poeticising and minimal abstraction join forces on the surface of a light and thin handling in a manner never seen before. Andreas Schulze's pictures are unmistakable, willful and original. His is a specific blend or unrealisation, meaninglessness, cosiness and minimalism, a poetically transfigured formalism expressly embedded in the tradition of German Romanticism and the romantic German. "The world must be romanticised", Novalis said in 1798. "This is the way to find original meaning again. Romanticising is nothing but enhancement of quality, in the process of which the lower self becomes indentified with a better self. Just as we ourselves embody such a qualitative progression". That is precisely

Andreas Schulze's approach when he pursues his startlingly aggressive positivity of the good and beautiful picture in the medium of a personal, modern beauty of form.

A lovable, silly dog is sitting on an elegant minimal-carpet à la Schulze while the long, mysterious path of romantic yearning fades into the horizon without, however, melodramatically exaggerating the purified form of the picture. There is even a touch of irony in Schulze's intentional simplicity as opposed to the shallow solemnity and foolish self-adulation of contemporary art. But although the surface impression of Schulze's pictures is very formal, decorative and conceptually artificial, his works are also authentic: a personal and individual statement. Andreas Schulze *is* the aesthetic position which he paints. His art is based on his idiocy. But idiocy is not to be misconstrued. Not until the bourgeois acquisition of this word did it become a synonym for pathological deviation, for insanity that had to be excluded and punished as deviating from the norm. In ancient Greece *Idiota* meant private person, the individual. Elaborating on this meaning, Sartre understood the idiotic to be the individual moment in the determinative thicket of institutional and signifying structures, effective only insofar as the individual tries to make something out of what he has been turned into. 'Idiotic' thus refers to the individual means of adapting to our social constitution. And in this sense, Andreas Schulze is indeed a great idiot in the post-fashionable uniformity of the art business. The idiotic lends his poetic formalism its whimsical and unique substance. And yet the quality of his pictures consists in sublimating himself, i.e. his life-style, in a minimalism of his own idiosyncracy to form. In fact much of what is portrayed in his pictures conveys his life-style, his own atmospheric identity, although it does enter into an unrealisation of content *per se* by formally and aesthetically overriding the personal. Private fetishes become form. The picture stands for itself and is simultaneously a romanticised self-portrait of the fortunate kind.

Schulze's works are informed with 'idiocy' and familiarity, with cosy lyricism and piquant/mannered formalism, abstract unreality and the picturesque thereness of nothing—all of which is clothed in the associative aura of German-romantic yearning. But enough said about pictures which say so much for themselves, especially if one does not want to apply the ante interpretation to the brilliant surface of non-sense. This is after all what these pictures have just succeeded in surmounting with supreme mastery. What remains is the idiot of the family in the manifestation of a romantic, ironic silence that may someday culminate in the aggressive positivity of art as ministry to the soul. We shall see.

Wilfried Dickhoff
translated by Catherine Schelbert

Reprinted from *Parkett* No. 8, Zurich (1986), by permission.

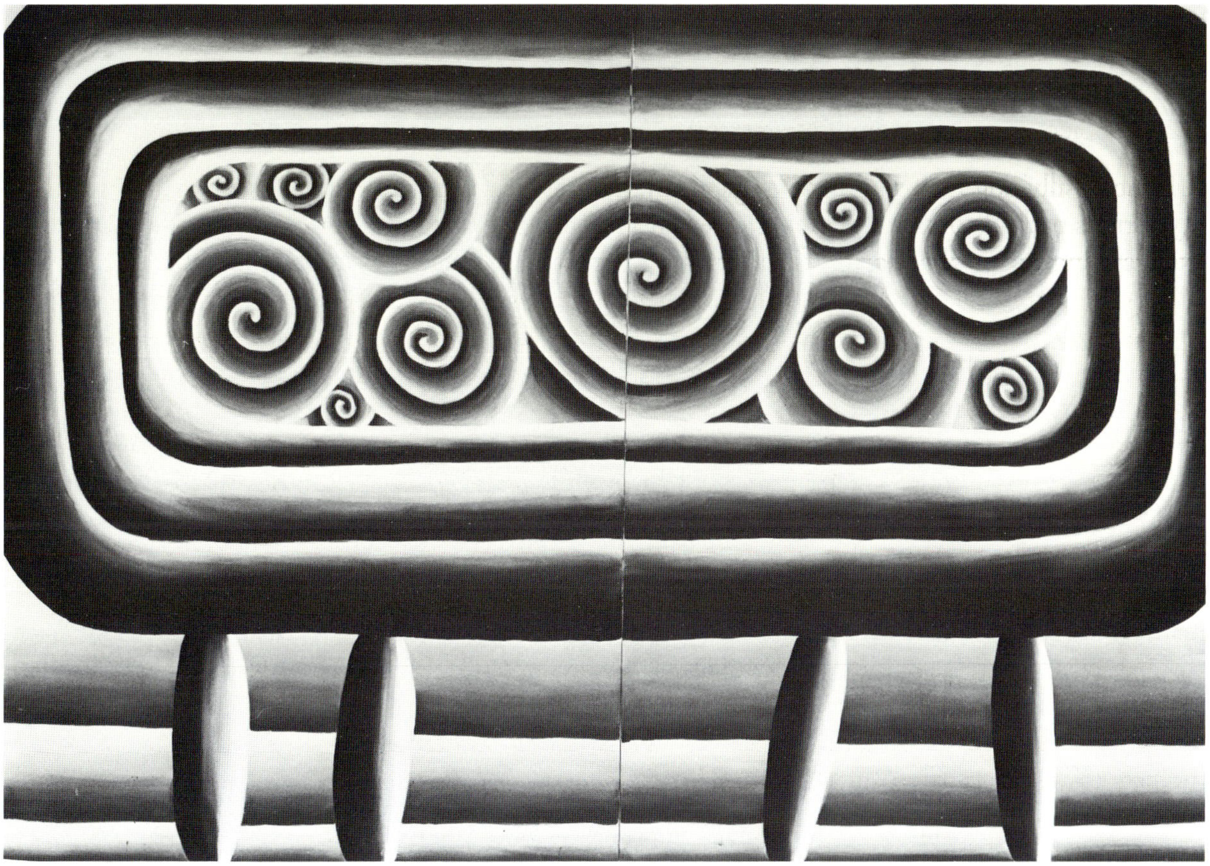

40 Andreas Schulze, *Untitled* 1984

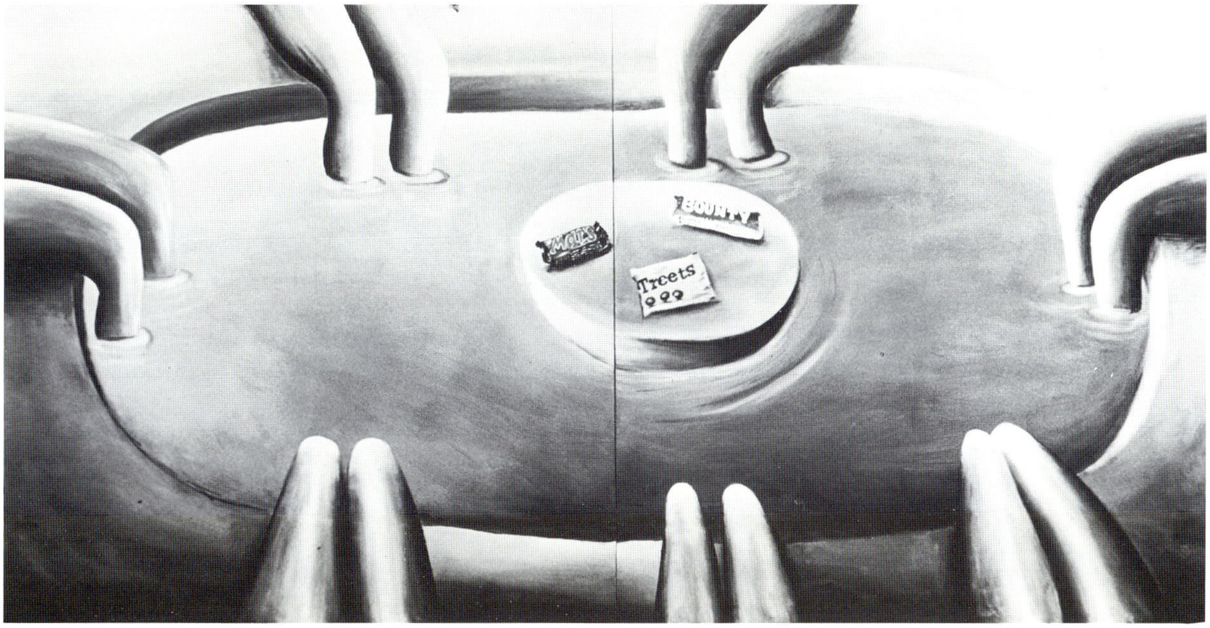

42 Andreas Schulze, *Untitled* 1985

CY TWOMBLY

The Great Mediator

''We are making it out of ourselves''. Barnett Newman made this claim for his generation, the first American artists to achieve a truly international status and to affect significantly the course of art. His statement reflects the pride and independence of the Abstract Expressionists, as well as their psychological courage in forging a radical art where before there had been very little. Cy Twombly is a member of the generation of American and European artists that emerged in the immediate wake of the Abstract Expressionists and that includes Jasper Johns, Robert Rauschenberg, Joseph Beuys, Yves Klein and the somewhat younger Jannis Kounellis. These artists reached maturity in the ten or so years after 1950, and to a very great extent, they have laid the foundation for the art of the second half of this century. They did not deny the Abstract Expressionist notion of selfhood: they too made their art out of themselves, but they also made it out of things that existed outside themselves. Each brought together in his art some combination of pre-existing materials, images, objects or language—things already charged with extra-personal meaning. All achieved a new, highly referential density in their work which functioned to explicate the larger world while it also explored the nature of art itself. It could be said that Newman's claim to be ''making it out of ourselves'' was replaced, or at least supplemented, by Rauschenberg's equally famous statement, that he desired to function ''in the gap between art and life''.

In a sense, it has been Cy Twombly's achievement to function in the 'gap' between these two statements. He has made art out of himself more openly and deeply than Barnett Newman ever imagined possible. By reducing painting to its essence—the mark and its inevitable extension, the line—Twombly found a visual mode capable of registering his most infinitesimal responses, both psychological and physiological. And, as the graphic mark opened his art to the possibility of language, and of actually writing on the canvas, he articulated these responses even more specifically. Broaching at times an almost excruciating vulnerability, his oeuvre is an intimate diary of his emotional life that has few equals within twentieth century art.

At the same time, Twombly has been faithful in his fashion to Rauschenberg's dictum. The other artists of his generation tended to convert aspects of life into art. One thinks of the found objects and images that Rauschenberg brought to his 'combine' paintings, of Johns' careful transformations of targets and American flags as well as his casts of such things as a flashlight, a lightbulb, etc.; of Beuys' prolonged involvement with fat and felt and of Kounellis' appropriation of both the animate and inanimate—from burlap bags, wood and bedsprings, to animals and even fire for his installations.

In contrast, Twombly has seemed more inclined to work in the opposite direction, starting out in the realm of the aesthetic and moving toward life. Primary among the 'materials' that Twombly has appropriated are other works of art, whether they are the classical myths set down by the Greek and Roman poets, or paintings from the Renaissance. Even when Twombly's art refers to the landscape, as it often does, it is a landscape infused with thought, mythological references, diagrams and poetry and it is after all, inspired by some of the most assiduously 'cultivated' vistas in the world; those of Italy, where he has made his home since 1957. At the same time Twombly often leavens his high culture with sturdy doses of the culture of the street. His highly developed erudition is always balanced by a visceral emotionalism which originates in his touch and in the suggestiveness of his marks.

A review of Twombly's titles from the late 1950s onward gives a dazzling reflection of his aesthetic knowledge and affections. Sometimes it seems that Twombly's goal is to show us, in painting after painting, what goes on in an artist's mind, to make visible, and visual, the extensive body of cultural knowledge he carries with him. Twombly repeatedly gives voice to the voices of other artists, other artworks which have challenged and sustained him as he has proceeded through his own work. Certain of Twombly's efforts seem to both honour and exorcise these influences. Elsewhere, it seems that Twombly simply wants to reiterate certain beloved masterpieces in his own hand and time.

Twombly's art could be said to articulate a highly personal psychology—and physiology—of culture. In making his art out of himself, he has also felt compelled to reveal exactly what that 'self' is made of and this desire has formed one of the major subjects of his art. His work tells us that, like most artists, Twombly is made of the art that came before him and that it remains very much alive to him—and within him. He carries within himself a body of knowledge that his own body, culminating in the gestures of his arms, hands and fingers, makes manifest in his art. His art repeatedly underscores the continuity of culture and aesthetic experience, proving that old themes can yield new interpretations, can be rejuvenated when they are made to leap to a different medium.

In all this Twombly is more a mediator, a conduit than an iconoclast. But Twombly is also an artist of extremes who achieves his own kind of iconoclasm and radicality in his extremes. By taking certain ideas to extremes, Twombly represents the culmination of an amazing array of modern styles. Because of his deep involvement with literary subjects, Twombly could be seen as a late, or perhaps the final Symbolist. The out-of-control quality of his drawing technique, which often convinces us that the artist's deepest unconscious is being expressed, makes him seem like the most sustained automatist, bringing to fruition effects only hinted at by Miró and the Surrealists. He can be taken as the truest of all the 'action painters' as the Abstract Expressionists were sometimes called, for he conceives of the canvas (or the sheet of drawing paper) in terms of Harold Rosenberg's concept, as "an arena in which to act".

Twombly's approach to Abstract Expressionism was deliberately anti-heroic. He deflated its bombast, scaled down its gestures and brought its inherently graphic character to the fore. He downplayed the paintbrush in favour of tools more precisely suited to his sensibility. After brushing on a monochrome field of white, cream or grey paint, he would switch to a small piece of graphite or crayon-harder, more pointed tools which functioned much more as extensions of his own fingers. He would then work across the field of paint, which was sometimes wet and sometimes dry, approaching the canvas as if it were a large drawing.

Twombly's line is indelibly his and instantly recognisable; it it more like handwriting than a typical painting touch. It has a certain quaver or vibration to it which keeps the surfaces of his art in a subtle—or sometimes not so subtle—perpetual motion, and this visual motion gives his work its irresistable emotional undertow.

Twombly's development since 1960 is a vast and many splendoured thing, proceeding in big rhythmic swings, making regular, rejuvenating shifts in gesture and line, subject matter and material and, above all, emotional tone. With line, Twombly has been able to say almost everything a painter could want to say; the richness of his achievement can only be alluded to here. The 1960s began with the extravagant episodic accumulations of *Leda and the Swan* and ends in another form of majesty, the 'blackboard' paintings. In these, Twombly empties most of the mythological subject matter from his work and takes line back to basics, expanding upon simple conceptually-determined gestures. In other 'blackboard' paintings, Twombly's graphic outbursts give way to an array of linear configurations which speak of measurement, calculation and mechanistic speculation, but are no less fervent.

Since the mid 1970s, Twombly has spent more and more time working on paper, which he has often implied is his preferred surface. Much of the art he has produced forms an extended examination of collage, taking it to new extremes and giving it a status equal to paintings. A good example is the untitled work on paper in which Twombly writes "I am Thyrsis of Etna blessed with a tuneful voice" beneath a photograph of a woodland scene reflected on rippling water. On two smaller pieces of paper, one separately framed, he reiterates abstract details of this scene in his own hand, creating visual echoes. In works such as this Twombly creates a compartmentalised, episodic surface which mirrors his sequential approach. In other works, the multiple surfaces are increased in number and left completely separate. This is the case with Twombly's late 1970s masterpiece *50 Days at Ilium* which consists of ten often enormous canvases, whose separate 'actions' of violently applied paint each recount a different episode of the epic battle from Homer's *Iliad*. And this extreme extension and fracturing of the painting surface also operates in the paintings on paper that we find among Twombly's most recent work and that consist of several sheets of paper covered with continuous brushwork and saturated colours.

These paintings may mark a completely new phase for Twombly. Never has he seemed to forsake the line so completely, never has his painterliness been so lush, so total. New antecedents, Turner and Monet among them, are alluded to. But often these surfaces read like extended linear strokes which have simply massed together. And Twombly's nervous energy, the subtle perpetual motion of his hand remains very much the same and, as always, it propels his art forward.

Roberta Smith

Edited version of Roberta Smith, *The Great Mediator,*
published in *Cy Twombly*, Kunsthaus Zurich (1987), by permission.

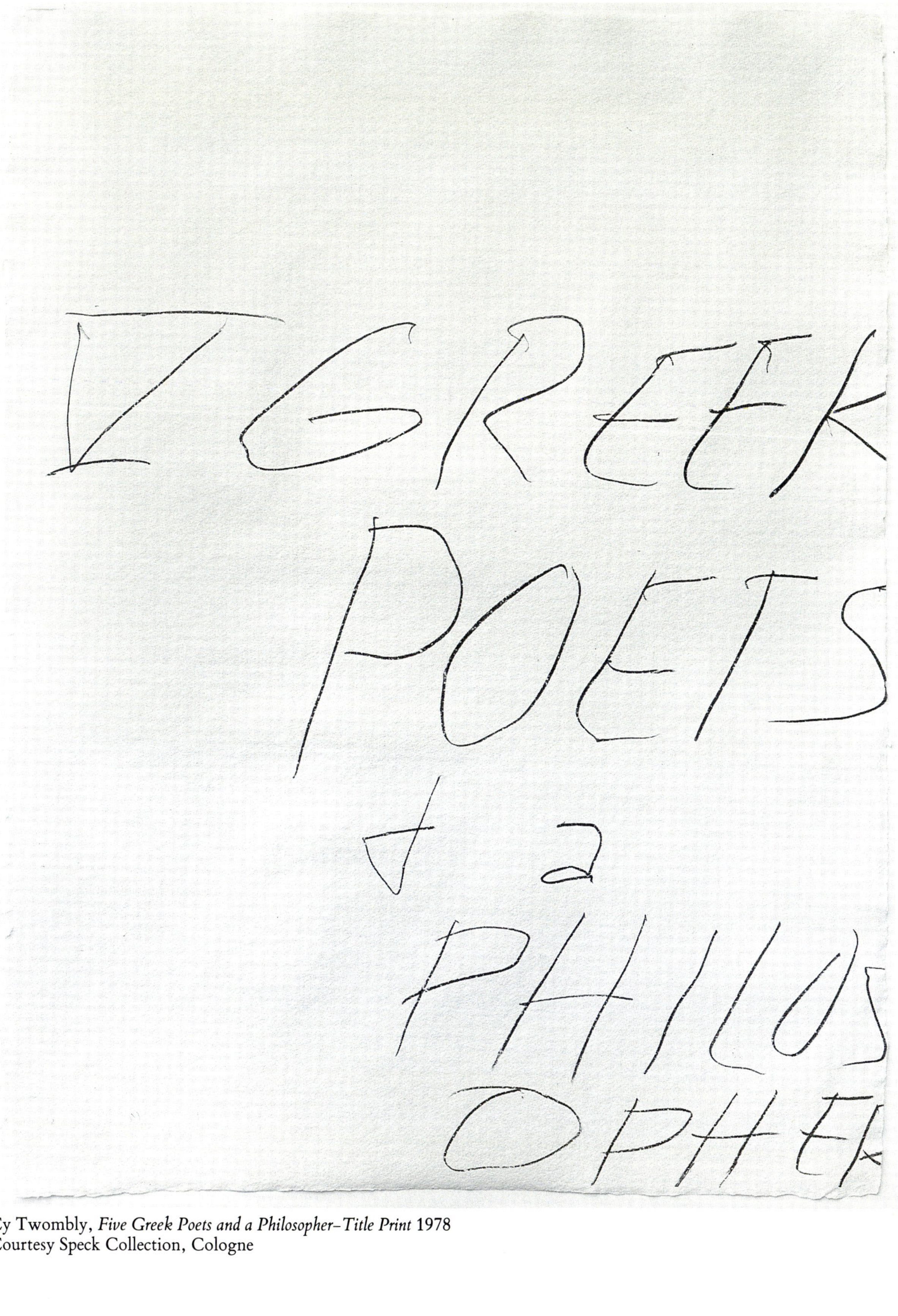

Cy Twombly, *Five Greek Poets and a Philosopher–Title Print* 1978
Courtesy Speck Collection, Cologne

ISOLDE WAWRIN

It's a pity. Out of all the scraps of language that I write I cannot make a text. Now it has become like doing homework—yet I have promised Dr Cumming a statement.

Edinburgh—it made me dream of Tristan and Isolde; I was Tristan. One can breathe in a landscape full of wind and sky. The moss-green and the sea-green over the rocks, I have never been there, but I remember it exactly.

It makes me almost hysterical that I cannot install my work myself, because I am just about to have a baby. I am used to doing everything alone, to being familiar with the wall, the space, in which my work is to be shown. Plans are of no use to me, I need the smell, the light, the temperature, I need to know what trees are growing outside, which bird I saw on the way there, what there is to eat and drink. What sounds, what music there is to hear. Does my art fit in with this or have I made a mistake—I have no conferral over any of these things as things are.

But I still dream. Mountains and valleys, dark names, lakes, which are all called lochs, hills with long-haired sheep and again and again the sea—I think that everything is fine, that my work will hang well there.

Isolde Wawrin

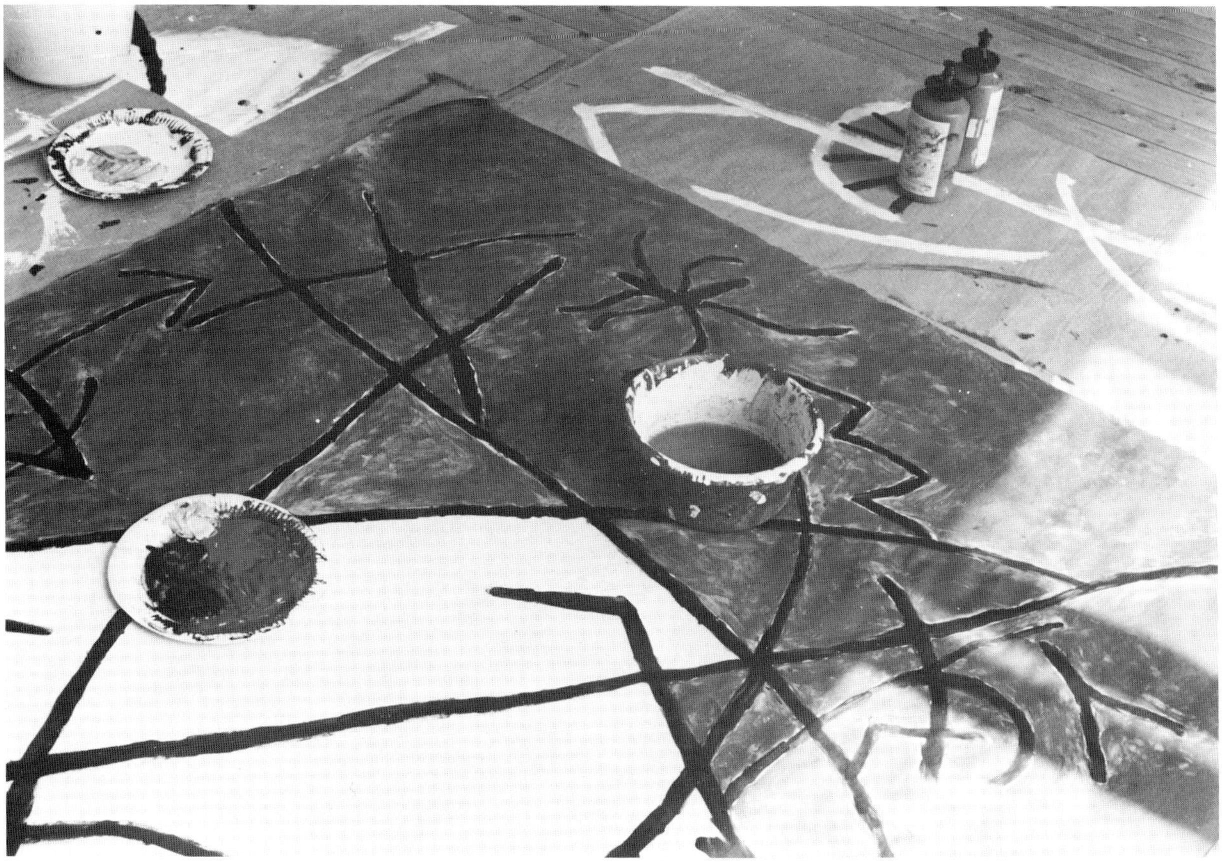

Isolde Wawrin's studio with detail of *Untitled Drawing* (49) 1987

Surveying the Territory

More than most artists, Isolde Wawrin wears her heart on her sleeve. From the directness of her technique—painting with her finger on the wall or on large sheets of laminated paper placed on the floor—to the directness of her speech, her personality is all of a piece. In the context of this exhibition, she is Nature. Not the nature of the *Wissenschaftlicher Naturbegriff,* the scientific conception of nature on which she pours scorn, but of the *Naturvolk,* the primitive people with whom she identifies. The primordial nature of the rituals of the classical world is evident from the epic poets and dramatists, and the dichotomy of the barbaric and polished aspects of classicism is important to any consideration of its role in contemporary art. Wawrin is a sort of exemplary protagonist in such a dichotomy. Not indeed for any barbarous or rebarbative quality capable of wounding or repelling but for the instinctual wholeness that is the key to her painting and her approach to life. This requires no classical formulations or stately sense of measure. In place of classical rhythms and regularity her paintings offer simple figurations drawn with the demonstrative urgency of the primitive artist and the sure sense of interval of the oriental.

Isolde Wawrin has presented herself to the public as well by her short pieces of writing as by her paintings—which plainly themselves have the character of pictograms. For the German language she uses the typewriter though she is not unwilling to replace both language and typewriter with her own signs-manual (see page 162). This is however a charming irrelevance, for only by using the ordinary language of common experience does Wawrin convince us of the identity of her thought-process and her painting. She is in fact a poet although she seems to renounce poetry as such.

Be that as it may, her verbal imaging is the stuff of good writing. The idea that drew itself on the wall opposite as she looked out of the window, and lay over her at night like a fish-net. Victor (*l'homme moyen sensuel,* it seems) narrowing his eyes and polishing his glasses to try to share her vision, then frustrated turning into a glaring, foaming, bull pawing the floor. The age-old living mummies with facetted eyes, their tiny gilded mouths mumbling on cheese that hangs from them like spiders' webs.

But the real content of Wawrin's statements confirms an instinctual exploration of life that finds a complete parallel in her finger painting. As she sees her life unfolding from childhood in a series of small highly objectified images, so the narrative of her pictograms extends in the great open spaces of white surface which she enters like some new territory, tentatively and armed with nothing but her colours. There she may encounter first the flight of a bird, then find a plain with a horizon, wherein are animal tracks, a snail shell, a tortoise, tufts of grass. A circle invites her to become a spider and spin filaments across its diameter, but many things she meets are unknown to her. All this and more we can see in the paintings.

Instinctual as she is, there is no place in her world for the exploiters or the polluters who in her scheme of things are to be identified with the ruling or ordering powers. In this she is perhaps no more than a particularly clear example of a stance many artists of her generation would take. Her extreme reductionism in ways and means, eliminating even the brush, emphasises it. The dichotomy between order as a constructive and as a destructive force, with the dilemma that that has always posed to artists, is sharply outlined by such artists as Isolde Wawrin.

Douglas Hall

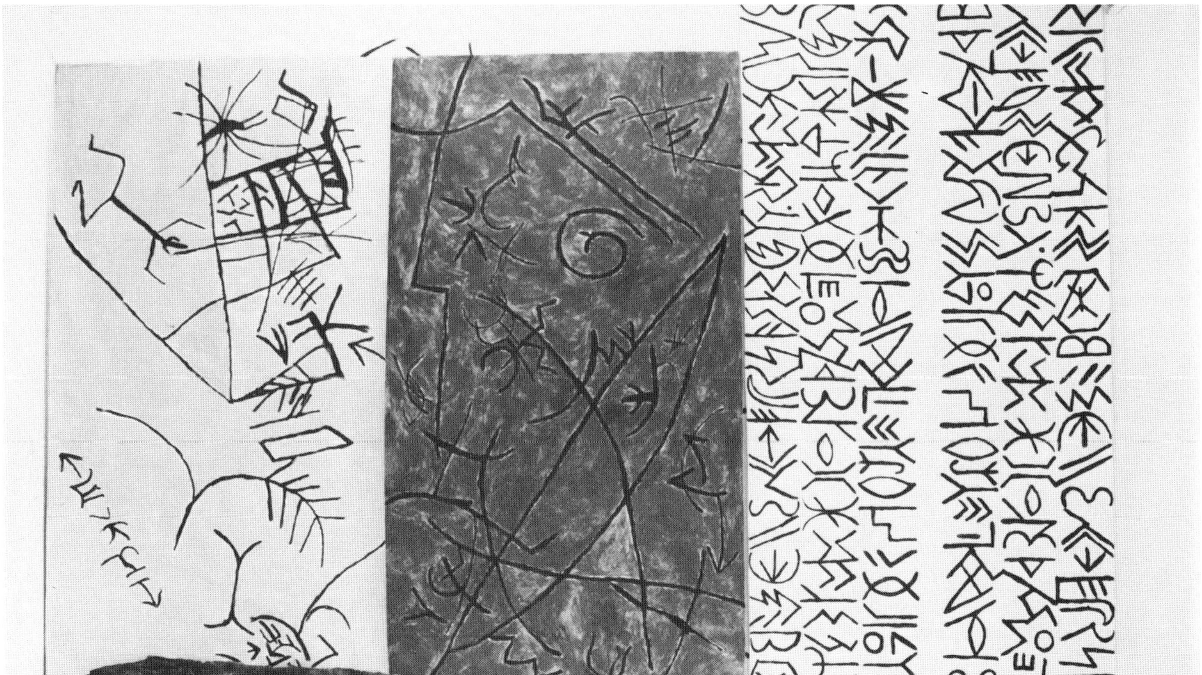

Isolde Wawrin, *Untitled Drawings* (47–49) with *Object* 1987

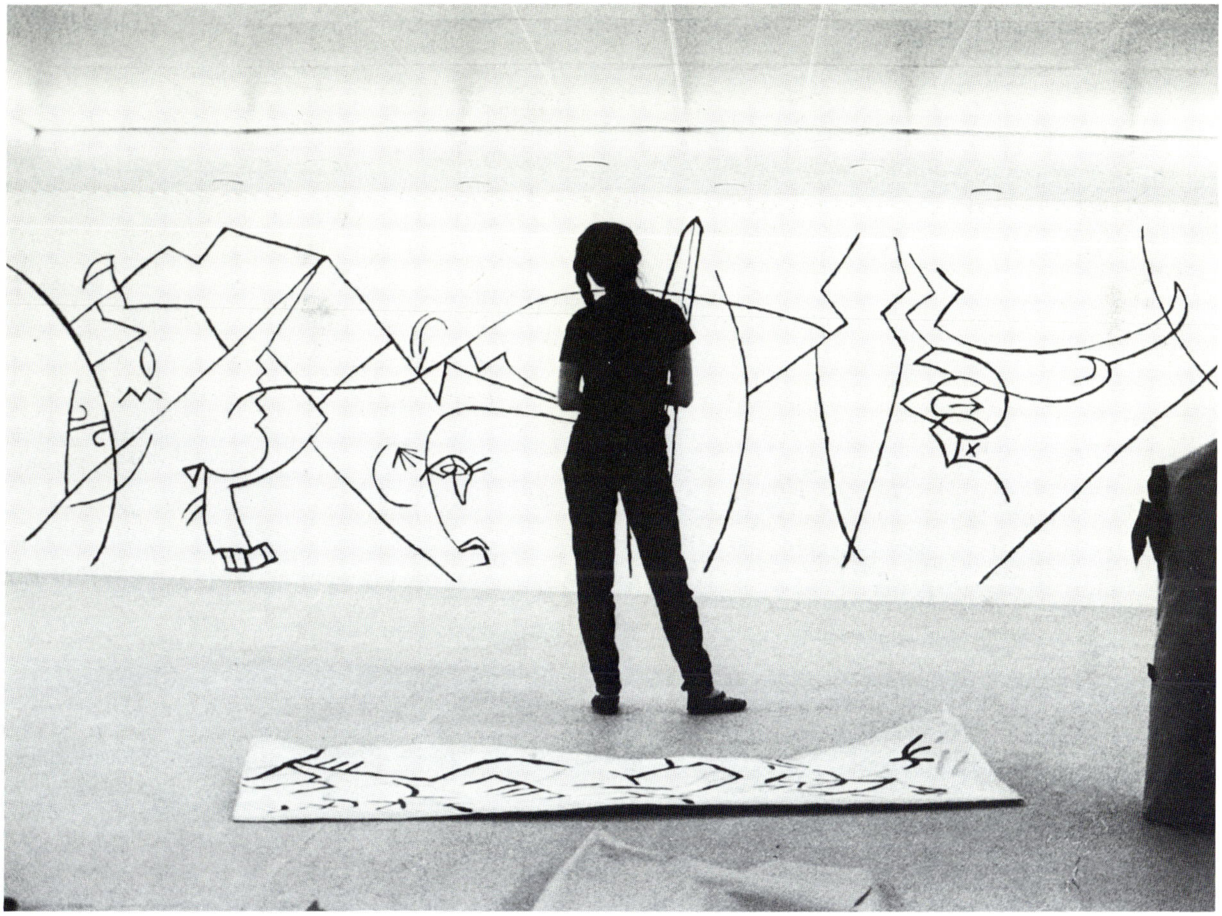

Isolde Wawrin, installation at Bonn (1986)

ALISON WILDING

Beneath the Skin

It is commonplace to complain that artists retreat to ivory towers. In fact very few have the courage and ruthlessness to do this, or to admit that making art which aspires to greatness is an occupation incompatible with the broken time of ordinary life. The compensation for isolation is that a rare, restorative aura transfers to the work, as it does with that of Alison Wilding. We, the viewers, examine her objects and their occupation of a wall or floor and realise that the person who made them is clearly feeding on a vivid inner life while pausing to question and make more precise her motives and structures. The sculptures rest lightly on the plane surface. Many seem to levitate, especially when light intrudes underneath or through or when they invite looking at from an eye-level other than five feet from the ground. The obvious corollary is that the viewer, troubled by the peculiarity of form and colour, becomes conscious of a distillation of feelings and concentrates and inspects what is seen as if he too were on trial in the sanctuary of the studio. Artists working in the Royal College of Art Sculpture Department (during its lively period, about 1968–75), were attracted to the idea of sculpture as a collective identity of things so distributed in space that partnered with the spartan studios there arose a metaphysical, rather staged ambience. The rationale of conceptual, minimal and constructured sculpture became familiar to the students (Wilding studied there from 1970–73); however, spareness and introspection rather than reform guided individual researches. Using simply-fashioned materials—sticks, blocks of wood, paper, plaster forms, found objects—connections were made through symbols, metaphors and alter-egos.

Verbal components often referred to an overpowering feeling of loss and impasse. One thinks of the memorable early work of Carl Plackman, Martin Naylor, Boyd Webb and John Cobb which surrounded Wilding. It contrasts with the more aggressive stances of the artists who had been studying at St Martin's School of Art. They pioneered the 'new art' in the face of the committed object-making of Anthony Caro and the New Generation sculptors. Two alternatives which dominated the official scene were Richard Long's particularly puritanical walking and signing programmes with their archetypal references, and the sacrilegious undermining of sculptural permanence and self-sufficiency realised so effectively by Bruce McLean, Barry Flanagan and Gilbert and George.

The options obviously worried Wilding and for various reasons, some practical, she made little work after leaving college until 1978. However, her 'formative' period had clearly produced a belief that discrete objects could be extremely potent if they came wholly out of one's isolated, and therefore responsible, self, placed in a cage with the escape route opening when the focus of analytic concerns exactly overlapped the shape and detail of the hand-fashioned object. Wilding seemed to draw away both from the discursive approach of her student associates and from an organisation of method on didactic lines. But this was not because she was converting to the ethics of artists like Tony Cragg and Bill Woodrow with whom she was grouped from 1982 onwards as a result of the shared Lisson Gallery affiliation. Her sensibility, unlike theirs, appeared when she tampered with virgin material, gently carving or cutting or bending, until what was created had absorbed a new identity, one as delicate, puzzling and structured as a Zen poem.

Those artists mentioned, and others very different like David Nash and Richard Deacon, drew attention to their actions. By appropriating, or taking on routine processes like splicing, laminating, riveting or sorting by colour or size, they introduced such issues as science versus nature, consumer expediency versus ecological principle.

Wilding's handling of pristine two-dimensional material has a rash aspect: the drawing potential of a knife or shears activates unequivocally what might have been roughly sketched in chalk on the studio floor. Sheet metal, she found, could be self-supporting and burnished or treated with chemicals to emit a dull lustre. The flat elements, with their parabolically-curved edges, have frequently been set in opposition to kernels of dense material. They feed each other during the making. While chiselling rivulets in wood or stone, in a meditative, therapeutic activity, Wilding's attention drifts to the problems of the more adventurous other half of the sculpture. *Blue Skies*, 1987, is an example of a two element, two activity work where one part seems a

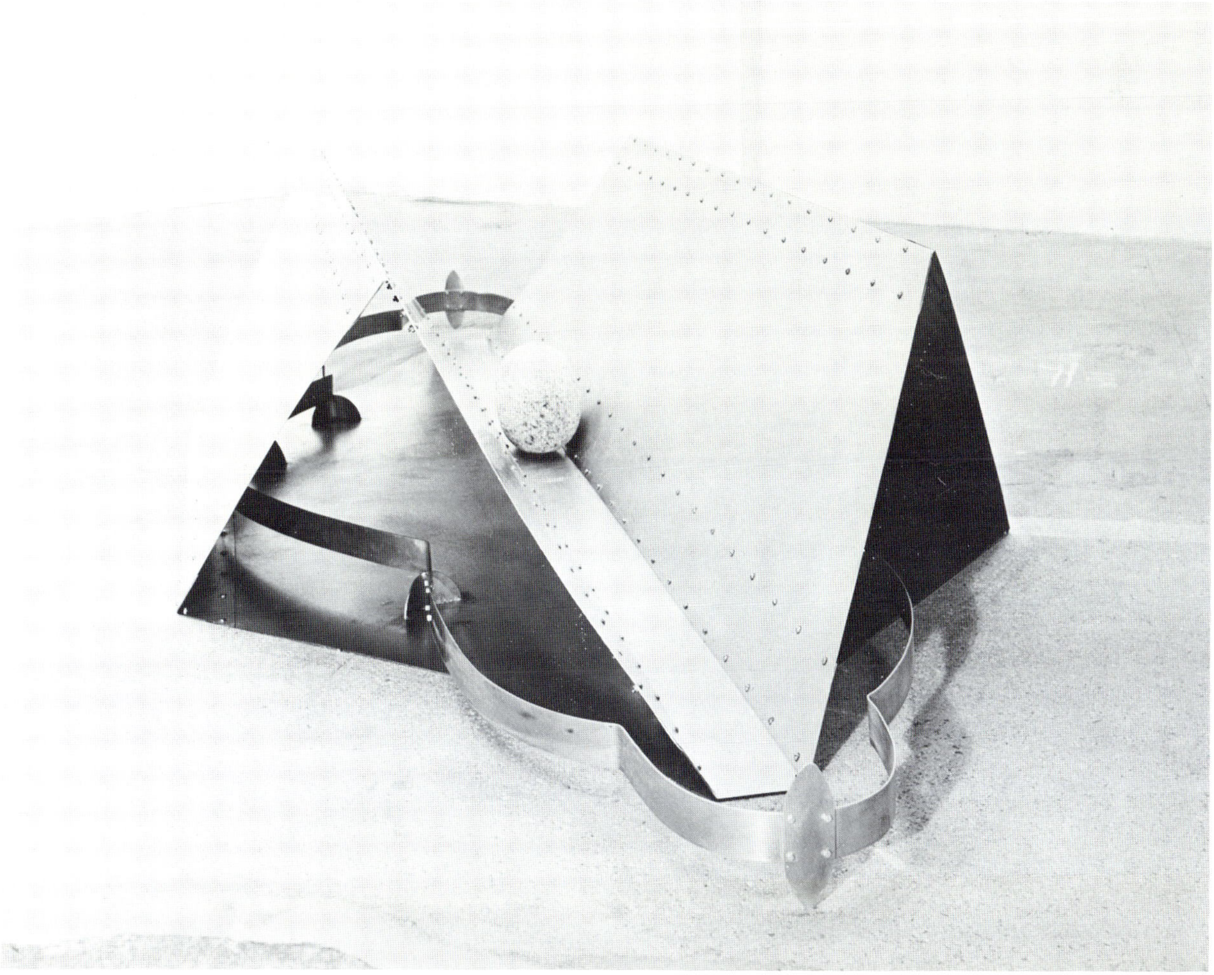

Alison Wilding, *Blue Skies* 1987
Courtesy Karsten Schubert Ltd., London

light-capturing foil or cape that offers itself to the ovoid-pure, reticent and dense. Here and elsewhere, balancing the virtues of unequal elements indicates the artist's tolerance within herself for conflicting aspirations and instincts; for female compassion, for ambition, for stoicism, for abstract quantities of space, balance and chemistry and finally for devoted embellishment. It was as if Wilding was remembering the sacramental feeling she experienced when making sculpture at the Royal College but was determined to move beyond the tempting clichés of egg/lingam or negative/positive. They were not accepted as self-sufficient polarities since polarity in itself perhaps seemed to her quizzical mind an axiomatic idea not adequately life-like.

The answer was to begin with something basically ordinary that would take on a character and dynamic during the experience of its making. Lately Wilding has asked a metal-working firm to duplicate her paper template in rigid material. Several times she has had two copper sheets rolled and welded; in *Her Furnace* a narrow cylinder is slid inside a funnel-shape or in *Slow Core*, 1985–87, the upright fenders hold a bronzed funnel. By modifications to the surface and edges, Wilding achieves something coherent and simple, reminiscent of the Shakers' functional and aesthetic objects. However, these things also have a humanistic pull. Looking down on *Her Furnace* from overhead, one reading might be a view into the soul through the womb, or abstractly a consideration of the difference between reflected light versus light windows or bright negative space within the inky dark interior. Since we sense that it is not the purpose of the work to be clever in the eyes of the viewer or critic, the potential interpretations seem pleasantly optional and inviting. The sculpture exists as a thing with its own identity which the artist grows to like and service.

There is something in Wilding's work which suggests she needs to surprise and refresh herself and be released from austerity and introspection. Matisse's flat dance-forms were motivated by a similar attraction to suspending in time a sudden revelation. The 1932–33 murals at the Barnes Foundation allow the dancers' bodies to conform to the apse-like curves of the wall. The late work, especially the large cut-outs and environment designed for the Vence Chapel show a sculptural sensitivity to light and space. The point of working irreversibly with flat colour and cut-shape was, in Matisse's words, to realise "feelings of release, of obstacles cleared . . . where thought is clarified, where feeling itself is lightened". Going further there is a comparison between his compulsion to make signs and Wilding's apertures and silhouettes and her ideas of inlaid substances. The parallel may be extended by his use of seemingly generalised forms in the maquettes for chasubles made of gouache on cut and pasted paper. On the front of a red apron-pattern in the *Maquette for Red Chasuble* (Nice 1950–52) he placed a yellow stem surrounded by tapering reeds over which are black crosses and on top a few smaller yellow ones.

Wilding's incisions in the metal sheet and additions to columns might at first glance appear rather restrained and classic being clearly derived from conventions for organic forms like oval eyes and tapering leaves. At present she is working on an angular monolith with cut holes through which will be pulled cloth, like reverse pockets. This unusual way of suggesting mass without resorting to modelling may launch an image luxurious, solemn and enigmatic.

Catherine Lampert
August 1987

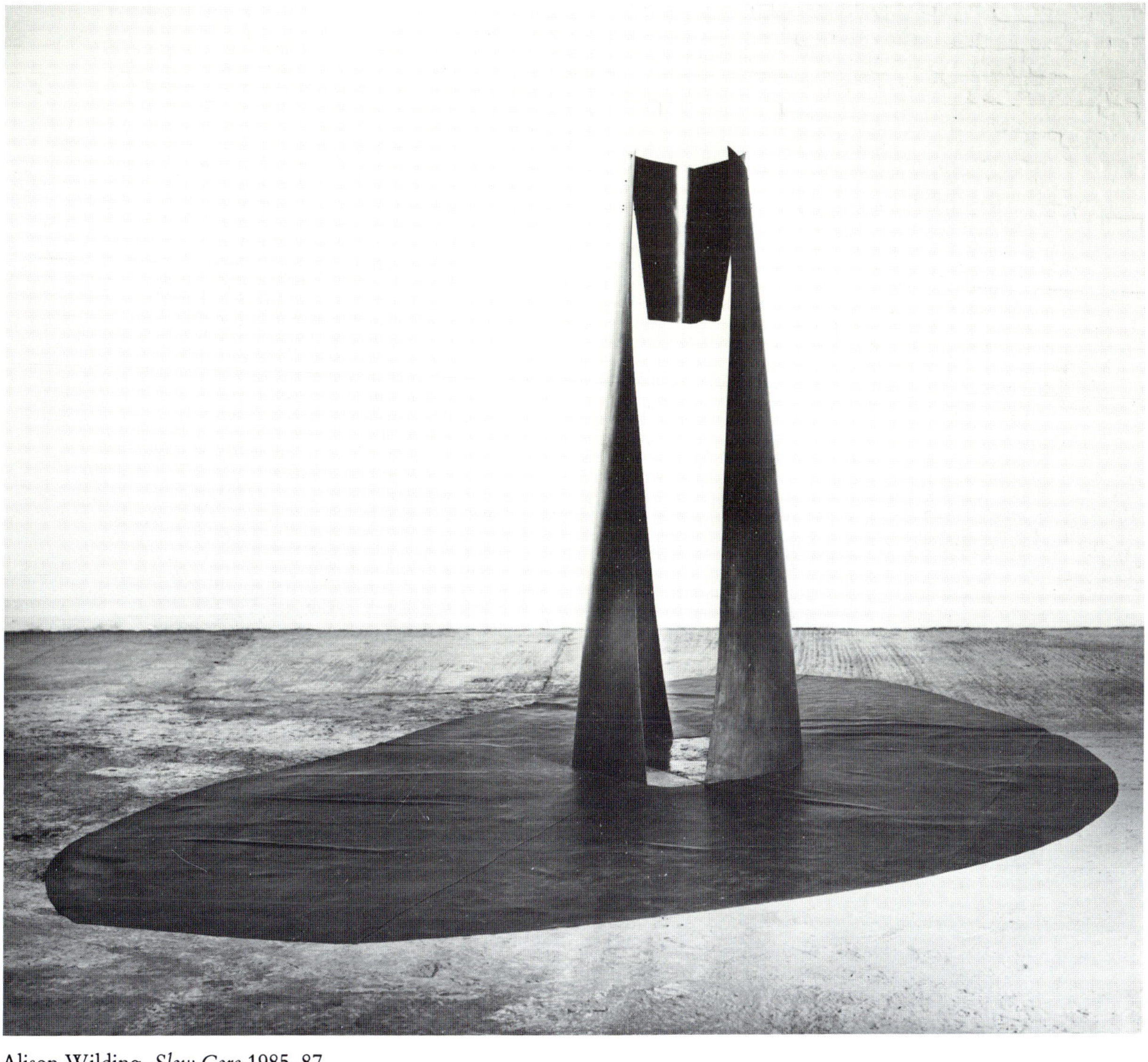

Alison Wilding, *Slow Core* 1985–87
Courtesy Karsten Schubert Ltd., London

TERRY WINTERS

Painting as Metaphor

In the tradition of Classical myth and literature a character bears a meaning greater than its literal manifestation. Oedipus is not simply a particular son of a particular mother and father but stands for all sons and his attributes and actions are universalised to the point where he becomes character, symbol and metaphor. Thus the Oedipus trilogy may be read both at face value as a dramatic narrative and on a second level as a presentation of more generalised ideas. The same can be said about many paintings in the history of art, for universality was traditionally a prerequisite of the grand manner. Artists chose themes from classical myth and history, or from the bible, which were subjects elevated beyond daily life. In the twentieth century, fewer artists have attempted to grapple with such distanced but pertinent themes but the spirit of classicism remains in the work of those artists who, looking beyond literal depiction, seek to present an image which has far reaching metaphorical connotations. Such an artist is Terry Winters.

Ostensibly Winters depicts forms of botanical and biological origin. The forms—generally mushrooms, pollen seeds, stamens, flowers, crystals, honeycomb or some such items from the world of flora and fauna and microbiology—are laid out across the surface of the canvas like specimens. They are enlarged in scale and thereby endowed with a greater, almost supernatural presence on the canvas. Winters has a strong interest in science fiction films of the fifties and the sense of the bizarre does sometimes enter into these works.

The diagramatic presentation of the 'figures', the disregard for relative scale and spatial relationships, at least in the paintings of 1982–83 such as *Fungus* (Saatchi Collection, London), are reminiscent of charts in scientific books to which Winters often has recourse. However, they are also suggestive of the concept of the rebus where words and images are combined to form sentences with a total disregard for relative scale. There is, at times, in Winters' paintings a sense of a build up towards a final image which parallels this 'primitive', pictographic concept.

The changes in scale within some of the paintings and the grid-like presentation of the 'figures' endow the paintings with a feeling of objectivity and of dispassionateness, which is consistent with Winters' earlier interest in Minimal Art and, in some senses, with the practice of Pop artists. In the late seventies Winters painted all-over, monochromatic canvases in which he displayed an interest in the way the paint was applied and in the brushstrokes, rather than in the field. His paintings of the early eighties manifest further strong links with such art; with Minimalism in his use of a restricted and often monochromatic palette; his emphasis on surface and flatness; on literalness of form and brushstroke; with Pop Art in the decontextualised image; the enlargement of scale and astonishing juxtapositions of forms. But this formal analysis and literal reading of the works belies the metaphorical implications with which these paintings resound.

Many of the forms in Winters' paintings are depicted at different stages of their life cycles, from embryo through nascence to death. On one level his work can be seen to relate to primeval notions of procreation, reproduction and fertility, as well as to notions of life patterns in general and, on another level, to the concept of the physical making of paintings. *Stamina 2,* 1982,

(Saatchi Collection, London), depicts stamens in different degrees of paintedness, some as complete forms, others in the process of becoming or perhaps fading away. The forms themselves were sometimes suggested by incidents in the paint surface which Winters then exploited. At other times images were overpainted while some were left as *pentimenti* both as a testament to the history of the making of the picture and as a suggestion of the notion of time. Thus time is evoked in the actual making of the painting and in the subject depicted. In this sense the painting is a unity in an almost classical sense.

The title of the work ensures that it is not interpreted simply as a manifestation of paint on canvas for it signals a number of more specific subjects. *Stamina* is the Latin plural of *stamen* (the title is deliberately classicising) which in archaic English use denoted the fundamental parts, elements or nature of something, especially an organism. It also denoted the innate capacities formerly regarded as conditioning or governing the duration of life. The painting may refer, therefore, to ideas about the essence of life as well as to the time span of the life cycle. In addition, in botanical terms a stamen is the male or fertilising organ of a flowering plant which consists of two parts, the anther, which is a double-celled sac containing the pollen, and the filament, a slender footstalk supporting the anther; hence the painting suggests notions of reproduction both in its title and in the phallic appearance of the imagery. Since Winters has deliberately chosen to classicise the title it should also be noted that in Latin a *stamen* is the warp or thread spun by the fates at the birth of a child to determine the length of his life. The Latin word derives from the Greek *stemon* meaning a warp or thread.

The manner in which the forms are drawn out of the paint surface, the almost accidental way in which Winters often creates form, mirrors, on the level of painting, this interest in primordialism and creation. In later works the interest in reproductive life is more overtly stated. For example in *Pitch Lake*, 1985, (Eli and Edythe L. Broad Collection, Los Angeles), the spore clusters can be read as spermatazoa creeping across the sticky, bituminous surface towards the leaf shape on the left, which is suggestive of a vagina. Within the 'vagina' rest the ova. There is a sense of expectancy in this work, a feeling that the spectator is witnessing the creation of the earliest living organisms, that fertilisation is taking place in a protoplasm. The depiction of other undeveloped, insect or molecular organisms floating in the ether reinforces this impression of primordialism. While *Pitch Lake* depicts a specific moment it also has an air of timelessness and a sense of myth and universality. The references to life are generalised in the tradition of the grand manner.

Although *Pitch Lake* was painted relatively recently it is unusual among Winters' recent works in its restricted range of colours. Here, as in earlier paintings, Winters employed only earth colours, an act which was consistent in some respects with the subjects depicted. The introduction of colour occurred gradually in 1984 and coincided with the making of more painterly, thickly impastoed surfaces. The earth tones became more intense and less neutral, so that sharp contrasts began to be pointed up and, in 1985, Winters increased his range to include colours of great luminescence and incandescence. Colour became less descriptive and more emotive, even more autonomous as in a work such as *Dumb Compass*, 1985, (Saatchi Collection, London), where spheres of orange-red, yellow, green and blue-purple are included because Winters wanted "to get some colour into the painting". The colours do not describe organic forms but are perceived as artistic devices intended to add a particular weight to counterbalance the pull to the left. They do, however, embody the colours of the spectrum and therefore denote the essential components of light. Like *Pitch Lake*, *Dumb Compass* has strong overtones of sexuality and reproduction in its biomorphic masculine and feminine forms. These two totemic configurations are strongly reminiscent of the biomorphism of Joan Miró and also, perhaps more relevantly, of the biomorphic paintings of 1943–44 of Mark Rothko, who was more overtly concerned with classical myth and history but whose works display an interest in primeval, organic forms. The bipartite and tripartite division of Rothko's paintings in this period is echoed in some of Winters' paintings such as *Insecta*, 1985, (Collection of Antonio Homem, New York), with its richly wrought ground of orange, green and brown across which specimens of insect life are spread, as though part of a display collection.

In one of his most recent paintings, *Monkey Puzzle*, 1987, Winters has renounced this tendency to construct diagrammatic compositions and portrays figures which appear to interact in a ritualised relationship. Here he has returned to a subdued palette perhaps because *Monkey Puzzle* represents a new development in his art, an increased dependence on line rather than mass and literal volume, in the form of thick impasto, to describe form. The artist imposes his will on the surface rather than exploiting what is suggested by the paint. In its graphic quality it is in some respects reminiscent of the late paintings of Miró, although Winters did not have them in mind. But like Miró, Winters handles the large scale with great breadth and abandon creating an image of great spontaneity and rhythm in which the brush flows across and into the wet paint in bold, sweeping movements. The forms retain their sexual and phallic overtones and there is more than a suggestion of the enactment of a ritual by two figures. There is something more liberated and lighter in *Monkey Puzzle* than in earlier, heavily worked paintings, as though Winters has overcome the problem of how to include figures in a painting and solved the problem of the figure ground relationship by not bodying out the forms but simply by differentiating them from the ground by contour. Winters has referred to his earlier works as a kind of 'choreography of form', thereby implying notation, charts and exactitude. *Monkey Puzzle* represents a release from the grid-like structure and might be described as the enactment of the dance.

Jeremy Lewison

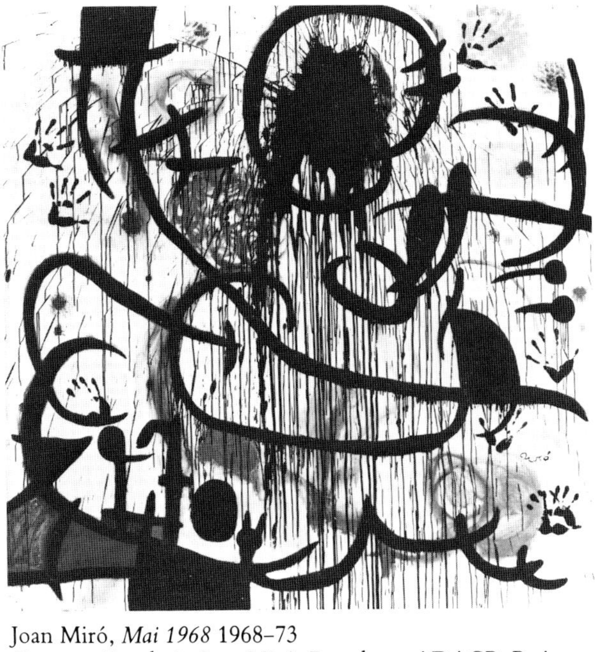

Joan Miró, *Mai 1968* 1968–73
Courtesy Fundacio Joan Miró, Barcelona, ADAGP, Paris and DACS, London

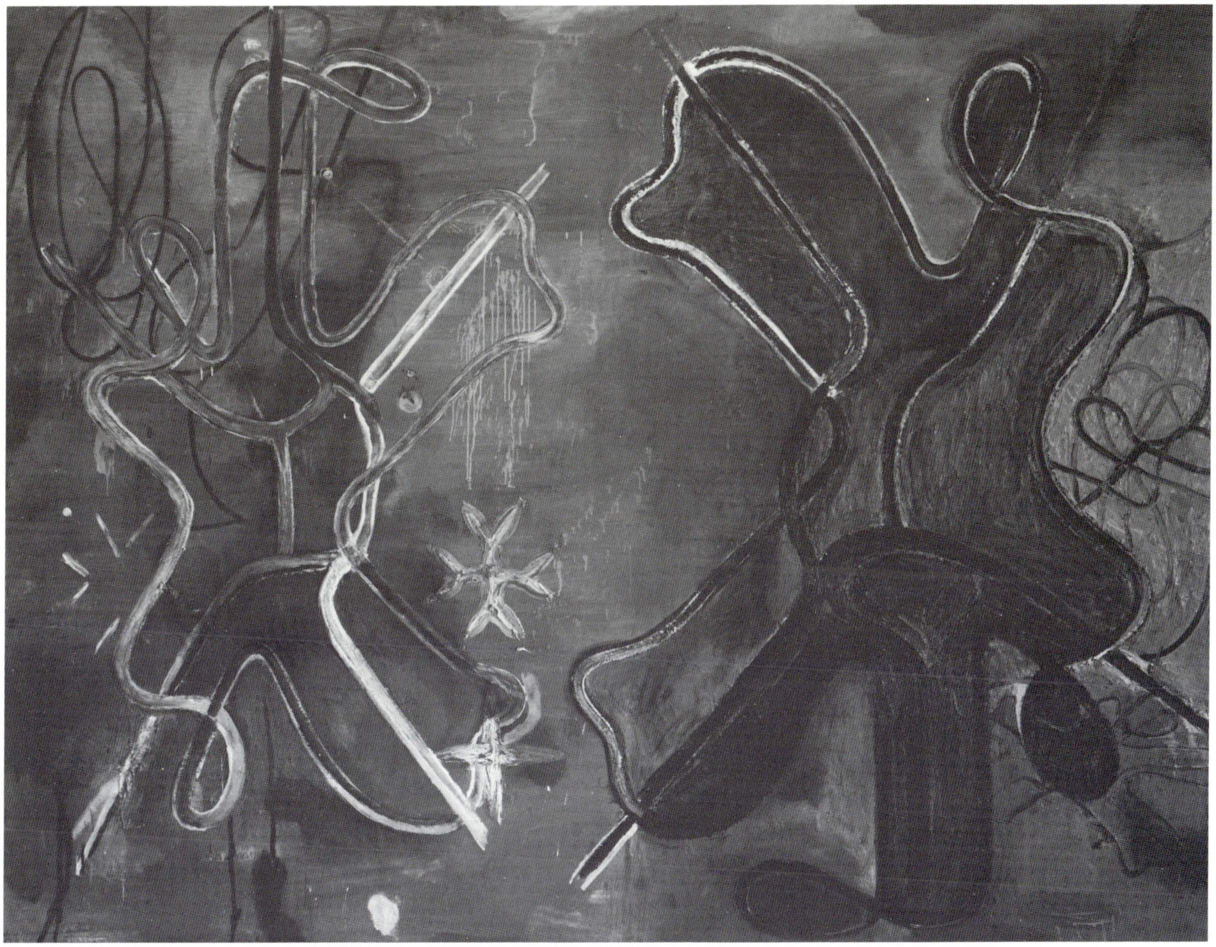

Terry Winters, *Monkey Puzzle* 1987
Courtesy Sonnabend Gallery, NYC

CATALOGUE

All dimensions are in centimetres, height precedes width precedes depth

James Lee Byars

1. *Figure of Death* 1986
ten blocks of basalt lava stone
70 × 70 × 70 each
Galerie Michael Werner, Cologne

Tony Cragg

2. *Eye Bath* 1986
cast iron
55 × 56 × 40
Saatchi Collection, London

3. *Instinctive Reactions* 1987
cast steel
240 × 350 × 450
Saatchi Collection, London

4. *Untitled* 1987
plastic
size according to installation
The Artist courtesy Lisson Gallery, London

Richard Deacon

5. *Troubled Water* 1987
wood and galvanised steel
310 × 100 × 140
The Artist courtesy Lisson Gallery, London

6. *It's Orpheus When There's Singing No. 3* 1978–79
pencil and crayon on paper
111.8 × 147.5
Collection of Jackie Poncelet

7. *It's Orpheus When There's Singing No. 4* 1979
pencil and crayon on paper
111.8 × 147.5
Private Collection

8. *It's Orpheus When There's Singing No. 5* 1979
pencil and crayon on paper
112 × 147
Private Collection

9. *It's Orpheus When There's Singing No. 6* 1979
ink and pencil on paper
107 × 141.5
Jack and Nell Wendler, London

Ian Hamilton Finlay

10. *Aphrodite of The Terror* 1987
plaster cast
200 × 90
Collection of the Artist

Gérard Garouste

11. *St Thérèse d'Avila* 1983
oil on canvas
200 × 300
Liliane and Michel Durand-Dessert, Paris

12. *Lucrèce* 1983
oil on canvas
200 × 235
Fondation Cartier pour l'Art Contemporain, Jouy-en-Josas

Rebecca Horn

13. *Black Bath* 1986
mixed media
30 × 220 × 440
Collection of the Artist

Stephan Huber

14. *Untitled* 1987
mixed media
size according to installation
Collection of the Artist

Axel Kasseböhmer

15. *Drapery* 1981
oil on canvas
206 × 232
Monika Sprüth Galerie, Cologne

16. *Column II* 1982
oil on canvas
291 × 65.5
Private Collection, Cologne

17. *Still Life IV* 1984
oil on canvas
40 × 150
Private Collection, Cologne
courtesy Monika Sprüth Galerie, Cologne

18. *Landscape XII* 1984
oil and wax on canvas
150 × 300
Monika Sprüth Galerie, Cologne

19. *Still Life with Ornament* 1987
oil on canvas
60 × 150
Monika Sprüth Galerie, Cologne

Sol LeWitt

20. *Wall Drawing* 1987
size according to installation
Collection of the Artist

Ann McCoy

21. *Daemon est Deus Inversus* 1980
pencil on paper on canvas
276 × 153
The Artist courtesy Karen Amiel, New York

22. *Coeur de Lion* 1985
pencil on paper on canvas
269 × 423
The Artist courtesy Karen Amiel, New York

23. *Barque with Lion Goddess* 1985
bronze
34.5 × 283.5 × 25.5
Collection of Jacqueline Sheinberg, New York

24. *Barque with Lion Goddess* 1986
bronze
98 × 218.5 × 46
Collection of Mr and Mrs Sidney Singer, New York

25. *Temple of Isis, Pompeii* 1987
pencil on paper on canvas
276 × 479
The Artist courtesy Karen Amiel, New York

Stephen McKenna

26. *The Tuscan Order* 1987
oil on canvas
203 × 152.5
203 × 305
203 × 152.5
The Artist courtesy Edward Totah Gallery, London

27. *The Acrobat* 1987
oil on canvas
183 × 122
The Artist courtesy Edward Totah Gallery, London

28. *Puchinello* 1987
oil on canvas
183 × 122
The Artist courtesy Edward Totah Gallery, London

29. *Fabio* 1987
oil on canvas
183 × 122
The Artist courtesy Edward Totah Gallery, London

30. *Isabella* 1987
oil on canvas
183 × 122
The Artist courtesy Edward Totah Gallery, London

Carlo Maria Mariani

31. *Castor and Pollux* 1982
crayon on paper
145.5 × 186
Gian Enzo Sperone, Rome

32. *To Look at Oneself in a Celestial Mirror* 1984
crayon and gouache on paper
200 × 175
Gian Enzo Sperone, Rome

33. *Prophetic Dream* 1984
oil on canvas
200 × 250
Gian Enzo Sperone, Rome

Michelangelo Pistoletto

34. *Venus of Rags* 1967
concrete, synthetic-resin,
mica and rags
130 × 100 × 100
Galerie Tanit, Munich

Salvo

35. *Untitled* 1984
oil on canvas
202 × 115
Galerie Paul Maenz, Cologne

36. *Ottomania* 1985
oil on canvas
78 × 51
Private Collection, Rottach-Egern

37. *Alba* 1985
oil on canvas
80 × 60
Private Collection, Milan

38. *Untitled* 1986
oil on canvas
218 × 122
Collection of Mr and Mrs Isler, Switzerland

39. *Untitled* 1986
oil on panel
168 × 71
Galerie Kaess-Weiss, Stuttgart

Andreas Schulze

40. *Untitled* 1984
oil on canvas
200 × 400
Galerie Six Friedrich, Munich

41. *Untitled* 1985
oil on canvas
200 × 400
Galerie Six Friedrich, Munich

42. *Untitled* 1985
oil on canvas
200 × 400
Private Collection, Milan

Cy Twombly

43. *Untitled* 1961
oil, crayon and pencil on canvas
165 × 200
Mayor Gallery, London

44. *Orpheus* 1975
oil, chalk and pencil on two sheets on card
140 × 100
Speck Collection, Cologne

45. *Untitled (Portrait of the Family Speck)* 1979
pencil, crayon, chalk and oil on two sheets on paper on card
120 × 149
Speck Collection, Cologne

46. *Naxos* 1982
paint stick, flat paint, crayon and graphite on paper
82 × 63.5
174 × 141.5
82 × 63.5
Private Collection, New York

Isolde Wawrin

47. *Untitled* 1987
acrylic on paper
333 × 150
Collection of the Artist

48. *Untitled* 1987
acrylic on paper
303 × 146
Collection of the Artist

49. *Untitled* 1987
acrylic on paper
273 × 150
Collection of the Artist

50. *Untitled* 1987
acrylic on paper
375 x 151
Collection of the Artist

Alison Wilding

51. *Beneath the Skin* 1986
pigment on limewood, beeswax
8.5 x 67 x 12.5
The Artist courtesy Salvatore Ala, Milan and New York

52. *Stormy Weather* 1987
galvanised steel and bronze
225 x 115.5 x 170
The Artist courtesy Karsten Schubert Ltd., London

Terry Winters

53. *Theophrastus Garden I* 1982
oil on linen
221 x 178
Saatchi Collection, London

54. *Stamina II* 1982
oil on linen
152.4 x 213.4
Saatchi Collection, London

55. *Station* 1987
oil on linen
180.5 x 150
The Artist courtesy Sonnabend Gallery, NYC

BIOGRAPHIES OF ARTISTS

JAMES LEE BYARS

James Lee Byars was born in 1932 in Detroit. In 1957 he made the first of seven visits to Japan. The following year he held his first exhibition at MoMA, New York, using emergency exits to show paper works. In 1959, the year Byars was awarded the Coply Prize by the Cassandra Foundation, he presented his first one-word plays and participation pieces in New York. The stone sculpture *Tantric Figures* was sculpted for the Whitney Museum in 1960. Exhibitions were presented in Japan from 1961.

The use of black, white or gold, combined with a pure simplicity of presentation both Oriental and Minimal, was established by the mid-sixties. A black exhibition, featuring a Balenciaga dress in the form of three spheres, was shown in New York in 1963. A performance featuring a one hundred-foot sheet of white Chinese paper was held in Kyoto in 1964. Fabrics, including single gold threads, began to be used in presentations, at first relating to architecture: the award in 1968 of the Prize of the Architectural League of New York was used to create the world's largest (pink) dress, worn to surround the League building. The following year Byars was 'the artist of the Hudson Institute' in Croton-on-the-Hudson where he established 'the World Question Center'. Exhibiting in *Prospect 69* in Düsseldorf he met Joseph Beuys with whose ideas he was particularly in sympathy. In 1986 Byars performed *The Perfect Death in Honour of Joseph Beuys* at the opening of *Hommage à Beuys* at Munich's Lenbachhaus and in 1987 contributed to *Brennpunkt Düsseldorf: Joseph Beuys—Die Akademie—Der allgemeine Aufbruch 1962–1987*.

The Berliner Künstlerprogramm of the DAAD awarded Byars a scholarship in 1974. During the seventies and eighties, in his search for perfection, Byars has presented a number of pieces and performances which in their concepts, titles and forms have reevaluated classical principles. These have included *The Perfect Kiss*, performed in Paris 1975, and by Byars himself in California 1977 and Amsterdam 1981, *The Perfect Performance is to Stand Still*, presented at Byars' first one-man exhibition in a museum, Antwerp 1976, *The Exhibition of Perfect,* Harvard 1980, and *The Perfect Death*, Philadelphia 1984. Byars has enjoyed a close association with the Michael Werner Gallery in Cologne over many years. Among important group exhibitions he has shown in *Documenta* at Kassel in 1972, 1977, 1982 and 1987, the Venice Biennale in 1979 and 1986, *Zeitgeist*, Berlin 1982 and *Kunst unserer Zeit in Berliner Sicht* in 1987. Byars retrospectives were held in Eindhoven and Paris in 1983 and at the Kunsthalle, Düsseldorf, in 1986.

James Lee Byars: The Philosophical Palace,
Kunsthalle Düsseldorf and Galerie Michael Werner, Cologne, 1987

TONY CRAGG

Tony Cragg was born in Liverpool in 1949, the son of an aircraft electrics designer. Between 1966 and 1968 he worked as a laboratory technician with the National Rubber Producers Research Association. In 1968–69 he studied at the Gloucestershire College of Arts and Technology and from 1969–72 at Wimbledon School of Art. During this period Cragg was experimenting with non-sculptural materials and soon after formed friendships with Richard Long, Bill Woodrow and Richard Deacon. Between 1973 and 1977 he studied at the Royal College of Art. Cragg made his first drawing piece, on a large paper bag, and his first stack in 1975. In 1977 Cragg settled in Wuppertal where he still lives. During the following year he participated in *JA-NA-PA* in Paris with a work of plastic elements arranged in the order of the spectrum: this established his emergent vocabulary of materials, objects and images, using floor or, from 1980, wall as a base. These materials, often found locally, are frequently used to provoke consideration of ecological issues and the materialist society. More recently, Cragg has used other materials and methods, including traditional bronze casting.

In 1979 Cragg started teaching at the Kunstakademie in Düsseldorf and held his first one-man shows with the Lisson Gallery, London, and Lützowstrasse Situation, Berlin. In the 1980s Cragg has held many one-man shows: in St Étienne, London, Wuppertal and Lyons (all 1981), Karlsruhe, Lyons, Otterlo, Munich and New York (1982), Berne, Amsterdam and St Gallen (1983), Louisiana, Cologne, Turin and Basle (1984), Winterthur, Munich, Brussels, and Paris (1985), Hanover, New York and Geneva (1986) and

London and Turin (1987). He has been selected to represent Britain in the 1988 Venice Biennale. Among important group shows to which he has contributed are *Europa Kunst der 80er Jahre*, Stuttgart (1979), *Aperto '80*, the Venice Biennale and *Kunst in Europa na '68* (1980), *Enciclopedia*, Modena and *British Sculpture in the Twentieth Century*, London (1981), *Aspects of British Art Today*, Tokyo, the Indian Triennale, New Delhi, *Kunst wird Material*, Berlin, *New Sculpture*, Edinburgh, *Documenta* 7, Kassel, *Lecons des Choses*, Berne and Paris (1982), *Terremoto*, Naples, *The Sculpture Show*, London (1983), *An International Survey of Recent Painting and Sculpture*, MoMA, New York, *Skulptur im 20. Jahrhundert*, Basle and ROSC, Dublin (1984), The Hayward Annual 1985 and *Aureola Borealis*, Oslo (1985), *Beuys zu Ehren*, Munich and *Spüren, Skulpturen und Monumente ihrer präzisen Reise*, Zurich (1986). In 1987 Cragg has shown in *Documenta 8* at Kassel, the *Skulptur Projekte* in Münster and *Anderer Leute Kunst* in Krefeld.

Tony Cragg, exh. cat., Palais des Beaux-Arts, Brussels, 1985
Tony Cragg, exh. cat., Hayward Gallery, London, 1987

RICHARD DEACON

Richard Deacon was born in 1949 in Bangor. He studied at St Martin's School of Art, the Royal College of Art, where he won the Penguin Book Prize in 1976, and the Chelsea School of Art. In 1978–79 he visited the United States where his interest turned particularly to ceramics and drawing. During this year Deacon made a series of drawings inspired by the *Sonnets to Orpheus* of Rainer Maria Rilke: in these he began to explore the relationship between language and the world. From 1980 Deacon made a related series of sculptures, using laminated wood, steel, linoleum and tarpaulin to introduce swelling forms echoing natural growth: image, surface and structure were expressed as one. A number of sculptures from 1981 onwards bear poetic titles. These have explored metamorphic relationships with the world in addition to developing the expression of organic form. A series of small sculpture, collectively titled *Art for Other People*, has at the same time developed a domestic scale and declared art as a social language.

Deacon held one-man exhibitions in 1983 at the Orchard Gallery, Londonderry and the Lisson Gallery, London (and in 1987), and Riverside Studios, London, Chapter Gallery, Cardiff, and the Fruitmarket Gallery, Edinburgh in 1984. In 1984–85 he showed in Lyons and in 1985 in Chicago, Aix-en-Provence, New York, and in London at the Tate and Serpentine Galleries. Important group shows include *Objects and Sculpture*, London and Bristol, 1981, *British Drawing* (the Hayward Annual), London, and *Englische Plastik Heute* in Lucerne in 1982, *The Sculpture Show*, London, *New Art* at the Tate Gallery and *Transformations—New Sculpture from Britain* (the XVIIth São Paolo Biennale) in 1983, *An International Survey of Recent Painting and Sculpture*, MoMA, New York, *Skulptur im 20 Jahrhundert*, Basle, and *The British Art Show* in 1984—the first year he was shortlisted for the Turner Prize—the 1985 Carnegie International in Pittsburgh, *Transformation in Sculpture*, New York, *The Poetic Object*, Dublin and Belfast, in 1985, *Falls the Shadow* (the Hayward Annual), London, *Prospect 86*, Frankfurt, and *Correspondence Europe*, Amsterdam in 1986. In 1987 he has contributed to *A Quiet Revolution: British Sculpture Since 1968* in Chicago, *Current Affairs: British Painting & Sculpture from the 1980s*, British Council, to the *Skulptur Projekte Münster*, and to *Anderer Leute Kunst*, Krefeld. Deacon has been awarded the 1987 Turner Prize.

Richard Deacon: Sculpture 1980–84, exh. cat, Fruitmarket Gallery, Edinburgh, 1985
'For Those Who Have Eyes': Richard Deacon Sculpture 1980–86, exh. cat, Aberystwyth Arts Centre, 1986

IAN HAMILTON FINLAY

Ian Hamilton Finlay was born in 1925 in Nassau, Bahamas, or in Rousay, Orkney. Such education as he had, took place in Scotland; at the outbreak of the War, when he was aged eleven, he was evacuated into the country and did not return to school. After being called up he served in the army for three-and-a-half years, and thereafter worked as a shepherd till, in the fifties, he began to publish short stories and plays. Towards the end of this decade he spent a period in Edinburgh, where, with Jessie McGuffie, he started the Wild Hawthorn Press, which introduced concrete poetry to Britain, as well as publishing the first poem-prints (poster poems) and poem-cards. In 1965 he moved to Easter Ross with Sue Finlay, producing his first 'environmental poems' in the garden of an old farmhouse, where he also made decorative interior poems—i.e. 'ajar', and others. He took part in the now famous *International Exhibition of Concrete Poetry* and was Scottish representative on the *comité internationale* of this movement. From this period also date his first poems in glass.

With Sue Finlay, his main collaborator, he now settled at Stonypath, on the Lanarkshire moors. The garden (see *The Oxford Companion to Gardens*) was embarked on, and Finlay began his collaborations with craftsmen working in stone, wood, glass, and other materials. In 1972 he held a one-man exhibition in the Scottish National Gallery of Modern Art, and since then has exhibited in the Serpentine Gallery, London; the Kroller-Muller Rijksmuseum, Holland; Kettle's Yard, Cambridge; the Graeme Murray Gallery, Edinburgh (etc., etc.). The adoption of the name 'Little Sparta' for the area surrounding Stonypath Cottage, and the transformation of the Stonypath Gallery into a Garden Temple, signalled the advent of Finlay's activist neo-classicism which has produced such events as The First Battle of Little Sparta (4 February 1983) and the Saint-Just Vigilante Raid on the Scottish Arts Council in the summer of the same year. This activism was given its considered commentary in the exhibition *The Third Reich Revisited*, toured by Southampton Art Gallery. In 1985 Finlay was shortlisted for the Turner Prize. From the time of his involvement in the major exhibition of international sculpture in Basel, in 1984, he has taken part in international sculpture exhibitions, this year participating in *Documenta 8*, Kassel as well as similar exhibitions at Münster, Antwerp, and in the Swiss Alps. He now has large-scale landscaped 'installations' at Stuttgart, Vienna (the Schweizergarten), the Kroller-Muller Sculpture Park, the French Government Sculpture Park in Brittany, San Diego (campus of the University of California), Celle (near Florence), Eindhoven (the Van Abbe Museum), and elsewhere. He has continued to write, and his plays are published (in German) in Vienna, while he is represented in such anthologies as *The Oxford Book of Scottish Short Stories, World's Classics Series, The Penguin Book of Scottish Short Stories*—and so on. The Bibliothèque Nationale is compiling a catalogue of all his published works. Among his latest commissions are those to celebrate the Bi-centenary of the French Revolution, taking the form of a garden on the site of the old Assembly building at Versailles (to be opened by the President on Bastille Day, 1989), and a large-scale landscaping project on the new Autoroute A.86 near Paris. Related to these projects are the four exhibitions he has held in Paris this year.

Finlay's publications are available through The Wild Hawthorn Press, Little Sparta, Dunsyre, Lanark. Books on his work include *Ian Hamilton Finlay*, by Francis Edeline, Hazan (in French), and *Ian Hamilton Finlay—A Visual Primer*, by Yves Abrioux, Reaktion Books.

GÉRARD GAROUSTE

Gérard Garouste was born in Paris in 1946. His first exhibition was held at the Galerie Zunini in 1969. Since he was interested primarily in figurative work which was out of fashion, his subsequent exhibitions were not mounted until ten years later, at the Galerie Travers, and with Enzo Cannaviello in Milan. He produced several stage décors—in 1977 for *Le Classique et l'Indien* at the Théâtre Le Palace (where he was to work as a set designer from 1979 until 1982), and for Jean-Michel Ribes' *Jack Parady* at the Théâtre de la Ville de Paris in 1979. In 1980 he held his first show with the Galerie Durand-Dessert, Paris, and designed the décor for *Privilège*: he also exhibited at the Vereniging voor het Museum van Hedendaagse Kunst in Ghent, and contributed to *Nueva Immagine* at the Palazzo della Triennale, Milan, *Après le Classicisme* at St Etienne and the XIth Paris Biennale. The following year a one-man show of designs 1974–81 opened at the Palazzo Ducezio in Noto, where he was also shown at the Musée des Beaux-Arts.

Although primarily associated with painting, Garouste has remained equally interested in sculpture. The theme of the exhibition *Mythe, drame, tragédie*, in which Garouste participated, underlined his dedication to the primary concepts of classical painting (among whose exponents he counts for example El Greco and de Chirico) and imagery: these he regards as both timeless and archetypal, and bonded with his interest in the lessons of history.

In 1982 he participated in the Venice Biennale and in

Zeitgeist in Berlin. In 1983 Garouste held his first exhibition in the United States with Leo Castelli and Sperone-Westwater, and also showed in the Biennale Nationale d'Art Contemporain, Tours, in *Sainte Thérèse d'Avila dans l'Art Contemporain* at the Musée du Luxembourg, Paris, in *Transfiguration* in Marseilles, and *New French Painting* in London. The commission to decorate the ceiling of the Palais de l'Elysée in that year marked official acceptance of his work. The last four years have seen his painting shown worldwide and included in group shows in France, Italy, Britain, Ireland, Hungary, Germany, Canada, Holland, Australia and Japan, and in one-man exhibitions in Düsseldorf, Rome, Bourbon-Lancy, Paris, New York and Montreal. In 1987 Garouste has shown at the Galerie Durand-Dessert in Paris and in group exhibitions in Munich, Mannheim, the São Paolo Biennale, and in *L'Epoque, La Mode, La Monde, Le Passion* at the Centre Georges Pompidou, Paris. Garouste lives and works in Paris.

Gérard-Georges Lemaire, Catherine Strasser, Bernard Blistene, *Gérard Garouste,* Paris, 1984

REBECCA HORN

Rebecca Horn was born in 1944 and studied at the Academy in Hamburg. Her earliest filmed performances already involved audience participation in explorations of time, space and experience. She first exhibited photography and film in *Documenta 5* in Kassel in 1972. In the following year she showed video film and drawings with René Block in Berlin. In 1974 her work in film was presented in *Projekt 74* at the Kunsthalle in Cologne, and in video at MoMA, New York, and the Institute of Contemporary Art, Philadelphia. She showed at the Edinburgh Film Festival in 1975, following presentations in Brussels, Vienna, the Paris Biennale and Hamburg. Her film *Berlin* won the critics' award during the Berlin Festival later that year.

Horn's book *Paradieswitwe* (Paradise Widow) was published in 1976: the film was shown in *Documenta 6* the next year. Also in 1977 a retrospective was mounted in Cologne and Berlin, her *Artist's Books* was shown at MoMA, New York, and a further exhibition presented at the Kunsthalle in Baden-Baden. Working in several related fields, an installation, objects and drawings relating to her film *Der Eintänzer* were shown in Genoa in 1978 after a showing at the videosymposium held in Tokyo. In 1979 Horn won the Kunstpreis der Böttcher-Strasse in Bremen and showed in Eindhoven, Münster and with Salvatore Ala in New York. *Goldenes Bad* was shown during the *Medicis* exhibition in Florence in 1980. Horn's film *La Ferdinanda* was shown at the Kunsthalle, Baden-Baden in 1981. Her most recent installation, *Der Zwinger*, was made for the 1987 *Skulptur Projekte Münster*.

In the eighties Horn's work has been seen in a number of festivals and large exhibitions, including the Spoleto Festival in 1980, the Sydney Biennale and *Documenta* 7, in 1982, *. . . von hier aus . . .*, Düsseldorf and the Japan Biennale, 1984, *The European Iceberg* in Toronto in 1985, the Musée d'Art Moderne, Paris and the Museum of Contemporary Art, Los Angeles, *Falls the Shadow* (the Hayward Annual), London, *Wien Fluss*, Vienna, *Sonsbeck 1986*, Arnhem, and the Venice Biennale, all in 1986, and *Wechselströme*, Bonn, 1987. Recent major solo shows have been presented at the Kunsthaus, Zurich in 1983 and with Eric Franck in Geneva, Marian Goodman in New York, Konrad Fischer in Düsseldorf, and Elisabeth Kaufman in Zurich.

Rebecca Horn, exh. cat., Kunsthaus, Zurich and Museum of Contemporary Art, Chicago, 1983

STEPHAN HUBER

Stephan Huber was born in 1952 in Lindenberg, West Germany. He has said that a strong formative influence on his work was the early experience of his father's factory. He studied at the Munich Academy from 1972 to 1978, holding his first one-man exhibition (the installation *Das Mehl*) at the Kunstforum in 1980. In 1980 he also contributed to *Künstlerbücher* held at the Produzentengalerie in Munich and the Bern Unibibliothek in Heidelberg, and *Performances* at Munich's Lenbachhaus. Huber was awarded a one-year scholarship to New York in 1980 which allowed him to exhibit twice at P.S.1. On his return to Munich he showed at the Lenbachhaus. His primary concern with installations using a specific range of objects such as hats, suitcases, chairs and light fittings stems from this period. Further important solo shows have been held regularly: at the Westfälischer Kunstverein in Münster in 1982, at the Kunstverein in Bonn in 1984, and at the Kunstraum, Munich, the Galerie Beatrix Wilhelm, Stuttgart, the Salone Villa Romana, Florence, and the Galerie Philomene Magers, Bonn in 1986. He has also shown regularly with Dany Keller in Munich, where he lives and works. A one-man exhibition of his work is being presented for the first time in Britain at Glasgow's Third Eye Centre in 1987–88.

Huber has continued to contribute to group shows, from *Noi altri* in Regensburg and *6 Münchner Künstler in Belgrad* in 1982 to *Im Theater* in Berlin and in 1983 to *Aktuell '83, 8 Münchner Künstler* in Alexandria, *Ansatzpunkte kritischer Kunst heute* in Bonn. Since 1984 although the majority of his group shows have been held in Germany several have taken place elsewhere in Europe. Among the most important have been his contributions to *Kunst in der BRD 1945–1985* at the Nationalgalerie, Berlin, *Alles und noch viel mehr* at the Kunsthalle, Berne, 1985, *Von Raum zu Raum* at the Kunstverein, Hamburg, and *Il Giardino d'Europa* at the Villa Demidoff, Florence in 1986, and, in 1987 *Wechselströme* at the Kunstverein, Bonn, *Documenta 8* in Kassel, and *Ateliers internationaux* at Fontevraud and *Trigon 87* in Graz.

Examples of Huber's sculpture are on permanent public display at Steiner-Design in Munich, and at Ruhrkohle AG and the Opera House in Essen. He has been awarded several prizes—the Kunstpreis in Munich in 1983, the Arbeitsstipendium Kunstfords in 1984, the Förderpreis Glockengasse, Cologne, and the Karl-Hofer-Preis, Berlin in 1985 and the Bayerischer Staatspreis in 1986.

Stephan Huber, Bonner Kunstverein [Stuttgart], 1984
Stephan Huber, Kunstraum, Munich [Stuttgart], 1986

AXEL KASSEBÖHMER

Axel Kasseböhmer was born in Herne, West Germany, in 1952, and has lived in Düsseldorf since 1976. He first exhibited in a group show at the Galerie Rüdiger Schöttle in Munich in 1981. In 1982 he showed with Rolf Ricke in Cologne, at the Kulturreferat der Stadt München, and held one-man shows with Schöttle and Ursula Schurr in Stuttgart. During the following year Kasseböhmer participated in a number of group exhibitions—in Maastricht, Portofino, Stuttgart, Regensburg, Rotterdam and Düsseldorf. In his paintings the exploration of modernism in terms of the essential spirit of past art, and in particular that of the sixteenth and seventeenth centuries, was fully established by this date. In 1984 he contributed to . . . *von hier aus* . . . in Düsseldorf, to other group shows in Darmstadt and Karlsruhe, and showed in the first of a series of regular exhibitions with Monika Sprüth in Cologne. Other exhibitions in which he has shown have included *Iterativismus* in Cologne in 1985, and *Der andere Blick* at the Wissenschaftzentrum, Bonn and *Europa-Amerika* at the Museum Ludwig, Cologne in 1986. In 1987 he has shown with the Galerie Grässlin-Ehrhardt in Frankfurt and Monika Sprüth.

. . . von hier aus . . ., exh. cat., Düsseldorf, 1984
Dreiundzwanzigste Ausstellung, exh. cat., Galerie Grässlin-Ehrhardt, Frankfurt, 1987

SOL LEWITT

Sol LeWitt was born in Hartford, Connecticut, in 1928, and educated at Syracuse University. In 1951–52 he served in Japan and Korea. Trained as a graphic artist and technician at the Cartoonists and Illustrators' School, from 1957 LeWitt practised both graphic design and painting. In 1960 he joined the non-curatorial staff of MoMA, where he met Lucy Lippard, Robert Mangold, Robert Ryman and Dan Flavin. His first three-dimensional work, included in a group show in New York in 1963, revealed the influence of the Bauhaus, de Stijl and Constructivism. LeWitt's first solo exhibition, of painted constructions, was held at the Daniels Gallery, New York, in 1965: this established him as an artist searching for and presenting a Conceptual (his own word) purity of statement through total and essential reduction of form.

Between 1964 and 1967 LeWitt taught at the People's Art Center attached to MoMA, in 1967–68 at the Cooper Union art school, in 1969–70 at the School of Visual Arts and in 1970–71 in the Education

Department of New York University. An exhibition in 1966 at the Dwan Gallery showed modules in serial form. In the late sixties he showed in a number of group exhibitions of minimal art in New York, including *Primary Structures* at the Jewish Museum, 1966, and *The Art of the Real* at MoMA and *Minimal Art* at the Gemeentemuseum in The Hague in 1968. Two important statements on Conceptualism were published in *Artforum* in 1967 and *Art-Language* in 1969. His definition of drawing as ''lines in four directions—vertical, horizontal, and the two diagonals'' was reflected in his first wall drawing shown with Paula Cooper in 1968: exploration of this medium, orchestrated by LeWitt with such precision that simplicity belies complexity, has continued to attract him, the final drawing frequently realised by assistants. In 1987 wall drawings have been made for the Musée d'Art Moderne de la Ville de Paris, the Cleveland Museum of Art, and the Westfälischer Kunstverein in Münster.

LeWitt is equally interested in book design: his first project, *Serial Imagery No. 1*, was made for *Aspen Magazine* in 1966. Subsequent books, their texts given to the principles and possibilities of wall drawing, have been published throughout the world. His designs have included books by Lippard, with whom he founded the group Printed Matter in 1976. In 1970, when LeWitt's serial concept was established, he took up printmaking as an additional medium: the range of his prints were shown at the Tate Gallery in 1986.

Sol LeWitt Wall Drawings 1968–84,
Stedelijk Museum, Amsterdam,
Stedelijk Van Abbemuseum, Eindhoven and
Wadsworth Atheneum, Hartford, Connecticut, 1984
Sol LeWitt, exh. cat., Tate Gallery, London, 1986

ANN McCOY

Ann McCoy was born in Boulder, Colorado in 1946, and studied at the University of Colorado and UCLA. Her first major exhibition was *15 Young Artists* at the Pasadena Art Museum in 1972. In that same year she was awarded the New Talent Award from the Los Angeles County Museum of Art. Since 1973 she has exhibited widely across America, with one-person exhibitions at the Fourcade, Droll Gallery and the Brooke Alexander Gallery in New York, the Wallraf-Richartz Gallery in Cologne, the Harkus Krakow Gallery in Boston, the Margo Leavin Gallery in Los Angeles, the Eugene Binder Gallery in Dallas, the Metropolitan Museum of Art, and the Kornfeld Gallery in Berne. Major group exhibitions have included *Second Sight* at the San Francisco Museum of Art, 1986, *Sacred Spaces* at the Everson Museum in Syracuse, *Art and Alchemy* (the Venice Biennale), *Myths and Symbols* at the Bruno Fachetti Gallery in New York and *Memento Mori* at the Tamayo Museum in Mexico City, all 1987. Her awards have included the Berliner Kunstprogramm at the DAAD and a National Endowment for the Arts grant.

McCoy has lived and taught in New York for ten years. She lectures at Barnard College and the School of Visual Arts and has also taught at Columbia University. Beginning in the mid-seventies with drawings of the sea, McCoy's chief interest has been in dreams, the collective unconscious and mythology. Forms related to alchemy, Graeco-Roman religious practices and funerary rituals fill the works. McCoy is a student of Jungian psychology and Celtic culture. She feels close to the tradition of William Blake and is a writer as well as a visual artist. Her writing has appeared in *Art International*, *Bomb* and the Dutch magazine *Museum Journaal*.

Ann McCoy, ''Meditations on the Red Mass'',
in *Bomb*, No. XIV, Winter 1986, pp. 38–41.

Thomas McEvilley, *Artforum,* April 1986

STEPHEN McKENNA

Stephen McKenna was born in London in 1939. In 1959 he left the Royal Military Academy at Sandhurst for the Slade School of Fine Art. He taught at art colleges, including Canterbury College of Art, for ten years from 1963. His first one-man exhibition was mounted in Germany at Olaf Hudtwalcker's Frankfurt gallery in 1964. From 1971 until 1979 he lived and worked in Bonn, presenting further solo shows at the Galerie Ostentor in Dortmund in 1971, the Städtische Sammlungen in Rheinhausen in 1973, and in the following year at the Galerie Rutzmoser in Munich.

He moved to Brussels in 1979. In paintings exhibited in Britain since the late seventies the works of Poussin and David, Courbet and Caspar David Friedrich, Magritte and de Chirico have been absorbed into his vocabulary: in his paintings the intrinsic importance of objects and their relationship to one another are of primary significance. McKenna has also written extensively on art.

Barry Barker in London and the New 57 Gallery in Edinburgh were among the first in this country to show McKenna's work, in 1978, followed in 1981 by the Orchard Gallery, Londonderry, in 1983 by MoMA, Oxford and in 1985 and 1986 by Edward Totah. Outside Britain the Sander Gallery in Washington DC exhibited his paintings in 1978 and 1980, the Museum van Hedendaagse Kunst in Ghent in 1980, followed by Patrick Verelst and Micheline Szwajcer in Antwerp in 1982 and 1983 and Isy Brachot in Brussels in the latter year. McKenna was given one-man exhibitions in Eindhoven and Berlin in 1984 and 1985, and the Sonder Gallery, New York, showed his work in 1985. Works dating from 1980–85 were shown at the Kunsthalle, Düsseldorf, in 1986. In the eighties large documentary group shows such as *British Art 1940–80*, Hayward Gallery, London, 1980, *Documenta* 7, Kassel, 1982, *New Art* and *The Hard Won Image*, Tate Gallery, London, 1983 and 1984, *Falls the Shadow: Recent British and European Art*, the Hayward Annual, London, 1986, and *Current Affairs: British Painting and Sculpture in the Eighties*, MoMA, Oxford and Hungary, Czechoslovakia and Poland, and *Avant-Garde in the Eighties*, Los Angeles County Museum of Art, both 1987, have put McKenna's work into a broad comparative perspective. McKenna divides his time between London, Co. Donegal and Italy.

Stephen McKenna, exh. cat., Museum of Modern Art, Oxford, 1983
Stephen McKenna 1980–85, exh. cat., Kunsthalle, Düsseldorf, 1986

CARLO MARIA MARIANI

Carlo Maria Mariani was born in 1931 in Rome where he studied painting at the Academy. His first one-man exhibition was held in Rome in 1968. The dominant influence on his early painting was the heroic style of the figural painters of sixteenth-century Italy. In 1973 he contributed to the exhibition *Mostra d'arte sacra* which opened at the Cenobino Visualità in Milan and held his second solo exhibition in Rome with Enzo Cannaviello. His discovery in *c.* 1973–74 of the philosophy, literature and art of the age of Neoclassicism has been the most formative influence of his career. Since 1974 paintings inspired by the spirit of the writings and paintings from this period—notably those of Goethe, Winckelmann, David, Mengs and Angelica Kauffmann—have been exhibited in Rome, frequently in the galleries of Cannaviello and Gian Enzo Sperone, and throughout Italy.

Mariana first showed in Germany in the solo *Pictor Philosophus* exhibition at Paul Maenz's gallery in Cologne in 1977. In 1978 he participated in the 12th Alexandria Biennale and in *Ipotesi 80* in Bari, and in *Image of Man in European Art since 1945* at the Fundatie Kunsthuis, Amsterdam, in 1979. These years marked a wider appreciation of his work, which was included in *Arte e critica 1980* at the Galleria Nazionale d'Arte Moderna, Rome, and in 1981 at *Linee della ricerca artistica in Italia 1960–1980* at the Palazzo delle Esposizioni in Rome, and the 16th São Paulo Biennale.

Studies for Mariani's major painting *The Constellation of Leo* (1981–82) were exhibited in one-man shows with Sperone in Rome in June 1981 and Sperone-Westwater, New York, in October. When the finished painting was shown in *Documenta* 7 in Kassel in 1982, Mariani expressed his debt to Goethe with whom he felt he shared a "mutual aspiration to a cosmic pantheism". His inclusion in *An International Survey of Recent Painting and Sculpture*, Museum of Modern Art, New York, *Content: A Contemporary Focus*, Hirshhorn Museum, Washington, and *Metaphor and or Symbol: A Perspective on Contemporary Art*, Tokyo as well as the Venice Biennale in 1984, emphasised the importance of Mariani's position within new figural painting worldwide.

In 1984 Mariani also showed in Canada, in *Via New York*, Musée d'Art Contemporain, Montreal, and in *Alibis* at the Musée Nationale d'Art Moderne in Paris, and *A New Romanticism: Sixteen Artists from Italy*, at the Hirshhorn Museum in 1985. In 1986, the year in which he executed a series of *Gigantic Heads*, where form became more purely abstracted, Mariani exhibited widely in group exhibitions. In 1987 solo exhibitions have been mounted with Sperone and Carlo Virgilio in Rome, Sperone-Westwater in New York, the Los Angeles County Museum and the Palais des Beaux-Arts, Charleroi. Mariani lives and works in Rome.

Italo Mussa, *Carlo Maria Mariani: Pictor Philosophus*, Rome, 1980
A New Romanticism: Sixteen Artists from Italy, exh. cat., Hirshhorn Museum, Washington, 1985

MICHELANGELO PISTOLETTO

Michelangelo Pistoletto was born in Biella, Italy, in 1933: as a young child he moved to Turin where he has since lived. Trained in both picture restoration and commercial advertising, his first solo exhibitions were with the Galleria Galatea in 1960 and 1963. In 1964 he held his first exhibition outside Italy, at the Ileana Sonnabend Gallery in Paris. The combination of life-size figures with mirrors in his paintings provided a unique environment to each showing and raised questions of identity, subjectivity and relationship. In 1966 his first major one-man exhibition in America, *A Reflected World*, shown at the Walker Art Center, Minneapolis, presented such works: he had already exhibited in the 1964 Carnegie International in Pittsburgh and in *Beyond Realism* at the Pace Gallery in New York, 1965, and contributed mirror paintings to a number of important European group exhibitions including *Nieuwe Realisten* at The Hague, *Figuration et defiguration: la figure humaine depuis Picasso* in Ghent, *Mythologies Quotidiennes*, Paris, and *New Realism and Pop Art* in Vienna, all 1964, and *Neuer Realismus und Pop Art*, Berlin and *Pop Art, Nouveau Realism Etc.*, Brussels in 1965. One-man exhibitions in Europe included those at the Palais des Beaux-Arts, Brussels in 1967 and the Museum Boymans van Beuningen in Rotterdam in 1969. The latter presented a group of works (including *Venus of Rags*, 1967) in which rags were used as an essential element. These fabrics were frequently combined with an assembly of various objects again of necessity relating to a particular venue and providing in their diversity a commentary on society. Works using rags were shown in a number of Arte Povera exhibitions including Bologna and Amalfi, 1968, *Land Art—Arte Povera—Conceptual Art*, Torino, 1970 and *Arte Povera*, Munich, 1971.

These ideas were explored in Pistoletto's *Manifesto of Collaboration* shown at the Venice Biennale (where he first exhibited in 1966) in 1968 and in major contributions to a number of other group shows presented from the late sixties, including *Documenta 4* at Kassel, *When Attitudes become Form*, Berne, 1969, and *Kunst van de 20 Eeuw*, Rotterdam, 1972. Pistoletto also showed at the Venice Biennale in 1978 and 1986, *Documenta* 7, Kassel, 1982 and in *The European Iceberg*, Toronto, 1985. Important solo exhibitions since the late seventies have been held at the National Gallery in Berlin, 1978, Rice Museum, Houston and the International Cultureel Centrum, Antwerp, 1979, the University Art Museum, Berkeley and the Museum of Modern Art, San Francisco in 1980, the Westfälischer Kunstverein, Münster in 1983, and at the Centre d'Art Contemporain, Geneva, 1984. Major retrospectives of his work were mounted in Madrid in 1983, in Florence in 1984, and in Oslo and Marseilles in 1986.

Pistoletto, exh. cat., Forte di Belvedere, Florence, 1984
Bruno Corà, *Pistoletto*, Ravenna, 1986

SALVO

Salvatore Mangione was born in Léonforte, Sicily, in 1947. His family moved to Turin when he was a child. Mangione began to paint in 1961, and received no formal art training. In 1963 work (which he later destroyed) was exhibited at the Palazzo del Promotrice delle Belle Arti. In 1967 he put aside painting to devote himself entirely to political interests. His friends at this time already included Gian Enzo Sperone, Giovanni Anselmo and Gilberto Zorio. Returning to art once more in 1969, he exhibited his work in 1970 with Sperone in Turin, and Francoise Lambert in Milan as well as at the Galleria Acme in Brescia, and, as a member of the 'young Italian avant-garde' at the Kunstmuseum in Lucerne. In the latter year he changed his name to Salvo. His work consisted of photographic pieces, engraved marble plates, handwritten books, neon works, etc. It thus related just as well to conceptual art as to arte povera. When taking up painting again, *c.* 1973, Salvo's art often followed very personal references to masters such as Raphael, Carpaccio, Cosimo Tura *et al*, in which autobiographical elements were present.

In 1971 Salvo showed with Guilio Paolini and Michelangelo Pistoletto at the Galleria Notizie in Turin and contributed to *Prospect 71* at the Düsseldorf Kunsthalle. Since 1971 he has shown in a number of other galleries in Europe—notably with Paul Maenz in Cologne, art & project in Amsterdam, Yvon Lambert in Paris, Marilena Bonomo in Bari, Gian Enzo Sperone in Turin. In 1972 Salvo exhibited in New York with the John Weber Gallery and in 1986 with Barbara Gladstone. Significant one-man shows were mounted in 1977 at the Museum Folkwang in Essen, and 1983 at the Kunstmuseum, Lucerne and the Nouveau Musée, Villeurbanne/Lyons and he will be the subject of a major retrospective at the Museum Boymans van Beuningen, Rotterdam, in early 1988. He was also selected for *Documenta 5* in Kassel. In the succeeding years his paintings were included in a number of important exhibitions including the 8th Paris Biennale, *Kunst aus Fotografie*, Hanover, 1973, *Die verlorene Identität*, Leverkusen, 1974, *Painting and Sculpture Today*, Indianapolis Museum of Art, 1974, and *Projekt '74*, Kunsthalle, Cologne, 1974. He showed in the Venice Biennale in 1976 and 1984, and in the Zurich exhibition *Malerei und Fotografie im Dialog von 1840 bis heute*, 1977.

During the eighties Salvo's painting has concentrated on poetic landscapes composed of simple, dreamlike and often classical elements. As a member of a new generation of Italian painters he was selected for the XVth Biennale at São Paolo, mounted in 1980, and London's *Arte Italiana 1960–82* at the ICA and Hayward Gallery in 1982, and more recently, in 1986 in *1960–85 Aspekte der italienischen Kunst* at the Frankfurter Kunstverein where he was also included in *Prospect 86*. Salvo lives and works in Turin.

Salvo, *Della Pittura, On Painting, Über die Malerei,* Cologne, 1986
Salvo, exh. cat., Museum Folkwang, Essen, 1977
Salvo, exh. cat., Kunstmuseum, Lucerne, 1983

ANDREAS SCHULZE

Andreas Schulze was born in Hanover in 1955. He studied art briefly in Kassel, completing his training in 1978–83 in Düsseldorf where he chose to study with Dieter Krieg. Between *c.* 1981 and 1983 Schulze painted a number of *Kugelbilder*—paintings of variously coloured balls (often eight in number to symbolise infinity) against shallow backgrounds where abstracted forms combined with contradictions in perspective—which have ranked him as a neo-surrealist. In 1981 he participated in the *Rundschau Deutschland,* two exhibitions which surveyed current developments in German painting, in Munich and Cologne. Since 1982 Schulze has lived and worked in Cologne, where he showed in that year in the *Herbstsalon.* He also held his first one-man exhibition at the Galerie Six Friedrich in Munich and contributed to *La giovane pittura in Germania* in Bologna and to *Tendenzen 82* in Ulm. In 1983 he was selected for *New Art* at the Tate Gallery, London, for *Supermix* with Paul Maenz in Cologne, and invited to show in Stuttgart, Munich and Ghent.

In 1983–84 Schulze was painting *Kastenbilder* where boxes, some with objects within, emphasised illusionist perspectives. Throughout his career Schulze's works have remained large in scale and commonly use the diptych format for both practical and aesthetic reasons. Since 1984 his paintings have been seen widely in much of Europe and in America: in . . . *von hier aus* . . . in Düsseldorf, *An International Survey of Recent Painting and Sculpture* at MoMA and in *Hand Painted Dreams* with Barbara Gladstone, both New York, and in *Paravents* at the Schloss Lörsfeld, Kerpen, in that year. In 1985 he contributed to the Paris Biennale and to *Wolfgang Amadeus Mozart—neue Bilder* at the Galerie Thaddeus Ropac in Salzburg, to *Künstliche Paradiese* in Essen and Munich, in 1986 to *Prospect 86* at the Kunstverein, Frankfurt, *Sie machen was Sie wollen: Junge rheinische Kunst* at the Galerie Shipka, Sofia, and, in 1987, to *Vom Essen und Trinken* at the Kunst- und Museums-verein, Wuppertal, and *Art from Europe* at the Tate Gallery.

An International Survey of Recent Painting and Sculpture, exh. cat., Museum of Modern Art, New York, 1984
Art from Europe, exh. cat., Tate Gallery, London, 1987

CY TWOMBLY

Cy Twombly was born in Lexington, Virginia, in 1927. He studied in Boston, Washington, New York and in North Carolina where he met Robert Motherwell, Franz Kline and Charles Olsen. In 1951 he travelled in Europe with Robert Rauschenberg, with whom he showed in New York in 1953 and Düsseldorf in 1960. Twombly first exhibited in New York in 1951 and in Europe at the Galleria d'Arte Contemporanea, Florence, in 1953, since when numerous one-man shows have been mounted on the Continent and in the United States. He has lived in Rome since 1957.

With Twombly, erudition partners emotionalism: from the early years of automatic writing in the fifties he has experimented with media while simultaneously reflecting and contributing to the classical tradition. In drawing in particular Twombly uses the surface to express the seeming unconscious. At the same time he has achieved a major progression of ideas: the attack and surface simplicity of his purely expressionist paintings of the fifties preceded a revelation of transitory form and space seen in the grey paintings of the late sixties and early seventies. In the mid-seventies his interest in collage produced paintings and particularly prints of varied technique and powerful complexity, of which some of the best known appeared in his *Natural History Part 1: Mushrooms* in 1974. Since this date Twombly has devoted much of his time to works on paper and, more recently, to a revived interest in sculpture as a medium, in which found objects are coated and sometimes cast in bronze.

During the 1980s many major exhibitions have included work by Twombly. Among these have been *A New Spirit in Painting,* London, *Westkunst,* Cologne, and *Amerikanische Kunst 1930–1980,* Munich, all in 1981, *Documenta 7,* Kassel, and *Zeitgeist,* Berlin, 1982, *La grande parade,* Amsterdam, 1984, *Italia aperto,* Madrid, *Spüren, Skulpturen und Monumente ihrer präzisen Reise,* Zurich, 1985, and *In Tandem, the Painter-Sculptor in the Twentieth Century,* London, and *Die Landschaft,* Bielefeld, in 1986.

Cy Twombly, exh. cat., Kunsthaus, Zurich, 1987
Cy Twombly, exh. cat., Whitechapel Gallery, London [Munich], 1987

ISOLDE WAWRIN

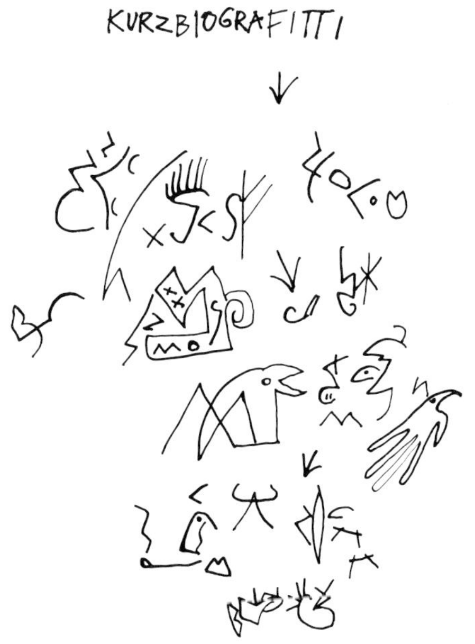

Isolde Wawrin was born in Altdorf im Schwarzwald in 1949. Wawrin studied at the Academy in Karlsruhe between 1971 and 1974 and at the Academy in Düsseldorf from 1974 to 1977, when she won a scholarship to study in Paris. She first exhibited in *Letzes Mal hast Du doch gesagt, dass Du keine Kunst machst* in Wiesbaden in 1976, and in 1978 held her first solo exhibition with the Galerie Hetzler und Keller, Stuttgart. She contributed to a number of group shows in Germany and Paris from the late seventies. In 1980 Wawrin received the Stipendium des Kulturkreises im Bundesverband der Deutschen Industrie (an art award from industry) and the local Förderungspreis des Landes Nordrh.-Westfalen für junge Künstler given to outstanding young artists, and also showed in *Art Allemand Aujourd'hui* in Paris. In the same year she held an important exhibition at the Bonner Kunstverein. Other major one-person exhibitions have been mounted at the Kunsthalle, Düsseldorf, in 1982, and the Westfälischer Kunstverein, Münster in 1983–84. Wawrin exhibited with Astrid Klein and Christa Näher at the Kunstmuseum in Lucerne in 1984. She showed in *Documenta* 7 in Kassel in 1982, *Hin und Her* in Düsseldorf in 1983, *Märchen, Mythen, Monster* in Bonn and Graz and *Kunst mit Eigensinn,* Vienna, both held in

1984, *Rheingold,* Turin and the *Friedenbiennale,* Hamburg in 1985, and in 1986 in *Sonsbeck '86* in Arnheim and *Sie machen was sie wollen* in Sofia.

Isolde Wawrin, exh. cat., Kunsthalle, Düsseldorf, 1982
Isolde Wawrin, exh. cat., Westfälischer Kunstverein, Münster, 1983

ALISON WILDING

Alison Wilding was born in Blackburn in 1948. Between 1968 and 1971 she studied at Ravensbourne College of Art and Design, and from 1971–73 at the Royal College of Art under John Panting and Peter Kardia. She presented a solo show with the Friends of the Tate Gallery in 1971. In the early seventies her sculpture took the form of installations utilising sound, text and photography. By 1976, when Wilding exhibited pieces at the AIR Gallery, conceptual work relying on text dominated her work. The move to a new London studio in 1977 announced a new phase in her career in which the textual basis of recent work was abandoned in favour of spare, more tightly controlled visual forms. Wall and floor pieces, often composed of carved elements and therefore of slower gestation, have since had equal importance.

During the eighties Wilding has contributed to a large number of group exhibitions in Britain and Europe, from *Eight Women Artists* at London's Acme Gallery in 1980 to *Current Affairs: British Painting and Sculpture in the 1980s* at MoMA, Oxford in 1987. Other group shows have included, in Britain, *The Sculpture Show,* Arts Council, 1983, *The British Art Show,* 1984, and abroad *Collazione Inglese,* Venice, 1982, the XVIIth Paris Biennale in 1982 and the XVIIth São Paolo Biennale, 1983, *Synonyms for Sculpture,* Graz, 1985, *Between Object and Image,* Madrid, 1986, *Art and Alchemy* (the 1986 Venice Biennale), and *Viewpoint: British Art of the 1980s,* Brussels, 1987. Solo exhibitions have been held in the eighties at Kettle's Yard, Cambridge (1982), with Salvatore Ala in New York in 1983 and 1985 (and Milan in 1985), at the Serpentine Gallery (also 1985), and with the Galleri Lang, Malmö, Karsten Schubert Ltd., London, and MoMA, New York, in 1987.

Alison Wilding, exh. cat., Serpentine Gallery, London, 1985
Alison Wilding, Sculptures, exh. cat., Karsten Schubert Ltd., London, 1987

TERRY WINTERS

Terry Winters was born in Brooklyn, New York, in 1949. He studied at the Pratt Institute, gaining his BFA in 1971. During the mid-seventies Winters' paintings displayed an allegiance to Minimalism. Since that date, however, he has become increasingly involved with the natural substances he uses in his art, and has conducted his own enquiry into the plant and mineral forms from which the pigments, some ground by the artist himself, originate. In the later seventies he was contributing to group shows at P.S.1 and the Drawing Center, New York. Notebooks from this time depicted detailed plant studies. Further concerned with unity of material and representation, Winters executed a series of paintings showing the outlines of pigment crystal structures in 1980–81. In the early eighties his work was seen more widely—in New York and Dallas in 1981, and in 1982 at the Detroit Institute of Arts, the Baltimore Museum of Art and the Sonnabend Gallery, New York, where he also mounted his first solo exhibition during the same year. In 1982 Winters' use of botanical images intensified, their forms arranged sequentially across the canvas.

Since 1985 Winters has used an increased diversity of surface textures, together with a wider range of natural subjects evoking entomological and by implication zoological and human forms. Although primarily shown in American galleries, his work has been seen in *New Art* at the Tate Gallery and *New York Now—Works on Paper* at the Nordjyllands Kunstmuseum, Denmark (both 1983), in *Vernacular Abstraction* at the Wacoal Art Center, Tokyo, and *Nuove Trame dele'Arte* with the Comune di Gennazzano, in 1985. Since 1985 his work has been very widely shown in America in both commercial galleries and museums including the Whitney Museum of American Art and the Brooklyn Museum (1986), and, in 1987, in the major *40th Biennial of American Contemporary Painting* at the Corcoran Gallery of Art, Washington and the 1987 Whitney Biennial. A series of one-man shows has culminated in exhibitions mounted at the Kunstmuseum, Lucerne (1985), the Tate Gallery (1986) and in 1987 at the University Art Museum, Santa Barbara.

Terry Winters, exh. cat., Kunstmuseum, Lucerne, 1985
Terry Winters: Eight Paintings, exh. cat., Tate Gallery, London, 1986
Terry Winters, exh. cat., University Art Museum, Santa Barbara, 1987

SELECTED BIBLIOGRAPHY

The bibliography has been largely restricted to catalogues of important group exhibitions in which the artists in the *Edinburgh International* have participated. For information on artists' individual exhibitions the reader is referred to the artists' biographies on the preceding pages.

Aktuell '83: Räume. Kunst aus Mailand, München, Wien und Zurich, exh. cat., Munich, Städtische Galerie im Lenbachhaus, 1983

Alles und noch viel mehr, exh. cat., Berne, Kunsthalle/Benteli Verlag, 1985

Der andere Blick, exh. cat., Bonn, 1986

Anderer Leute Kunst, exh. cat., Krefeld, Museum Haus Lange, 1987

Ansatzpunkte kritischer Kunst heute, exh. cat., Bonn, 1983

Après le Classicisme, exh. cat., Saint-Etienne, 1980

ARS 83, exh. cat., Helsinki, The Art Museum of the Ateneum, 1983

Art from Europe, exh. cat., London, Tate Gallery, 1987

Arte Italiana 1960-82, exh. cat., London, Arts Council of Great Britain, 1982

Arte povera, exh. cat., Turin, Museo Civico, 1970

arti visive '82: La Biennale di Venezia, exh. cat., Venice, 1982

1960 85 Aspekte der italienischen Kunst, exh. cat., Frankfurt, Frankfurter Kunstverein, 1985

Avant-Garde in the Eighties, exh. cat., Los Angeles, County Museum of Art, 1987

Between Object and Image: Contemporary British Sculpture, exh. cat., London, British Council, 1986

Beuys zu Ehren, exh. cat., Munich, 1986

40th Biennial of American Contemporary Painting, exh. cat., Washington DC, Corcoran Gallery of Art, 1987

Brennpunkt Düsseldorf 1962-87, exh. cat., Düsseldorf, Kunstmuseum, 1987

The British Art Show: Old Allegiances and New Directions, exh. cat., London, Arts Council of Great Britian/ORBIS, 1984

British Sculpture in the Twentieth Century, exh. cat., London, Whitechapel Gallery, 1981

1985 Carnegie International, exh. cat., Pittsburgh, Museum of Art, Carnegie Institute, 1985

Chambres d'Amis, exh. cat., Ghent, Museum van Hedendaagse Kunst, 1986

Correspondence Europe, exh. cat., Amsterdam, Stedelijk Museum, 1986

Current Affairs: British Painting and Sculpture in the Eighties, exh. cat., Oxford, Museum of Modern Art, 1987

Documenta 7, exh. cat., Kassel, Museum Fridericianum/Dierichs GmbH & Co, 1982

Documenta 8, exh. cat., Kassel, Museum Fridericianum/Weber & Weidemeyer GmbH & Co, 1987

Englische Plastik Heute, exh. cat., Lucerne, Kunstmuseum, 1982

L'Epoque, La Mode, La Monde, Le Passion: Aspects de l'Art d'Aujourd'hui 1977-87, exh. cat., Paris, Centre Georges Pompidou, 1987

XLI Esposizione Internazionale d'Arte: La Biennale di Venezia, exh. cat., Venice, Electa Editrice, 1984

XLII Esposizione Internazionale d'Arte: La Biennale di Venezia. Arte e Scienza, exh. cat., Venice, Electa Editrice, 1986

Europa Kunst der 80er Jahre, exh. cat., Stuttgart, 1979

The European Iceberg: Creativity in Germany and Italy Today, exh. cat., Toronto, Art Gallery of Ontario/Mazzotta, 1985

Falls the Shadow: Recent British and European Art: The Hayward Annual, exh. cat., London, Arts Council of Great Britain, 1986

Il giardino d'Europa, exh. cat., Florence, 1986

La giovane pittura in Germania, exh. cat., Bologna, Galleria communale d'arte moderna, 1982

The Golden Thread: Classical Mythology in Contemporary Art, exh. cat., Preston, Harris Museum and Art Gallery, 1986

La Grande Parade, exh. cat., Amsterdam, Stedelijk Museum, 1984

Hin und Her, exh. cat., Düsseldorf, 1983

Image of Man in European Art since 1945, exh. cat., Amsterdam, Stedelijk Museum, 1979

An International Survey of Recent Painting and Sculpture, exh. cat., New York, Museum of Modern Art, 1984

Die 60er Jahre: Kölns Weg zur Kunstmetropole, exh. cat., Cologne, Kunstverein, 1986

Junge Kunst in Deutschland, exh. cat., Berlin, Edition Kunstbuch Berlin im Rembrandt Verlag, 1982

The Knot: Arte Povera at PS1, New York, PS1, 1985

Kunstliche Paradiese, exh. cat., Essen, Museum Folkwang, 1985

Malerei in Europa, Positionen, Teil 1, exh. cat., Zaragossa, 1987

La Memoria del Tempo, exh. cat., Verona, Quartiere Fieristico/Bologna, Grafis Editione, 1986

New Art, exh. cat., London, Tate Gallery, 1983

The New Metaphysical Dream, exh. cat., New York, Jack Shainman Gallery/Rome, De Luca Editore, 1986

A New Romanticism: Sixteen Artists from Italy, exh. cat., Washington DC, Hirshhorn Museum, 1985

New British Sculpture: Objects and Figures, exh. cat., Edinburgh, Scottish Arts Council, 1982

A New Spirit in Painting, exh. cat., London, Royal Academy of Arts, 1981

Nouvelle Biennale de Paris, exh. cat., Paris, Electa Moniteur, 1985

Paravents, exh. cat., Kerpen, Schloss Lörsfeld, 1984

Projection, Prospect 71, exh. cat., Düsseldorf, Kunsthalle, 1971

Projekt '74, Aspekte Internationaler Kunst am Anfang der 70er Jahre, Cologne, Kunsthalle, 1974

Prospect 86, exh. cat., Frankfurt, Frankfurter Kunstverein, 1986

The Sculpture Show, exh. cat., London, Arts Council of Great Britain, 1983

Skulptur Projekte Münster, exh. cat., Münster 1987

Skulpturen im 20. Jahrhundert, exh. cat., Basle, 1984

Sie machen was Sie wollen: Junge rheinische Kunst, exh. cat., Sofia, Galerie Shipka, 1986

Sonsbeck 86, exh. cat., Arnhem, Gemeentemuseum, 1986

Spüren, Skulpturen und Monumente ihrer präzisen Reise, exh. cat., Zurich, Kunsthaus Zurich, 1986

Tendenzen 82, exh. cat., Ulm, Ulmer Museum, 1982

Der Traum Des Orpheus: Mythologie in der italienischen Gegenwartskunst 1967 bis 1984, exh. cat., Munich, Städtische Galerie im Lenbachhaus, 1984

Die verlorene Identität, exh. cat., Leverkusen, 1974

Visual Arts 80: La Biennale di Venezia, exh. cat., Venice, 1980

. . . von hier aus . . ., exh. cat., Düsseldorf, Messehallen, 1984

Wechselströme: Kontemplation—Expression—Konstruktion, exh. cat., Bonn, Kunstverein/Edition Wienand, 1987

Westkunst: Zeitgenossiche Kunst seit 1939, exh. cat., Cologne, DuMont, 1981

When Attitudes become Form, exh. cat., Berne, 1969

Wien Fluss, exh. cat., Vienna, Wiener Festwochen, 1986

Zeitgeist: International Kunstausstellung Berlin 1982, exh. cat., Berlin, Martin-Gropius-Bau/Verlag Frolich & Kaufmann, 1982

PHOTOGRAPHIC ACKNOWLEDGEMENTS

Jon Abbott, New York
C. Cantini, Florence
F. Català-Roca, Barcelona
Hans Doering, Munich
Chris Felver, New York
Franz Fischer, Bonn
Jean-Marie Francuis, Paris
Maria Gilissen, Brussels
Marion Gray, San Francisco
Jacques Hoepffner, Paris
Michael Hooymann, Cologne
Sean Hudson, Edinburgh
Scott Hyde, New York
ISO, Bordeaux
Mimmo Jodice, Turin
Galerie Kaess-Weiss, Stuttgart
Verna Klüser, Munich
Salvatore Liaitra, Turin
André Marin, Paris
Heinz-Günther Mebusch, Düsseldorf
Il Milione, Milan
Elio Montanari, Venice
Christian Philipp Müller, Münster
Monika Nikolic, Kassel
Sue Ormerod, London
P. Pellion, Munich
W. Penkert, Stuttgart
Paulo Pellion di Persano, Naples
Vincenzo Pirozzi, Rome
Pucci, Rome
Antonia Reeve, Edinburgh
Adam Rzepka, Paris
San Francisco Museum of Art
Paolo Mussat Sartor, Turin
Bernhard Schaub, Cologne
Philipp Schönborn, Munich
Joachim Schumacher, Essen
Christian Stein, Turin
Stuart Collection, San Diego
Ivan Dalla Tana, New York
Ben Taylor, Norwich
Achim Thode, Kiel
Rodney Todd-White and Son, London
Isolde Wawrin, Düsseldorf
John Weber Gallery, New York
Westfälischen Landesmuseum für Kunst und Kulturgeschichte, Münster
Gareth Winters, London

CATALOGUE AUTHORS

Yves Abrioux
Art critic and member of the Group René Tadlov for the study of contemporary American fiction, Maison des Sciences de l'Homme, Paris. Author of the monograph, *Ian Hamilton Finlay—A Visual Primer*, published by Reaktion Books, Edinburgh (1985).

Stephen Bann
Reader in Modern Cultural Studies, University of Kent. Author of articles and books on Ian Hamilton Finlay over a period of twenty years including, with Yves Abrioux, *Ian Hamilton Finlay—A Visual Primer* (1985).

Barry Barker
Director of Arnolfini, Bristol. Organiser and author of a number of exhibitions of contemporary art, including (with Jon Thompson) *Falls the Shadow—Recent British and European Art* (Hayward Annual, London) published by the Arts Council of Great Britain (1986).

James Bustard
Exhibitions Organiser, Scottish Arts Council. Author of various exhibition catalogues.

Michael Compton
Until recently, Keeper of Museum Services, Tate Gallery, London. Organiser of many exhibitions for the Tate Gallery, including *New Art at the Tate* (1983): has written extensively on modern art.

Elizabeth Cumming
Freelance art historian and exhibition organiser. Keeper of Fine Art Collections, City of Edinburgh Art Centre (1975–84).

Bice Curiger
Art critic and editor of the journal *Parkett*.

Jan Debbaut
Director, Societé des Expositions in the Palais des Beaux-Arts, Brussels.

Wilfried Dickhoff
Art critic and author of several books, including works on Jiri Georg Dokoupil, Rosemarie Trockel and Walter Dahn.

Walter Grasskamp
Professor of Fine Art at the Münster Academy.

Douglas Hall
Keeper of the Scottish National Gallery of Modern Art in Edinburgh (1961–86) and author of numerous articles and exhibition catalogues.

Martin Kunz
Director, Kunstmuseum, Lucerne. Organiser of numerous exhibitions and author of several publications.

Catherine Lampert
Senior Exhibitions Officer for the South Bank Centre, London. Recent publications include *Rodin—Sculpture & Drawings* (Hayward Gallery, London) published by the Arts Council of Great Britain (1987).

Jeremy Lewison
Curator, Tate Gallery, London and author of several publications, including *Terry Winters—8 Paintings*, published by the Tate Gallery (1986).

Demetrio Paparoni
Art critic and publisher of the Italian journal *Tema Celeste*.

Karel Schampers
Curator, Boymans-van Beuningen Museum, Rotterdam and curator of the forthcoming *Salvo* retrospective (1988).

Roberta Smith
Art historian and critic, New York.

Alexander Stoddart
Scottish neoclassical sculptor and leading Saint-Just Vigilante.

Published by The Scottish Arts Council
on the occasion of the exhibition

Edinburgh International:
Reason and Emotion in Contemporary Art

Royal Scottish Academy, Edinburgh
19 December 1987 to 14 February 1988.

Edited by Douglas Hall
Designed by McIlroy Coates, Edinburgh
Typesetting and printing by
Blackwood, Pillans & Wilson Ltd.,
Edinburgh and London

2000 copies printed December 1987

Volume I ISBN 1-85119-024-4